Hedge Funds Demystified: A Self-Teaching Guide

SCOTT FRUSH

New York   Chicago   San Francisco   Lisbon
London   Madrid   Mexico City   Milan   New Delhi
San Juan   Seoul   Singapore   Sydney   Toronto

1 2 3 4 5 6 7 8 9 0 FGR/FGR 0 9 8 7

ISBN-13: 978-0-07-149600-1
ISBN-10:   0-07-149600-9

This publication is designed to provide accurate and authoritative information in regard to the subject matter covered. It is sold with the understanding that the publisher is not engaged in rendering legal, accounting, or other professional services. If legal advice or other expert assistance is required, the services of a competent professional person should be sought.

—From a Declaration of Principles Jointly Adopted by a Committee of the American Bar Association and a Committee of Publishers and Associations

McGraw-Hill books are available at special discounts to use as premiums and sales promotions, or for use in corporate training programs. For more information, please write to the Director of Special Sales, Professional Publishing, McGraw-Hill, Two Penn Plaza, New York, NY 10121-2298. Or contact your local bookstore.

This book is printed on acid-free paper.

Library of Congress Cataloging-in-Publication Data

Frush, Scott P.
   Hedge funds demystified / Scott Frush.
      p. cm.
   Includes index.
   ISBN-13: 978-0-07-149600-1 (pbk. : alk. paper)
   ISBN-10:   0-07-149600-9
   1. Hedge funds–United States. I. Title.

HG4930.F756 2007
332.64'5–dc22   2007013906

To Gabriella Anne

All My Love

CONTENTS

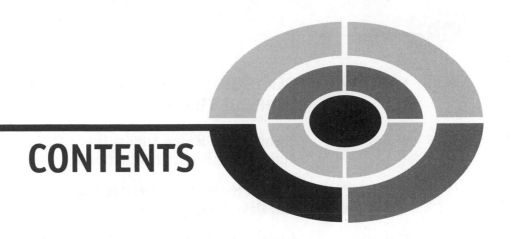

CONTENTS

Acknowledgments

Once again I am extremely grateful to the people at McGraw-Hill for giving me the opportunity to continue my passion for writing. To all involved in the production of my third McGraw-Hill book, I say thank you. For their vision and commitment to publishing this book, I thank Dianne Wheeler, executive editor, and Herb Schaffner, publisher, at McGraw-Hill. It has been a distinct pleasure pursuing our passion together.

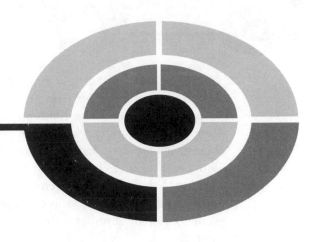

INTRODUCTION

Sowing the Seeds of Hedge Fund Discovery

Imagine an investment where money managers target attractive positive returns in both bull and bear markets. Now envision that same investment with higher returns than the market over time. Sounds rather enticing, doesn't it? To top it off, this investment also has lower volatility risk than the overall market. Now imagine that this investment were available in the financial marketplace—ready for those accredited investors willing, able, and ready to make an investment. Of course, what I am talking about is hedge funds. Yes, what you just read is very true about hedge funds from a macro point of view. Research has shown that hedge funds have outperformed the overall market in terms of long-term performance with less volatility risk. Moreover, hedge funds' primary objective is to generate attractive positive returns on a consistent basis regardless of how well or poorly the market is performing. This is an aim most other investments cannot accomplish. These are some of the primary reasons why hedge funds have been gaining in popularity over the

years. This book will demystify what many people consider one of the most mysterious and often misunderstood investments available today.

Let me be direct, hedge funds are not for everyone. The Securities and Exchange Commission restricts who can invest directly in hedge funds, and hedge funds themselves typically have high investment minimums, generally around $1 million. Funds of funds have much lower requirements. We will get into that and more later on. No worries, however, if you do not qualify or do not want to invest in hedge funds because the tools managers employ are available to you as well. If you want to employ leverage or sell short, you can do just that—within reason, of course.

Hedge Funds Demystified is written to arm you with the information and tools you will need to invest in hedge funds with success. Significant emphasis is placed on how to include hedge funds in your existing investment portfolio rather than simply investing exclusively in hedge funds. Perhaps you are not interested in investing in hedge funds but are looking to gain knowledge about hedge funds out of curiosity or for your job. This book will deliver exactly what you need to know in these cases as well. Lastly, this book is aimed at those readers who have little knowledge of hedge funds but have the intellect and appetite for a solid grounding in the fundamentals of hedge funds. Accordingly, my guiding principle was not to insult any reader's intelligence but instead to build on it constructively.

The Hedge Fund Universe

Throughout this book you will read about the different types of hedge funds in the marketplace. Hedge funds are defined not only by the investment style of hedge fund managers but also by the tools and strategies managers employ to generate profits. Unfortunately, some people in the hedge fund trade use the words *strategy, style,* and *tools* interchangeably to mean the same thing. This is not really the case because there are differences. As the hedge fund industry grows and matures, more standardized terminology will be used. Nevertheless, this book will use *style* to represent the guiding investment purpose of a particular hedge fund—be it tactical, event-driven, relative value, or perhaps hybrid. *Strategy* will be used to describe the specific actions hedge fund managers follow to profit within their investment style. Finally, *tools* will be used to describe the common everyday practices hedge fund managers use to implement their desired strategies. Some of these tools include selling short, employing leverage, and trading derivatives. Chapter 8 will delve into tools of the trade in detail. Figures I–1 and I–2 illustrate the universe of investing opportunities and the hedge funds universe, respectively.

Figure I-1. Universe of investing opportunities

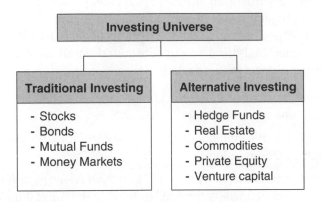

Figure I-2. Hedge funds universe

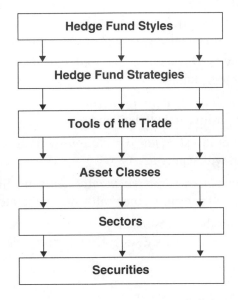

Executive Summary: The 10 Defining Characteristics

Most investors are very comfortable with and have good knowledge of traditional investing, particularly mutual funds. Practically all investors at one time or another have invested in mutual funds either on their own or through their employer's

retirement program. In many ways, hedge funds operate the same way. But they also differ in some very important areas. This section presents a brief introduction to the 10 defining characteristics of hedge funds, an executive summary of sorts. Note that Chapter 18 provides detailed descriptions of each defining characteristic, and each is mentioned and discussed in substantial detail throughout this book. The top 10 defining characteristics include

- Hedge funds have *minimal organizational structures* and are typically operated by one or two key decision makers.
- Hedge funds receive *minimal oversight and regulation* by the Securities and Exchange Commission (SEC).
- Hedge funds are restricted by the SEC to *accept fewer than 100 accredited investors,* a term defined by the SEC to include only investors with substantial wealth and income.
- Hedge funds offer their investors *limited liquidity* and impose restrictions on withdrawing invested capital.
- Hedge funds are severely *limited on the type of marketing and promotions they can make* to potential clients, a restriction imposed by the SEC.
- Hedge funds have *extensive strategies and tools available* to them for the management of their funds.
- Hedge funds passionately *aim to generate attractive absolute returns,* or returns that are positive in both bull and bear markets.
- Hedge funds offer investors *low correlations* with the total market and, more important, with equity assets.
- Hedge funds have *incentivized fee arrangements* in which they charge an industry average 20 percent on the profits they generate for their investors.
- Hedge funds offer their investors *performance safeguards* to ensure that performance-incentive fees are suitable and appropriate.

Sports Cars and Minivans

The investing marketplace consists of many different traditional and alternative methods of investing, with the pooling of funds being one of the most popular. Two of the most popular vehicles of pooled funds are hedge funds and mutual funds. A good way to think about the differences between hedge funds and mutual funds is to consider the differences between a sports car and a minivan. If mutual funds

resemble minivans, then hedge funds resemble sports cars. Both minivans and sports cars are conceptually the same—they transport one or more people from location A to location B. But, as we all know, minivans and sports cars are classic examples of how two things with similar purposes differ. This is the beginning of the great divide between mutual funds and hedge funds. Going back to our analogy, sports cars are faster off the line, have higher top speeds, are more nimble, are significantly more maneuverable, and can go where many other vehicles dare not venture. At the same time, however, sports cars are limited in the number of passengers they can carry, attract the attention of the police more frequently than do minivans, require a somewhat more polished driver, and have substantially fewer safety features in the case of a crash. The same positives and negatives can be said of hedge funds and mutual funds.

By far the greatest drawback to hedge funds is the potentially higher risk involved. This risk can be controlled by the driver, or manager, as is the case with hedge funds. Moreover, it is not a forgone conclusion that investing in hedge funds is going to be any riskier to an investor than investing in mutual funds. Going back to our analogy, the driver and the actions he or she takes are what dictate risk. Driving fast, darting in and out of traffic, and going through red lights can be done by drivers of either sports cars or minivans. This means that hedge fund risk is often the result of manager-specific actions. However, one can argue that different types of drivers select different type of vehicles. More conservative drivers typically will not drive, let alone buy, a sports car. Thus hedge funds probably attract managers that prefer the higher risk and are comfortable with taking that risk. Furthermore, regardless of the type of driver who is behind the wheel of a sports car, at some point that driver is going to open things up to see what the vehicle can do. The same can be said for hedge fund managers. Regardless of their view of risk taking, hedge fund managers may feel motivated at some point to assume more risk than they ordinarily would assume.

The final part to this analogy involves how each vehicle protects passengers in the case of an accident. There is no arguing the fact that minivans simply provide substantially greater protection than do sports cars. The same difference can be applied to mutual funds and hedge funds as well. Mutual funds tend to safeguard investor assets more so than hedge funds. However, regardless of the vehicle, passengers are at greater risk traveling on expressways and major streets than they are traveling side streets. For example, if small-cap stocks are expressways and blue-chip stocks are side streets, then it is the type of street you are traveling on rather than your vehicle that determines the risk. By applying this same logic to hedge funds, it is therefore the investments or assets held in the fund—mutual fund or hedge fund—that dictates overall risk. We will explore all these topics later in this book.

Before Getting Started

Time and time again I tell people to manage their portfolio before it manages you. Managing your portfolio always begins with you. Never rely on someone else to do what you should be doing. When it comes to your investments, you really have two options: accomplish those tasks that will help you to manage your portfolio or simply forgo them and let your portfolio manage you. Since you are already reading this book, you have demonstrated your ability and willingness to be proactive in managing your portfolio. Consider this book an invaluable tool to help you with your endeavor.

Self-Assessment

Before embarking on your endeavor of investing in hedge funds, I highly encourage you to complete a self-assessment. Since hedge fund investing is a personalized process and will change over time as your situation changes, understand as much as you can about your current position, what you are hoping to accomplish, and how best to bridge the gap. Different investors not only have different goals and obligations but also have varying financial circumstances and preferences. As a result, investors need to exercise care, skill, and patience to reap the benefits of investing in hedge funds.

How to Get the Most from This Book

Hedge Funds Demystified is divided into four parts, and the chapters in each part address similar subject matter. No one part is of greater importance than the others. All parts are of equal value. Consequently, reading this book from Chapter 1 to Chapter 20 is your best route. The book is structured to provide maximum benefit, ease of learning, and quick and simple referencing. As such, the book begins with a discussion of the essentials of hedge funds and is followed by a detailed discussion of the different types of hedge funds, including common practices of hedge fund managers. Part III shows how to set in motion your own plan for investing in hedge funds. The final part helps to reinforce and enhance the first three parts with special considerations and important peripheral material.

What You Will Not Find in This Book

Hedge Funds Demystified presents hedge funds in an easy-to-understand manner using a very specific format in which you will learn the basics first and how to

invest in hedge funds second. This book will not teach you about the highly complex mathematics of hedge funds nor drill down so deep into a topic that you lose sight of the big picture. Although the difficult technical information was deliberately excluded from this book, you will still encounter enough of the simple technical information to learn and grasp the big picture of hedge funds. If after reading this book you still want to immerse yourself in the highly technical aspects of hedge funds, I encourage you to investigate some of the books mentioned in Appendix A.

A Review of the Chapters

Hedge Funds Demystified is divided into four parts to help you find and learn what you want quickly and easily. Included in these four parts are 20 chapters covering all things hedge funds from the basics to the peripheral issues. The chapter structure of this book is as follows:

PART I: DEMYSTIFYING THE FUNDAMENTALS

The first chapter in this book sets the groundwork for your exploration and understanding of hedge funds, including the present state of the hedge fund industry, and covers many of the important topics with a broad overview. The second chapter is all about the history of hedge funds and why investment managers pursued this type of investing to gain a performance edge over other investors. Chapter 3 focuses on the reasons and benefits of hedge fund investing and answers the proverbial question of "Why hedge funds?" Chapter 4 takes a somewhat contrasting viewpoint and presents the various types of risks associated with hedge fund investing. Be prepared; there are many of them. Following the chapter on risks is a chapter that presents some of the biggest hedge fund failures to date. This chapter discusses the two largest fund failures in history—the fall of Long-Term Capital Management and the fall of Amaranth Advisors. Moving away from the risks and failures, Chapter 6 talks about the key players in the hedge fund trade from the perspective of both investor and hedge fund professional. Chapter 7 provides a solid introduction to investment risk, return, and market dynamics, all important considerations for the hedge fund investor. The final chapter in Part I, Chapter 8, presents the common practices of hedge fund managers or what are typically called their tools of the trade. Here you will get a greater understanding of leverage, derivatives, and selling short—all common techniques of hedge fund managers.

PART II: DEMYSTIFYING THE DIFFERENT TYPES OF HEDGE FUNDS

The second part of this book focuses on the different types of hedge funds found in the marketplace today. Each of the four chapters in Part II present one of the different styles. Chapter 9 presents event-driven hedge funds, or those that attempt to profit from specific events or happenings. This is followed in Chapter 10 by a discussion of tactical hedge funds, or those employed to profit from price bets on the movement in more macro investments. These types of hedge funds are quite popular. Chapter 11 talks about relative-value hedge funds, or those that employ arbitrage to capitalize on small but more certain opportunities. Leverage is often used by these hedge fund managers to magnify the small gains. Chapter 12 discusses hedge funds that are really just a mix of the other hedge fund types. These hybrid hedge funds either employ more than one strategy to manage their funds or become a pool of money and invest in other stand-alone hedge funds. These are call *funds of funds*—the fastest growing type of hedge fund. The last section in this chapter talks about values-based hedge funds, or those managed with a higher calling.

PART III: DEMYSTIFYING HEDGE FUND INVESTING

The third part of this book takes you inside the process of building your own hedge fund portfolio. Chapter 13 begins with a solid introduction to what peak-performance investing and winning portfolios are all about. That being the foundation for successful hedge fund investing. Chapter 14 looks at hedge funds from the perspective of your financial goals and obligations and how best to align them with hedge funds. Chapter 15 takes this idea to the next level by presenting a process you can use to find and pick a suitable hedge fund. Presented are multiple questions you can ask while investigating hedge fund managers for possible investing engagements. Chapter 16, on hedge fund benchmarking, wraps up Part III by discussing how to monitor and measure your investing progress with hedge funds and how to evaluate for continued proper fit.

PART IV: DEMYSTIFYING SPECIAL CONSIDERATIONS

Part IV is all about special considerations and important peripheral topics of hedge funds. Chapter 17 presents the leading misconceptions and fallacies that abound in the hedge fund trade. Knowing these will help you to better avoid some of the pitfalls involved in investing in hedge funds. Chapter 18 highlights the key attributes of hedge funds in an executive summary format. These attributes define exactly what hedge funds are all about. Investors looking to invest like a hedge fund without

actually investing in a hedge fund will find Chapter 19 very interesting. This chapter discusses the latest inventions in alternative investing from the perspective of mutual funds and exchange-traded funds. Chapter 20 provides a brief outlook on what's ahead for hedge funds and how the industry might change and evolve. The Appendices offer some helpful resources to jump-start your endeavor of researching and investing in hedge funds.

PART

I

Demystifying the Fundamentals

CHAPTER 1

Getting Started in Hedge Funds

Understanding the Basics

For investors looking to gain a performance edge, hedge funds could be the answer. Hedge funds are a powerful way for investors to build wealth. But what exactly is a hedge fund? In simple terms, a *hedge fund* is an actively and alternatively managed private investment fund that seeks to generate attractive positive returns in good and bad markets. To accomplish this aim, hedge funds employ many different strategies, financial instruments, and tools of the trade. Some strategies are aggressive, and some are conservative. Hedge funds are managed by professional investment managers and are limited to a small number of "accredited investors." Hedge fund managers receive a percentage of the profits earned by the fund as an incentive to generate performance and drive investor wealth. Unlike most traditional investment managers, hedge fund managers usually have a significant amount of their own wealth invested in their hedge fund. This minimizes conflicts of interest and

gives a substantial amount of comfort to the investor in knowing that the manager's interests are aligned with the investor's interests for protecting and growing the investment.

Today, use of the term *hedge fund* generally is considered to be a misnomer. Many hedge funds do not hedge risk at all, whereas many create more risk. The term was introduced in the 1940s when Alfred Winslow Jones established the first hedge fund by employing long and short strategies enhanced with leverage. Since those early days, hedge funds have grown in both number and complexity. Although the types of hedge funds and the tools of the trade may have changed over the decades, the use of the catchy name has not.

Inside the Hedge Fund Trade

Hedge fund data source companies track anywhere from 4,000 to 6,000 hedge funds, although many experts estimate that there are over 9,000 hedge funds in the world today. Many hedge funds are not tracked owing to their small size and thus are not represented in the numbers.

The hedge fund industry is dynamic in so many ways. Each hedge fund manager and, more specifically, each hedge fund differs greatly. Some of the more important differences include size, composition, structure, culture, performance, and strategies employed. Furthermore, these differences change over time as the market fluctuates or a manager's objectives change. In the investing marketplace, change will create opportunities for growth and return, thus keeping everything in balance.

The hedge fund business has growth by leaps and bounds over the last couple of decades owing to increased investor interest attributed to solid performance. For instance, in 1990, hedge funds managed nearly $40 billion in assets, whereas 15 years later in 2005, assets under management had grown to more than $975 billion, a head-turning growth rate. Much of this increase in assets is attributed to new money, or cash inflows, with the rest of the growth from appreciation of principal. Growth rates for net inflows of new assets into hedge funds have averaged in the high teens per year, with some years experiencing nearly 50 percent growth in assets. Today, the growth rate of new assets is approximately 10 to 11 percent per year.

At the same time as assets were flowing into hedge funds, so too were new hedge funds being established to capitalize on the growth trend. Since 1990, the number of hedge funds has increased dramatically to over 9,000 worldwide with—according to Chicago-based Hedge Fund Research—assets under management of $1.4 trillion. Note that London-based HedgeFund Intelligence estimates total global hedge fund assets at the end of 2006 to be $2 trillion, a 30 percent year over year increase.

Between 2001 and 2004, over 600 new hedge funds were established on average each year.

Hedge funds and mutual funds differ substantially in the amount of assets they manage. There are some hedge funds that are quite large and some that are quite small. Typically, however, the average hedge fund is much smaller than the average mutual fund. Much to the surprise of many investors, there are numerous hedge funds with assets under management of less than $10 million and only a select few with assets under management of greater than $5 billion. With hedge funds, smaller is considered more ideal because smaller means that hedge fund managers can take investment action much faster and without artificially moving the market, as some mutual funds often do. In addition, smaller hedge funds allow managers to take positions in smaller investments and generate opportunistic gains, whereas mutual funds cannot, given that even a small position on their part would equate to a large investment, thus artificially moving the market and drying up gainful opportunities. The performance-incentive fee for hedge funds is used to support this kind of activity to capitalize on smaller opportunities. To further complicate the matter for mutual funds—and thus presenting opportunity to hedge funds—the Securities and Exchange Commission (SEC) established a rule in 1998 that prohibits mutual funds from engaging in short-term trading. Hedge funds are not required to follow this rule, the so-called short short rule.

Specifically, over two-thirds of hedge funds have assets under management in the range of $25 million to $100 million. As for the smaller hedge funds, or those with assets under management of less than $25 million, approximately 22 percent are represented here. The biggest hedge funds, or those over $100 million in assets under management, represent only a fraction of the total number of hedge funds at approximately 10 percent. Hedge funds with over $1 billion in assets under management can be considered "monster" funds. However, fewer than 5 percent of all hedge funds have asset levels this high (see Figure 1–1).

Figure 1-1. Hedge funds by approximate asset size

Assets Managed	% of All Funds
< $10 million	22%
$10 - $25 million	16%
$25 - $100 million	33%
$100 - $200 million	11%
$200 - $500 million	11%
$500 - $1000 million	4%
> $1 billion	3%

The age of hedge funds is as varied as the types of hedge funds. Given the large number of hedge funds that have entered the field within the recent past, the vast majority of hedge funds, approximately 75 percent, have not been in existence for more than 10 years. The newest hedge funds make up approximately 15 percent of all existing funds, and the average age is in the 3- to 8-year range (see Figure 1–2).

Figure 1-2. Hedge funds by approximate age

Age	% of All Funds
< 1 Year	14%
1 to 2 Years	16%
2 to 3 Years	15%
3 to 5 Years	18%
5 to 7 Years	13%
> 7 Years	24%

Hedge Fund Objectives

The primary objective for most hedge funds is to generate attractive absolute returns with long-term growth of capital. This is not always the case because some hedge funds may target other objectives, such as a highly focused risk-reduction strategy. Nevertheless, hedge funds typically strive to achieve a return that exceeds the rate of inflation over the period in question. Doing so will protect what is called *real purchasing power*, or the ability to purchase goods and services with a stable and specific amount of money. Depending on the hedge fund, the strategies employed may be aggressive, whereas other strategies may be less aggressive and sometimes conservative. Protecting purchasing power without placing the portfolio at substantial risk is of primary consideration for most hedge fund managers. Hedge funds looking to accomplish this aim will invest nearly all their assets in the U.S. equity market, as well as international equity markets. Given strong performance track records over time, equity markets provide the best means to achieve this aim.

As with mutual fund managers, hedge fund managers also measure themselves against certain performance benchmarks. Mutual fund managers measure themselves against their peers and, as a result, attempt to deliver solid relative returns.

Relative returns are returns that beat other managers in their peer group. With hedge funds, managers also measure their performance against other hedge fund managers; however, they place significantly more emphasis on what is called *absolute performance* or *absolute returns*. Here, managers first will attempt to deliver positive returns rather than attempt to beat their peers. Delivering performance that surpasses that of similar hedge funds is not the prime directive, only a secondary consideration to delivering positive returns.

As mentioned, relative performance and measurement involve attempting to surpass your peers in performance. Little consideration is given to benchmarks that fall outside the style and strategy of the manager in question. Comparing against a benchmark that tracks investments that are not in the same style or strategy as the manager is a fruitless endeavor. Comparisons must be made using apples to apples and oranges to oranges. For example, large-cap equity managers will measure themselves against the Standard & Poor's (S&P) 500 Index, whereas small-cap equity managers will measure themselves against the Wilshire 5000 Index. Doing so will give the managers and their investors perspective into the value the managers are creating or losing.

For example, if a manager earns 12 percent when the passive index returns 9 percent, then the manager is delivering good relative performance. However, if another manager earns a 6 percent return when the same passive index returns 9 percent, then that manager is losing value. Furthermore, when a manager delivers a return of −4 percent, but the index delivers a −7 percent, then that manager still is delivering good relative performance. With relative performance, no consideration is given to whether or not the return is positive or negative as long as it surpasses the return of the peer group, as measured by the index. Comparing a manager against a benchmark is a solid way to measure the value he or she is adding. However, in down markets, a good relative performance still can be negative—and this means losses. As we all know, you cannot fund your retirement with losses.

Absolute returns are returns that are positive regardless of whether the return is 25 percent or 1 percent. Depending on the amount of risk a manager is willing and able to take, an aggressive fund might target returns of 15 percent or more annually, whereas a moderate-risk fund might target returns of 10 percent annually. Regardless of the degree of positive returns sought by the manager, simply earning positive returns is the primary aim of most hedge fund managers. Delivering a certain level of positive return is the secondary goal. Putting them together, the industry goal is to generate attractive positive returns on a consistent basis. The more attractive, the better, because hedge fund managers receive most of their compensation from performance-incentive fees.

To generate absolute returns, hedge fund managers will employ strategies and tools that take into account existing investments, such as Treasuries. Consequently,

one hedge fund manager may say that he or she wants to generate a premium to five-year Treasury notes, whereas another manager may want to generate a premium to the London Interbank Offered Rate (LIBOR). Given markets that move both up and down, generating absolute returns is not always a forgone conclusion. Thus hedge fund managers will need to manage in such a way that the traditional market does not matter. If a hedge fund is able to accomplish this goal, then it is said to be an *all-weather fund*. Regardless of how well the market does, such funds can weather the market storms.

There is one final note on the aim of generating absolute returns rather than relative returns—that being the elimination of a protective shield for hedge fund managers. When relative return is used to measure performance, a mutual fund manager can use it to defend his or her track record even if the good relative performance is negative. Nevertheless, the manager still has lost money. In contrast, hedge fund managers cannot hide behind this shield. Hedge fund managers are charged with the aim of generating attractive absolute returns, thus giving their investors more comfort in knowing that the manager is looking after their investment with the best of intentions.

Historical Performance

Over the last 20 years or so, hedge funds have performed quite nicely, particularly against the overall equity market, as measured by the S&P 500. At the same time, the aggregate volatility in hedge funds was lower than that of the overall equity market, and lower volatility translates into less investment risk. When you dissect the performance of the market and the performance of hedge funds, you will find that the market outperformed hedge funds during the period of strong equity returns in the late 1990s to early 2000s. However, with the markets losing steam and equities falling precipitously, hedge funds began not only to make up the lost ground but also to surpass the market in total returns.

What is more important than the level of absolute returns of the market and of hedge funds is the number of months, or consistency, that each generates positive performance. During this same time period, the market generated positive returns about two-thirds of the time, whereas hedge funds generated positive returns about three-quarters of the time. Although the market did enjoy a higher average monthly gain over this time period, the market also experienced a higher average monthly loss over the same period. In other words, hedge funds outperformed the market on both an absolute return basis and a risk-adjusted return basis. In aggregate, performance data clearly hedge funds.

One final point to note about performance before moving on is that performance within hedge funds was varied depending on the type of strategy employed by the manager. Over any particular time period in question, one strategy may do well, whereas another may not do so well. For instance, during 1994, merger arbitrage strategies delivered the best hedge fund returns. However, the following year that same strategy underperformed many other hedge fund strategies, even though all were decisively positive. Hedge funds called *funds of funds* provide a solid solution because they typically invest in a number of different hedge funds, and this means enhanced diversification. The end result is lower volatility and higher risk-adjusted returns for the typical hedge fund investor.

Risk and Return Profile

Investment risk and return are inextricably linked. There is no free lunch when it comes to generating returns. If you want to earn a high return, you must accept a corresponding high-risk investment. Any promise of a high return with little to no risk is a sure sign of investment fraud. Nevertheless, generating an attractive positive return is the goal. But what are the sources of risk and the corresponding factors that determine return potential?

With traditional investing, risk and return are determined by three distinct factors. The first is the performance of the market or asset class. The second is the investment strategy (e.g., asset allocation, security selection, or market timing) employed to capture returns in a market or asset class. The third is the skill of the investor or investment manager to implement, monitor, and manage the strategy employed. This means that the return of a mutual fund is subject to the market or asset class performance, which is not typically under the control of the manager— thus the reason for emphasizing relative returns instead of absolute returns. In a traditional market, it is the strategy employed to capture the return of the market or asset class that is the leading determinant of portfolio performance. Study after study has proven that properly allocating your assets is the leading determinant of portfolio performance over time.

Given the ability of hedge funds to go both long and short, the risk of the market or asset classes can be minimized or eliminated. Thus the two factors that determine risk and the corresponding return for the hedge fund investor are the strategy employed by the hedge fund manager and the skill of the hedge fund manager in implementing, monitoring, and managing that strategy. Therefore, the emphasis is on generating absolute returns rather than relative returns. As with traditional investing, it is again the strategy employed by the hedge fund manager than determines the majority of portfolio performance over time. Such strategies could involve selling short large-cap stocks and buying Treasury bonds, buying small-cap stocks using significant leverage, or implementing a strategic asset allocation approach. It is the selection of the strategy that is vitally important.

Hedge fund managers go long, or buy an investment, in order to take advantage of forecasted price advances. Likewise, hedge fund managers go short, or sell a borrowed investment, to take advantage of forecasted price declines. Having the ability, or at least the opportunity, to profit when markets are either advancing or declining is what makes hedge funds so unique and attractive. As a result, hedge fund managers can take pride when generating solid returns, for they exercise significant influence over investment decisions and actions that affect the performance of their fund. On the contrary, traditional managers are handcuffed on what they can do. Thus they have less impact on the performance of their funds. This relationship is simply the nature of the business (see Figure 1–3).

Figure 1-3. Broad sources of risk and return

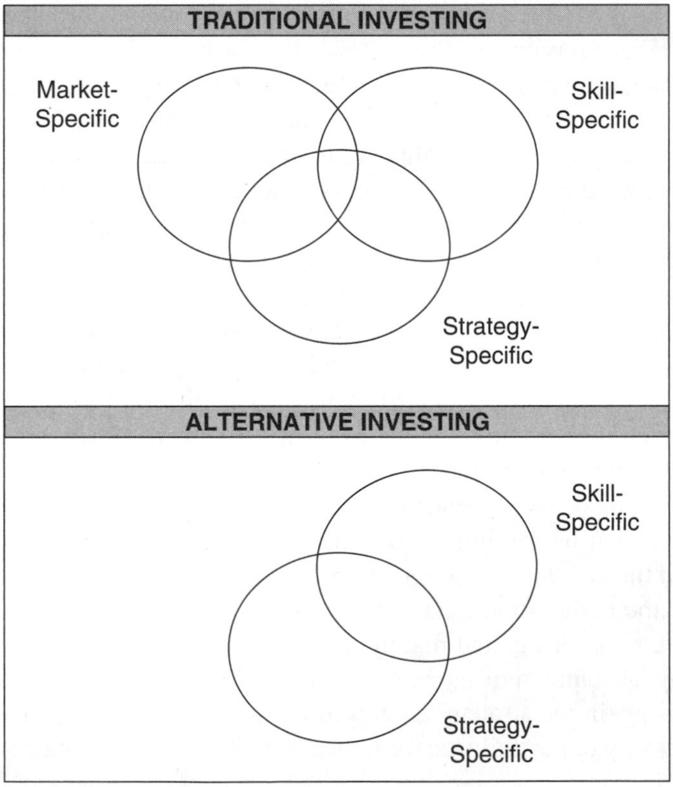

Structure, Organization, and Culture

In hedge fund lingo, a *drawdown* is a period of time that begins with a loss in a hedge fund and continues until that loss is earned back and subsequent new gains are generated. As a whole, hedge funds have achieved solid returns over the long term with low volatility, meaning that there are few drawdowns. This translates into the optimal wealth preservation and accumulation scenario. As a result, allocating a portion of an investment portfolio to hedge funds can be a wise move.

Hedge funds assist investors with achieving their investment goals and objectives by placing those investors with investment managers who take advantage of market inefficiencies in varied and unique ways. The hedge fund structure provides investors with the means to pool their capital together and have that capital invested the right way by a professional manager. Obviously, you will want to do a thorough investigation of a manager to ensure that he or she has the talent to generate solid returns and meet your expectations. Pooling funds with other investors is ideal not only for investors but also for hedge fund managers because it gives them ease in making investment decisions, in taking investment action, and capitalizing on investment opportunities. This structure creates a win-win situation for all involved.

Hedge funds are legally organized in several different ways depending on where the hedge fund is located, what type of investor the hedge fund is targeting, and what the hedge fund is attempting to accomplish. Given the desire to create a pass-through of gains and losses to investors—rather than pay taxes from the hedge fund itself—hedge funds in the United States are formed primarily as either limited partnerships, trusts, or limited liability companies (LLCs). Offshore registration is also commonplace with hedge funds.

STRUCTURE

Under the limited partnership arrangement, hedge funds register with the appropriate state agencies, similar to how other limited partnerships are registered. With a limited partnership, there is a general partner or partners, who are responsible for the decision making, and numerous limited partners. Limited partners are liable only to the extent of their investment in the hedge fund; however, general partners have no such protection and are thus liable above and beyond the amount of their investment. Limited partners are the investors in the hedge fund, whereas general partners are the managers of the hedge fund that assume this role as either an individual or a corporation. Many hedge fund managers operate as general partners through another company as a way to avoid the unlimited personal liability, thus only exposing themselves to unlimited liability given the company serving as the general partner.

Limited partners are held liable only for losses up to the amount of their investment. These limited partnership interests cannot be sold to other investors but can be sold to, or redeemed by, the hedge fund partnership provided that certain established guidelines are met and followed.

With offshore hedge funds, the corporate tax structure typically is employed. Although this form of legal organization provides taxation on the corporate level, this usually does not occur with offshore funds, given where the hedge fund is specifically organized. Tax-friendly locations such as the Cayman Islands and the Bahamas do not tax on the corporate level. This provides the motivation and justification for organizing hedge funds offshore. Offshore hedge funds tend to consist of non-U.S. investors, although certain U.S. tax-exempt institutions do participate. Many hedge fund companies operate both an onshore, or U.S. organized, hedge fund and an offshore hedge fund that mirror one another. This expands the client base, provides for additional hedge fund assets, and keeps open the limited number of slots each hedge fund is able to provide to domestic investors in domestic hedge funds. Hedge fund assets remain segregated even under this scenario, however (see Figure 1–4).

Approximately 80 percent of all hedge fund managers in the world work somewhere in the United States. However, only about 35 to 40 percent of all hedge funds are legally organized in the United States, with most registered in tax-friendly Delaware. Thus 60 to 65 percent are organized outside the United States as offshore funds. The majority of the offshore funds are organized in the Cayman Islands, followed by the British Virgin Islands, Bermuda, Ireland, and the Bahamas (see Figure 1–5).

Hedge fund companies themselves also differ from company to company. However, the typical hedge fund company is significantly smaller and with a flatter organizational structure than a typical mutual fund company. This design enables hedge fund managers to quickly and easily respond to changes in the market and the introduction of new information that can influence the price of an investment. Some hedge funds are designed around one or two key people, thus making the decision

Figure 1-4. Domestic versus offshore hedge funds

CATEGORY	DOMESTIC	OFFSHORE
Liquidity	Less	More
Structure	As limited partnership	As corporations
Number of Clients Permitted	Limited number	Potentially unlimited
Accredited Investor Limitations	Commonly done	Generally none
U.S. Investors Permitted	Yes	Typically no
U.S. Institutions Permitted	Yes	Typically yes
Fixed Set of Regulations	Yes	No, depends on country

Figure 1-5. Approximate domicile of hedge fund registration

Registration	% of All Funds
Delaware	30%
Cayman Islands	28%
British Virgin Islands	10%
Other	9%
Bermuda	8%
Ireland	3%
California	2%
New York	2%
Bahamas	2%
Guernsey	2%
Luxembourg	2%

making even more robust. Mutual fund organizations are not designed with this flexibility.

Many hedge fund managers have quite varied and diverse backgrounds that provide hedge funds with highly specialized knowledge and experience. Most hedge fund managers come from an investment background, and many come with an entrepreneur attitude. Their typical first foray into hedge funds is to establish an investment company, launch a hedge fund, and invest a significant portion of their assets in their hedge fund. Rarely will you find a hedge fund where the manager, or general partner, does not have some stake in the returns. Often managers will manage assets of friends and family as the fund grows and gains exposure. When managers run hedge funds with their own money and that of their friends and family, they have an extra incentive to generate attractive absolute returns. Generating attractive absolute returns is the name of the game for hedge funds, and in doing so, the time and effort needed to market the hedge fund are minimized. Given hedge fund regulation, managers are handcuffed in the marketing and advertising activities they can do to promote their funds to prospects. This is one of the trade-offs with hedge funds. Mutual funds are not handcuffed by these same marketing restrictions and can advertise and promote much more freely, within certain boundaries, of course. On a side note, many mutual fund organizations are entering the hedge fund trade and are training their traditional mutual fund managers on how to run a successful hedge fund.

SEPARATE ACCOUNTS

Most hedge funds are formed as one big pool or account. All the assets from investors are commingled in the one account and managed by the hedge fund team.

However, on certain occasions, hedge funds will establish what are called *separate accounts* for large hedge fund investors, typically institutions. Institutions prefer this format because they are the only investor with assets in the account. This provides for greater access to the hedge fund management team, enhanced transparency, and ability to better monitor the investment. Many hedge funds do not like this format because it means greater burdens on the fund. Some hedge funds will accept this relationship, and some will require that the assets be commingled with the assets of the other investors.

Investor-Manager Relationship

Investing in a mutual fund is quite different from investing in a hedge fund. Although there are many similarities, there are sharp contrasts. One of the primary contrasts involves the investor-manager relationship. With mutual funds, an investor becomes a shareholder of the manager. The same cannot be said for hedge funds because the investor and the manager become business partners. This is evidenced by the legal arrangement they enter into with the limited partnership. A mutual fund manager may have no material personal assets in the fund he or she manages, but a hedge fund manager will have a material investment that sometimes makes the manager the single largest investor in the fund. Furthermore, the hedge fund manager is encouraged to not have investments outside the fund. Activities such as *front running*—where the manager places trades in his or her personal account outside the hedge fund and then makes trades in the same security in the hedge fund to create favorable price movement—are eliminated when all the manager's investments are in the fund. Doing so will provide the manager with added incentive and the investor with added comfort regarding aligned interests and the pursuit of performance. The key point here is that investors should investigate the level of personal assets that the hedge fund manager has invested in the hedge fund. If a certain hedge fund manager is unwilling to invest in the hedge fund he or she manages, why would you invest in that fund?

Typical individual hedge fund investors are affluent to ultra-affluent individuals and families. However, this is beginning to change as more people invest in funds of funds partially due to their lower contribution requirements. In addition, it used to be commonplace for the majority of hedge fund investors to originate from inside the United States. However, this trend is changing as more hedge funds are established around the globe, thus opening up opportunities to foreign investors. At the same time, hedge funds have become more enticing to institutional investors such as pension funds, insurance companies, and endowments. Hedge funds are responding to this increased interest from institutions and disclosing more information on the assets held and the strategies employed by their managers. This, in turn, motivates more institutions to invest in hedge funds, creating a giant

Figure 1-6. Approximate minimum initial hedge fund investment

$ Investment	% of All Funds
< $10,000	4%
$10,000 to $50,000	8%
$50,000 to $100,000	16%
$100,000 to $250,000	18%
$250,000 to $500,000	18%
$500,000 to $1,000,000	29%
> $1,000,000	7%

disclosure-investing circle. Given that institutions tend to be much larger than the average affluent investor, hedge funds are more than willing to accommodate them. This is not always the case, but it holds true most of the time.

Given the limitations imposed by the SEC on the number of investors allowed to invest in any one hedge fund, hedge funds aim to maximize their assets under management by establishing minimum initial investment requirements. The minimum typically ranges from $100,000 to $5 million, but the most popular range is between $600,000 and $1 million. More than 25 percent of hedge funds have this requirement (see Figure 1–6).

During the startup phase, most hedge funds have lower minimum initial investment requirements as a way to entice investment. However, as the hedge fund grows in both asset size and number of investors, it will raise its requirement with the goal of maximizing total assets under management.

Much to the disappointment of investors, hedge funds typically limit, or restrict altogether, the amount and type of information on the various assets held in the hedge fund and the specific strategies employed by the hedge fund management team. Disclosure of information has become the latest crusade of the SEC, and before long, we probably will see a balance struck. Doing so will help investors to make more informed decisions, to better monitor hedge fund investments, and, unfortunately, drive up hedge fund costs and homologize the hedge fund trade.

Liquidity Considerations

Mutual funds and hedge funds differ in the degree of liquidity they provide to investors. Mutual funds are required to provide daily liquidity, whereas hedge funds are not. With mutual funds, investors can deposit and withdraw cash from the fund quite easily. The same cannot be said for hedge funds given their minimal liquidity. With hedge funds, investors are permitted to withdraw their cash only at certain prescribed intervals. Some hedge funds allow contributions and withdrawals only once per year or even once every couple of years. More flexible hedge funds allow for monthly or quarterly contributions and withdrawals. The most common provision allows for annual contributions and withdrawals. Given that hedge fund investors typically are wealthy individuals or institutions, liquidity restrictions are not especially burdensome.

In the hedge fund industry there is a term that describes this lack of liquidity and restrictions on investments and withdrawals. This term is *lockup*. Lockup also can be the period of time new investors must wait before their investment can be withdrawn, subject to standard liquidity provisions, of course. The most common lockup period is one year.

Lastly, hedge fund investors must provide notice to hedge fund managers regarding their intent to withdraw invested capital. These notice periods are often required to give the hedge fund manager sufficient time to deliver the required liquidity for withdrawal. This can take anywhere from a couple of weeks to a couple of months depending on the assets held in the fund.

Some hedge funds will institute longer lockup periods to give investors the impression that the hedge fund is more private and exclusive than other hedge funds. The concept of the lockup is not necessarily a bad thing. Lockups give the hedge fund manager the ability and freedom to employ typical hedge fund strategies that otherwise would be hampered given no lockup. These strategies include selling short, high leverage, and most important in the case of lockups, holding illiquid investments. Being forced to sell illiquid investments to satisfy investor withdrawals may require the hedge fund manager to sell at unfavorable prices and sometimes create losses.

Depending on the hedge fund, some funds will deliver securities rather than cash to satisfy investor withdrawals. This is not done commonly, but it is possible for hedge funds that hold sizable positions in illiquid or private investments. A fund's offering memorandum will state if this is possible.

Lastly, hedge funds typically require holding back a certain amount of withdrawals, commonly 10 percent, for investors who want to withdraw 100 percent of their investment. This is called the *holdover provision*. The 10 percent held back will be paid to the investor once the year-end audit is complete.

Strategies and Tools of the Trade

What makes hedge funds so unique and powerful? The answer is the strategies and tools they employ. Hedge funds are managed by intelligent, hardworking managers who can employ complex merger arbitrage strategies or simple long position strategies. Many traditional money managers also employ strategies and give them fancy names to provide them with life in the hope of attracting investors. Nevertheless, the availability and use of the varied investment strategies and tools by hedge fund managers provides them with a significant advantage over traditional managers. This does not mean that it is a forgone conclusion that hedge fund managers will outperform traditional money managers, but the opportunity to do just that is greater—with the opportunity for greater risk as well. Hedge fund strategies are called *alternative strategies*, whereas the other strategies, used by mutual fund managers, are called *traditional strategies*. For example, fixed-income arbitrage is an alternative strategy commonly employed by hedge fund managers but not employed by traditional investment managers. The SEC restricts mutual funds from employing alternative strategies under most conditions.

Mutual fund managers invest in stocks and bonds that they believe will increase in price, and surpassing an appropriate benchmark is the aim. Hedge fund managers, on the other hand, typically employ alternative strategies and tools either to leverage existing opportunities or to take advantage of new opportunities. These strategies can be complex or simple, with many somewhere in the middle.

There are four broad categories, or styles, of hedge funds, which can be divided into multiple hedge fund strategies. The strategies hedge fund managers often employ at times will deviate slightly from the following strategies, but those strategies still will resemble one of those in the broad category. Combining strategies in multiple categories is also common. Regardless of the strategy, each has the aim of generating attractive absolute returns. The following are the primary strategies employed by hedge fund managers, grouped by style:

- *Tactical (also called directional)*
    - *Macrocentric*. Strategy whereby the hedge fund manager invests in securities that capitalize on domestic and global market opportunities.
    - *Managed futures*. Strategy whereby the hedge fund manager invests in commodities derivatives with a momentum focus, hoping to ride the trend to attractive profits.
    - *Long/short equity*. Strategy whereby the hedge fund manager capitalizes on opportunities by either purchasing equities or selling short equities.
    - *Sector-specific*. Strategy whereby the hedge fund manager invests in specific markets by going long, short, or both.
    - *Emerging markets*. Strategy whereby the hedge fund manager invests in less developed, but emerging markets.
    - *Market timing*. Strategy whereby the hedge fund manager either times mutual fund buys and sells or invests in asset classes that are forecasted to perform well in the short term.

- *Selling short.* Strategy whereby the hedge fund manager sells short borrowed securities with the aim of buying them back in the future at lower prices thus making a profit.

- *Relative value (also called arbitrage)*

  - *Convertible arbitrage.* Strategy whereby the hedge fund manager takes advantage of perceived price inequality with convertible bonds and the associated equity securities.

  - *Fixed-income arbitrage.* Strategy whereby the hedge fund manager purchases a fixed-income security and immediately sells short another fixed-income security to minimize market risk and profit from changing price spreads.

  - *Equity-market-neutral.* Strategy whereby the hedge fund manager buys an equity security and sells short a related equity index to offset market risk.

- *Event-driven*

  - *Distressed securities.* Strategy whereby the hedge fund manager invests in the equity or debt of struggling companies at often steep discounts to estimated values.

  - *Reasonable value.* Strategy whereby the hedge fund manager invests in securities that are selling at discounts to their estimated values as a result of being out of favor or being relatively unknown in the investment community.

  - *Merger arbitrage.* Strategy whereby the hedge fund manager invests in merger-related situations where there are unique opportunities for profit.

  - *Opportunistic events.* Strategy whereby the hedge fund manager invests in securities given short-term event-driven situations considered to offer temporary profitable opportunities.

- *Hybrid*

  - *Multistrategy.* Strategy whereby the hedge fund manager employs two or more strategies at one time.

  - *Funds of funds.* Strategy whereby the hedge fund manager invests in two or more stand-alone hedge funds rather than directly investing in securities.

  - *Values-based.* Strategy whereby the hedge fund manager invests according to certain personal values and principles (see Figure 1–7).

Figure 1-7. Characteristics of hedge fund styles

HEDGE FUND STYLE	STRATEGIES	CORRELATION	VOLATILITY	LEVERAGE	RISK
Tactical	Macrocentric, Managed Futures, Emerging Markets, Sector Specific, Selling, Short Long/Short Equity	High	High to Very High	Moderate	High
Relative-Value	Fixed-Income Arbitrage, Convertible Arbitrage, Equity Market Neutral	Low	Low	Very High	Low
Event-Driven	Distressed Securities, Merger Arbitrage, Reasonable Value, Opportunistic Events	Low	Low	Exceptionally High	Medium
Hybrid	Multistrategy, Fund of Hedge Funds, Values-based	Low	Low to Moderate	Low to Moderate	Low to Medium

Some of the preceding strategies are used to take advantage of long-term opportunities, whereas others are defensive in nature and can be thought of as simple insurance. Each strategy is discussed in much greater detail in Part II of this book. Many hedge fund strategies are more risky than traditional strategies; however, some hedge fund strategies actually are less risky than traditional strategies.

One last thought on the strategies employed by both hedge funds and mutual funds. Even though hedge funds have the opportunity to engage in risky strategies, it is possible for a hedge fund to build a low-risk portfolio. At the same time, mutual funds can be quite risky, even though they adhere to each and every guideline and requirement of the SEC. Do not be fooled into thinking that hedge funds are always more risky than their traditional counterpart, mutual funds (see Figure 1–8).

Funds of Funds

Funds of funds, also referred to as *funds of hedge funds*, are very much what they appear to be—hedge funds that invest in other hedge funds. Funds of funds create pools of capital and then invest that capital in attractive stand-alone hedge funds. They are typically organized using the same limited-partnership or LLC method as other hedge funds. As such, there are general partners who make all the investment decisions and assume unlimited liability, and there are limited partners who assume risk to the level of their investment only.

Figure 1-8. Assets under management by strategy

Strategy	% of All Funds
Selling Short	29%
Equity Hedge	19%
Event-Driven	13%
Macrocentric	11%
Managed Futures	6%
Distressed Securities	5%
Convertible Arbitrage	5%
Sector Specific	4%
Emerging Markets	3%
Fixed-Income Arbitrage	3%
Equity Market Neutral	2%
Merger Arbitrage	1%
Market Timing	0%

Unlike other hedge funds, funds of funds managers do not make direct investments in securities. Rather, they invest in two or more stand-alone hedge funds. The primary decisions each fund of funds manager must make involves risk management, market analysis and direction, appropriate hedge fund strategies, and selecting hedge funds that are expected to generate attractive absolute returns. Good managers will build funds of funds that exhibit low correlations with the equity market, generate solid performance, and exhibit low volatility. As a result, these funds maximize returns for the risk they incur.

As with mutual funds that pool money from investors and provide enhanced diversification, hedge funds do quite the same. Fund of funds managers allocate to multiple hedge funds to enhance the diversification benefit to their investors. In addition, funds of funds also provide investors with the ability to invest in other hedge funds that they might otherwise be restricted from investing in given their high contribution requirements. A fund of funds will pool its invested capital and essentially become one investor, thus meeting the requirement to invest in other hedge funds. In addition, funds of funds also give individual investors more comfort in knowing that they will not need to monitor multiple hedge fund managers to evaluate performance and ensure proper fit. The fund of funds manager will accomplish this task. Funds of funds provide for greater hedge fund access, enhanced diversification to the masses of investors, and reduced manager oversight. However, these benefits do not come free. There is an added cost.

The cost of gaining these benefits is an extra layer of fees. The first is the funds of funds fee, and the second is the fees charged by the hedge funds in which the funds of funds invest. Some fund of funds managers charge a performance incentive fee, whereas others do not. Funds of funds without the performance-incentive fee or with a reduced version of it may offer excellent ways for investors to enter the hedge fund market. Funds of funds are quickly becoming the leading way for the mass of investors to take advantage of hedge funds.

The bottom line with funds of funds is to do your homework on the fund to ensure that the extra layer of fees is offset by the three primary benefits—enhanced diversification, reduced manager oversight, and greater access to other hedge funds.

Management Fees and Performance-Incentive Fees

Hedge funds typically charge two types of fees—an investment-management fee and a performance-incentive fee. In contrast, mutual funds typically only charge one type of fee—an investment-management fee. With an investment-management fee, investors pay a fee based entirely on the amount of assets under management. Traditional equity mutual funds charge a fixed percentage fee of anywhere between 1.00 and 1.75 percent of the assets under management. Some will charge even more. Many investors will not see this fee being deducted from their account because it is deducted each trading day whereas the price of the fund is adjusted for the amount of the daily fee. Charging a fee based on the dollar amount of assets under management is ideal for money managers because fee income will rise at a faster rate than will expenses given increasing assets under management. The drawback of this arrangement to the investor is that the money manager may be more focused on gaining additional assets through new business than on generating solid performance. This is an unfortunate conflict of interest.

This potential disconnect is minimized significantly with hedge funds. Tying compensation to performance thus is emphasized. As with mutual funds, hedge funds also charge an investment-management fee based on the assets under management. This fee typically runs around 1 percent, with some hedge funds charging a higher fee and some charging a lower fee.

Hedge funds add a new element to the traditional fees in that they charge a fee based on how well your investment performs. This is called a performance-incentive fee. This annual fee is rather standardized at 20 percent of profits earned by the fund. Some hedge funds charge quarterly and some monthly, but an annual charge is the norm. Funds of funds charge a lower performance-incentive fee, if they charge one at all. Performance-incentive fees can be quite lucrative to a successful hedge fund manager, and when the manager benefits, so too will the investors because this means that their portfolios would have increased in value. This is a true win-win situation for both partners. Moreover, performance-incentive fees highly motivate hedge fund managers to be diligent in their research, make smart decisions, initiate wise investment actions, and manage positions with the utmost care and skill.

There are two safeguards that hedge fund managers put in place to protect investors and make them feel more comfortable with performance-incentive fees. First, some hedge funds charge performance-incentive fees only if the return of the fund is above a specified hurdle rate. This hurdle can be the rate on Treasury bills or the LIBOR. Fund performance below a hurdle will not trigger a performance-incentive fee.

Example

In year one, the Discovery Hedge Fund generates a 3 percent return but has a 4 percent hurdle-rate safeguard. As a result, no performance-incentive fee is charged. However, in year two, the Discovery Hedge Fund generates a return of 20 percent. Since the return generated is higher than the 4 percent hurdle rate, the performance-incentive fee is triggered. In this case, a performance-incentive fee will be charged on the difference between the return generated and the hurdle rate, or 16 percent (20 – 4 percent).

The second way that hedge funds protect investors is by instituting a safeguard where performance-incentive fees are triggered only when new profits are generated. In other words, if an investor earns a profit that is only returning the value of the fund to a previous level, then a performance-incentive fee is not charged. This is called the *high-water mark*. Covering the same ground twice and being charged twice for profits that were gained, lost, and regained is simply not appropriate. Portfolios must venture to new highs before new performance-incentive fees are triggered.

Most hedge funds do not have hurdle-rate safeguards; however, most do have high-water-mark safeguards. Each hedge fund details how and when fees are charged in their offering and disclosure documents. Any fees charged are used by the hedge fund to pay salaries and expenses related to legal, accounting, audit, administration, and operations.

Tax Considerations

As investments that pool funds, mutual funds and hedge funds are very similar in regard to tax issues. Both are considered *pass-through entities*. This means that hedge funds do not pay taxes but instead pass all gains and losses to the investors.

If certain requirements are not met, then mutual funds are forced to pay taxes, but as you can imagine, this rarely, if ever, occurs. Hedge funds are not forced to pay taxes at the fund level.

The frequency and amount hedge fund investors pay in taxes depend on the specific hedge fund and, more important, on the type of strategy employed by the manager. The actions of the hedge fund manager are the leading determinant of tax consequences. For instance, hedge fund strategies that emphasize significant trading typically will result in higher capital gains taxes than will strategies where little trading is executed. Capital gains taxes are incurred when an investment is sold for a profit. The two types of capital gains taxes are *short term*, meaning gains generated within one holding year, and *long term*, meaning gains generated from holding an investment for longer than one year. Short-term capital gains are taxed at the investor's federal income tax rate, whereas long-term capital gains are taxed at a somewhat more favorable rate.

The other tax consideration to be aware of is the tax incurred on dividends and interest payments. This income is received from stock dividends and interest payments from bonds. Depending on the type of hedge fund, an investor may or may not be exposed to this tax consideration. Many stocks do pay dividends, and this will create taxable consequences.

Not only does the type of hedge fund make a difference regarding tax consequences, but so too does the type of investor. Individual investors generally hold taxable portfolios, whereas many institutions hold tax-exempt portfolios. Thus tax considerations do not make a material difference to tax-exempt institutions because they do not incur tax consequences. However, individual investors need to care about taxes because taxes can take a series bite out of earnings. It is not what you earn when the day is over but rather what you keep.

Regulatory Considerations

Hedge funds are limited in both the number and type of investors they can have by the SEC and the well-known Investment Company Act of 1940. This act provides very specific guidelines as to what type of investor hedge funds can accept and the total number of people permitted in the fund. The act also restricts hedge funds from publicly marketing their hedge fund. This act restricts the number of investors in any one stand-alone hedge fund to 99 accredited investors. In December of 2006, the SEC increased the level of net worth investors must have in order to qualify for accredited investor status. Prior to this time, investors needed to have a net worth of $1 million after excluding their personal residence and any automobiles owned.

The following are the new requirements that must be met to qualify for accredited investor status:

- Earned at least $200,000 annually in income for the past two years and have a reasonable expectation of doing so into the future
- Earned, with the spouse, at least $300,000 annually in income
- Has a net worth of at least $2.5 million after excluding the personal residence and automobiles

Many financial professionals do not foresee any material impact on the hedge fund industry from this rule change. Given that most hedge fund investors already have a net worth far greater than the $2.5 million required, these same investors will qualify as accredited investors. Capital inflows to hedge funds should be relatively unaffected.

HOW THE SEC VIEWS HEDGE FUNDS

Although not statutorily defined by the SEC, the entity charged with regulating the securities markets and investment activities of the nation, statements made by the SEC provide a look at how it views hedge funds. The SEC has described hedge funds in the following ways:

> *"Hedge fund" is a general, non-legal term used to describe private, unregistered investment pools that traditionally have been limited to sophisticated, wealthy investors. Hedge funds are not mutual funds and, as such, are not subject to the numerous regulations that apply to mutual funds for the protection of investors—including regulations requiring a certain degree of liquidity, regulations requiring that mutual fund shares be redeemable at any time, regulations protecting against conflicts of interest, regulations to assure fairness in the pricing of fund shares, disclosure regulations, regulations limiting the use of leverage, and more.*
>
> —SEC, INVEST WISELY: AN INTRODUCTION TO MUTUAL FUNDS

> *Like mutual funds, hedge funds pool investors' money and invest those funds in financial instruments in an effort to make a positive return. However, unlike mutual funds, hedge funds are not registered with the SEC. This means that hedge funds are subject to very few regulatory controls. In addition, many hedge fund managers are not required to register with the SEC and therefore are not subject to regular SEC oversight. Because of this lack of regulatory oversight, hedge funds historically have been available to investors and large institutions, and have limited investors through high investment minimums (e.g., $2.5 million).*

Many hedge funds seek to profit in all kinds of markets by pursuing leveraging and other speculative investment practices that may increase the risk of investment loss.

—SEC, HEDGING YOUR BETS: A HEADS UP ON HEDGE
FUNDS AND FUNDS OF FUNDS

REPORTING, DISCLOSURE, AND DOCUMENTATION

In the past, hedge funds reported their performance on a monthly or quarterly basis. However, given the increased interest in hedge funds by investors, performance is now being calculated more frequently. This creates extra burdens for hedge funds, but it is well worth the effort to gain top investors. Nevertheless, monthly reporting of performance is most common, although no standardized reporting is available. The CFA Institute, the most prominent industry association for investment professionals, highly encourages standardization of performance measurement and analysis. In situations where the investor does not know the composition of the portfolio with a hedge fund manager, then he or she will be solely responsible for the performance measurement. The trend is positive, however, because more and more hedge funds provide asset holdings and thus improve transparency and performance measurement and reporting.

New potential investors will receive three different documents prior to investing in a hedge fund. These documents include the following:

- Offering memorandum

- Limited-partnership agreement

- Subscription agreement

An *offering memorandum*, sometimes referred to as a *price placement memorandum* or *prospectus*, is the primary source of information to the investor about the hedge fund. This document details such key points as the manager's background, risks involved, conflicts of interest present, limited-partnership agreement points of interest, fees and charges, redemption provisions, and how fees and charges are calculated. Other information specific to the hedge fund is also provided, all with the objective of giving the investor more information to make a sound investment decision. As regulatory requirements and oversight increase, the offering memorandum will become more detailed in both breadth and depth of disclosure.

The limited-partnership agreement is the formal contract between the investor and the hedge fund manager. This document outlines how the relationship will be structured—limited and general partners—and the rights and responsibilities of each partner. How the hedge fund is to be operated is also fully documented in the limited-partnership agreement.

The subscription agreement is essentially an application for an investor to become a limited partner of the hedge fund. This "petition," so to speak, requires certain disclosures from the investor to ensure that he or she satisfies the accredited investor requirements as established and mandated by the SEC. On this form an investor will find questions relating to annual income, total net worth, liquid assets, trading experience, and risk tolerance. Each investor is required to submit a completed form along with a check for the initial investment, which typically is around $1 million (significantly lower for funds of funds, however). Simply accepting the application does not obligate the hedge fund to permit the investor to become a limited partner. However, if the investor is accepted, the initial check is invested into the hedge fund, and a confirmation letter is generated from the hedge fund manager to the investor.

Only onshore hedge funds have the limited-partnership agreement because off-shore hedge funds are not typically structured as such. Additionally, mutual funds provide prospectuses that detail the investment objectives, costs, holdings, and other material disclosures of the fund. Hedge funds provide similar disclosures in the *offering memorandum.*

SEC DOCUMENTS COMMONLY FILED

The SEC requires hedge funds to file certain documents if they reach specific asset thresholds. These documents include the following:

13-F

All investment firms, hedge fund and traditional, must file a 13-F form when they manage over $100 million in assets. This document details the specific holdings of the investment manager, and clues as to his or her strategy can be identified with this form. Short positions are not included because they are borrowed shares and not owned by the investment firm.

13-D

The SEC requires all investment firms to file a 13-D form when that firm owns more than 5 percent of the total outstanding stock of a company and is considered an active investor. As a result, some hedge funds will need to file a 13-D form, and some will not.

13-G

Much like the 13-D form, a 13-G form is required by the SEC when an investment firm owns more than 5 percent of the total outstanding stock of a company and is considered a passive investor. This is in contrast to the 13-D, where the investor is considered active. This form does not have to be filed for equity stock positions that constitute less than 5 percent of the total outstanding market value.

ADV

The ADV is the official application for investment advisor registration. All traditional investment advisors who are not associated with a broker-dealer must file this form. Investment advisors with less than $25 million under management do not file with the SEC and instead file with their state of domicile. As of late 2006, hedge funds do not have to file this form because U.S. courts struck down the requirement as imposed by the SEC. The SEC has made this a priority because it wants to register all hedge fund managers. New regulations are being planned and are not far off from being implemented. The courts may strike down similar future regulations, but that will not stop the SEC from trying.

Winning Hedge Fund Investing: The 9-P Process

The entire process of investing in hedge funds can be illustrated in nine steps called the 9-P process. This process covers everything from formulating your initial ideas and plans to monitoring your hedge fund portfolio for performance and continued strategic fit. Please note that this process is only a snapshot of what you will learn in the rest of this book, specifically Part III, which is dedicated to hedge fund investing from a personal vantage point. The 9-P process is as follows:

1. *Prioritize.* In this step, investors need to identify exactly what they are hoping to accomplish by investing in hedge funds. In addition, they need to ensure that allocating portfolio assets to hedge funds is suitable and appropriate for their goals and risk profile.

2. *Plan.* In this step, investors establish and formalize their investment policy in a written plan. Such things as number of hedge funds, how much to invest in hedge funds, and which types of hedge funds are included in the plan.

3. *Pinpoint.* In this step, investors will take a proactive approach to investigate and source hedge fund alternatives. Investors can obtain this information from a friend or family member, through their financial advisor, by

conducting online searches, or perhaps after reading a story in the financial news.

4. *Pursue*. In this step, investors will perform initial screening and identify hedge funds that meet their criteria. Investors then will pursue all hedge funds that pass this filtering.

5. *Probe*. In this step, investors need to be diligent in their evaluation of hedge funds and key people. To remain consistent, I have included four areas, each beginning with the letter P, that investors should investigate.

   a. *Performance*. Investors should conduct a quantitative investigation of the hedge fund by targeting such areas as level of historical returns, volatility of historical returns, and dispersion of historical returns. Risk measurements should be conducted.

   b. *Pedigree*. Investors should conduct a qualitative investigation of the hedge fund by targeting such things as the educational background, investment experience, and possible disciplinary history of the hedge fund manager.

   c. *Partnership*. Investors should conduct due diligence on the operational aspects of the hedge fund. Some of the key areas to investigate include liquidity and lockup provisions, performance safeguards, and quality of the technology systems.

   d. *Process*. Investors should conduct investigations into the investment process employed by the hedge fund manager. This includes such items as investment strategy, use of derivatives and leverage, and buying and selling methodology.

6. *Ponder*. In this step, investors will review and evaluate all the information obtained during the probing step. This step is best thought of as the final assessment and filtering before selecting one or more hedge funds with which to invest.

7. *Pick*. In this step, investors will make the formal selection of one or more hedge funds that meet their criteria and provide the investor with the greatest degree of comfort in knowing that the investment will go well.

8. *Position*. In this step, investors will make the initial hedge fund allocation and position that investment within the context of their overall portfolio.

Investment decisions for the total portfolio will now include the hedge fund allocation regardless of whether or not the money is combined under one investment manager or reported on the same monthly account statement.

9. *Police*. In this step, investors will monitor, measure, and evaluate the hedge fund investment for continued strategic fit and satisfactory performance. If the investment is doing well, then nothing needs to happen. However, if either strategic fit or performance has weakened since the initial investment, then perhaps a discussion with the hedge fund manager is appropriate or maybe a termination of the engagement is needed (see Figure 1–9).

Figure 1-9. The 9-P process

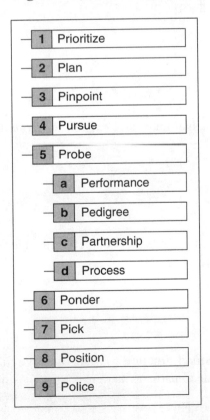

Quiz for Chapter 1

1. Approximately how many hedge funds exist today?

    a. 1,000

    b. 5,000

    c. 9,000

    d. 15,000

2. The short short rule says that hedge funds cannot sell short more than 200 percent of their equity assets.

    a. True

    b. False

3. Approximately what percent of all hedge funds have assets under management of over $1 billion?

    a. 5 percent

    b. 20 percent

    c. 50 percent

    d. 70 percent

4. What percent of hedge funds have existed for more than 10 years?

    a. 10 percent

    b. 25 percent

    c. 40 percent

    d. 65 percent

5. Which island nation is the leading choice for hedge fund startups?

    a. British Virgin Islands

    b. Cayman Islands

    c. Ireland

    d. Bahamas

6. The typical hedge fund structure consists of hedge fund managers, considered the general partners, and investors, considered the _____ partners.

    a. Mutual

    b. General II

    c. Capital

    d. Limited

7. Most hedge funds in the United States are organized as sub-Chapter C corporations.

    a. True

    b. False

8. There are four types of hedge fund management styles. Which style emphasizes directional price bets?

    a. Tactical

    b. Arbitrage

    c. Relative-value

    d. Strategic

9. Which of the following hedge fund styles does not invest directly in securities but rather invests in stand-alone hedge funds?

    a. Event-driven

    b. Relative-value

    c. Funds of funds

    d. Multistrategy

10. The Securities and Exchange Commission mandates that only certain investors can invest in hedge funds. What are these investors called?

    a. Certified

    b. Accredited

    c. Permitted

    d. Approved

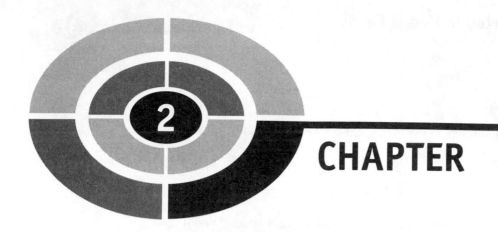

CHAPTER **2**

History of Hedge Funds

In Search of the Performance Edge

Origins of Hedge Funds

Hedging risk began in the nineteenth century when commodity producers and merchants began employing forward contracts to lock in prices and ensure the delivery of a standardized product. This was the forerunner of the modern-day hedge fund.

Most investment professionals would agree that the first recorded hedge fund was established in the late 1940s by Alfred Winslow Jones, a 1923 Harvard graduate, 1941 Ph.D. graduate from Columbia University, and a journalist with *Fortune* magazine early in his career. During his days with *Fortune* magazine, Jones became a student of the financial markets and engrossed himself with its inner workings. While researching and writing an article in 1948 on the current investing landscape and on how hedging can enhance returns and reduce risk, Jones concluded that he could design a better way to manage money and achieve abnormal returns over time. As a result, in 1949 Jones established what many consider the first recorded hedge fund to take advantage of market swings, both up and down, to generate the enhanced returns and reduce risk that he previously wrote about. To establish this hedge fund, Jones pooled together $60,000 from investors with $40,000 of his own money. Soon afterward, he was employing the tools he hypothesized would deliver returns in both up and down markets. The two primary tools he employed in his hedge fund were selling short and leverage. These are the same two tools that many hedge fund managers use today.

His investment general partnership, A.W. Jones & Co., sought to take long positions in individual equity securities when the market was rising and to take short positions in individual securities when the market was falling. Betting correctly, regardless of the change in the market, would, of course, produce a positive return. In times of greater confidence in which direction he thought the market would move, Alfred Jones employed leverage—or borrowing from a prime broker to buy more of an investment—thus magnifying the returns of his long or short positions. Jones called the use of selling short and leveraging "speculative tools used for conservative purposes." In 1952, Jones changed the legal structure of his hedge fund from the established general partnership into the more advantageous and commonly used structure of today, the limited partnership. About the same time as the change in legal structure, Jones introduced for the first time a performance-incentive fee that he set at 20 percent of profits. Jones also was the first hedge fund manager to place a significant amount of his own money in the hedge fund he managed. Most hedge fund managers today follow these same two concepts—performance-incentive fees and investing manager money in the fund—introduced by Alfred Jones.

Given Jones' stellar track record, in 1966, *Fortune* magazine published an article on Jones and his hedge fund entitled, "The Jones' That Nobody Can Keep Up With." The article praised Jones and his track record and revealed that his performance bested even the top-performing mutual fund by 44 percent and the top five-year-performing mutual fund of the day by 85 percent, returns net of fees. Jones' popularity skyrocketed. The *Fortune* article grabbed the attention and interest of numerous investors and investment professionals alike. The allure of earning 10 to 20 times what they were earning in traditional investments resulted in the creation of 140 new hedge funds between 1966 and 1968. The Jones hedge fund, in one shape or another, existed into the 1970s and continued its solid track record.

Although the Jones hedge fund is considered to be the first recorded hedge fund, it actually may not have been the first. Earlier and more basic versions may have existed. For instance, the father of value investing, Benjamin Graham, was known to have established an investment fund in the mid–1920s. This would have given Graham the opportunity and motivation to employ hedge fund tools, such as leverage, to enhance the returns of his value picks. Other investment professionals may have used hedge fund tools prior to Alfred Jones establishing his hedge fund. Such simple and common tools included leverage and arbitrage, especially with commodities.

Hedge Funds Gain Momentum

By the 1950s, more and more investment players began to enter the hedge fund arena, attracted by the greater flexibility and potential compensation. At around the same time, legendary investor Warren Buffett became involved in hedge funds with his company, Buffett Partnership, Ltd. His hedge fund gave investors a 24 percent annualized return for the 13 years his fund was in existence. Prior to dissolving his fund in 1969, he used his new wealth to acquire Berkshire Hathaway, then a run-down textile company and risky investment. Today, Berkshire Hathaway is synonymous with investing greatness and Warren Buffett is considered one of the greatest money managers of our time.

Other investment players who made names for themselves early in their careers by participating in hedge funds include George Soros and Michael Steinhardt. Soros began his career in hedge funds at the same time Warren Buffett was exiting the trade in 1969. Soros' first fund was with the investment firm of Bleichroeder & Company. Nearly five years later, Soros left Bleichroeder & Company to establish his own hedge fund, the well-known Quantum Fund.

Michael Steinhardt, through his Steinhardt Partners hedge fund, is widely recognized for his outstanding long-term performance using investments with short-term time horizons. Over his 28 year tenure, Steinhardt achieved a 24 percent compounded average annual return, more than double the return of the S&P 500 over the same time period. What is most impressive about his performance is that the time horizons he employed for each investment ranged from only 30 minutes to 30 days. Few hedge fund managers employ such short-term time horizons and achieve such stellar out-performance of the S&P 500 consistently over the long-term.

Another hedge fund company, established by Julian Robertson, a stockbroker with Kidder Peabody, gained substantial fame. His hedge funds were named for the big wild cats, with his signature fund so named the Tiger Fund. The offshore sister fund was named the Jaguar Fund. These funds gained him much fame and fortune and helped to produce many subsequent hedge funds managers. These hedge fund managers were appropriately called "Tiger cubs."

Most of the new hedge funds did not use the same two tools—selling short and leverage—to the degree that Alfred Jones did. The new managers did emphasize the use of leverage, but they declined to employ selling short. This decision exposed them to the impact of falling market prices, which happened in the late 1960s. Given that most of the hedge funds held long equity positions, more than 70 percent of the total value held by hedge funds was lost in consequence. Ouch! By 1970, there were about 150 hedge funds in existence with assets of nearly $1 billion.

Thereafter, hedge funds began to gain traction with investors—at the expense of traditional investments—as equity and fixed-income returns suffered under the weight of weak economics. Hard assets or commodities, considered *alternative assets* in the world of asset allocation, performed quite well. This occurrence is relatively common during times of inflation and economic hardship. As trading in commodities escalated, so to did the number of investment firms in the business. Within a short time, specialized funds, commodity pools, and futures funds were established by the mega-brokerage companies to take advantage of the new trading phenomenon. Some of these investment professionals gave birth to *commodity trading advisors* (CTAs). Early pioneers in this area include Paul Tudor, John Henry, Julian Robertson, Bruce Kovner, and Louis Bacon. Many of the initial trading strategies targeted stocks of companies that operated in the commodity space rather than purchasing the physical commodities outright. For instance, many early funds purchased or sold short the stocks of companies that mined gold rather than selling short gold itself directly on a mercantile exchange.

Unfortunately, the 1970s also saw its share of hedge fund challenges. With the markets advancing in the late 1960s and early 1970s, many hedge fund managers reverted to long-only positions and abandoned many of the common hedge fund practices. The bear market of 1973 to 1974 saw severe hedge fund losses, causing many hedge funds to exit from the business altogether. Tremont Partners, a hedge fund research company, concluded that there were less than 75 hedge funds in existence by 1984.

The Modern Era

As hedge funds entered the mid–1980s, the landscape began to change, with inflation coming under control and the economy gaining momentum. This resulted in rising equity prices in both the U.S. and global markets. Soon thereafter, hedge fund managers began to create portfolios without borders and opened their offerings to include global assets. At the same time, more standardized futures contracts began to emerge, as did the breadth and depth of the specific commodities traded. Foreign exchange (FX) trading of currencies gained momentum, as did the trading of bonds from developed nations across the globe. Hedge funds became a truly global business, and the number of hedge funds soared. This resulted in fewer hedge funds employing the traditional long/short model and instead incorporating FX and financial derivatives such as futures and options. By the late 1990s, Tremont Partners recorded over 4,000 hedge funds of various sizes, cultures, and strategies employed. Total assets in these funds amounted to over $38 billion (see Figure 2–1).

Figure 2-1. Number of hedge funds

YEAR	FUNDS
1990	530
1991	694
1992	937
1993	1,277
1994	1,654
1995	2,006
1996	2,392
1997	2,563
1998	2,848
1999	3,102
2000	3,335
2001	3,904
2002	4,598
2003	5,065
2004	5,900
2005	7,110
2006(e)	9,000

The 1980s also saw the beginnings of one of the largest cases of insider trading Wall Street had ever seen. Enter Michael Milken of Drexel Burnham Lambert, Ivan Boesky, and the emergence of the junk bond market, including junk bond investing. Note that *junk bonds* is the less appealing title for what are commonly called *non-investment-grade bonds*. The original purpose of the junk bond market was to finance the acquisition of distressed companies. The age of leveraged buyouts (LBOs) had begun. Unfortunately, these LBOs created significant conflicts of interest, and before long, Michael Milken and friends were accused of insider trading. To save their necks, Milken and Boesky pledged to stay out of the investment business for life. So ended their popularized careers.

One of the more modern inventions with hedge funds is the *fund of funds*. This style of hedge fund allows for greater flexibility in the number of investors permitted to invest in any one hedge fund. Investors no longer need to have significant wealth to quality for investing in hedge funds. Furthermore, funds of funds provide enhanced diversification owing to investing in multiple stand-alone hedge funds.

Since 1990, the number of hedge funds has increased dramatically to over 9,000 worldwide, including assets under management of approximately $1.4 trillion.

Historical Performance of Hedge Funds

Figures 2–2 through 2–4 are presented to give you a better understanding of how well some hedge fund strategies have performed over the past 25 years compared with the Standard & Poor's (S&P) 500 Index. You also will notice a chart with returns and standard deviations. Each simply provides another way of looking at the historical performance data, complied by Greenwich Alternative Investments. Other providers of performance data include Morningstar and Standard and Poor's. With hedge funds gaining momentum, more and more performance data suppliers will enter the market, making comparisons of different funds much easier. The end of Chapter 16 examines hedge fund performance benchmarking.

Figure 2-2. Hedge fund performance by strategy

CATEGORY	AVERAGE ANNUAL RETURN	STANDARD DEVIATION	SHARP RATIO
Aggressive Growth	19%	22%	0.9
Convertible Arbitrage Index	-1%	3%	-0.2
Distressed Securities	18%	15%	1.2
Emerging Markets	24%	28%	0.9
Equity Market Neutral Index	16%	8%	2.0
Fixed Income Arbitrage Index	6%	0%	33.2
Macrocentric	19%	20%	0.9
Market Neutral Arbitrage	13%	8%	1.7
Market Timing	18%	18%	1.0
Merger Arbitrage Index	5%	2%	2.7
Opportunistic	21%	16%	1.3
Short Selling	4%	19%	0.2
Special Situations Index	18%	13%	1.4
Value Index	18%	12%	1.5
S&P 500	13%	17%	0.7

Figure 2-3. Select risk/reward profiles (1999–2005)

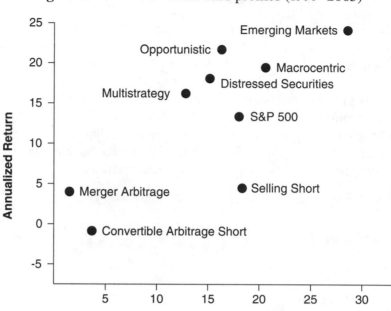

Figure 2-4. Growth of $1,000 (1986–2006)

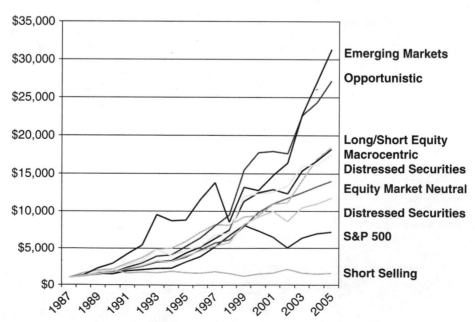

Quiz for Chapter 2

1. The first recorded hedge fund employed which two tools?

   a. Selling short and arbitrage

   b. Leverage and derivatives

   c. Selling short and leverage

   d. Arbitrage and emerging markets

2. Alfred Winslow Jones is credited with establishing the very first hedge fund.

   a. True

   b. False

3. Which hedge fund manager purchased Berkshire Hathaway and turned it into a major investing powerhouse?

   a. Sydney Armstrong

   b. Alfred Jones

   c. Arnold Armistead

   d. Warren Buffett

4. Julian Robertson, one-time stockbroker with Kidder Peabody, gained fame as a hedge fund manager with which fund?

   a. Tiger Fund

   b. Manhattan Fund

   c. Greenwich Fund

   d. Greentree Fund

5. The Quantum Fund was established by which well-known financier from Bleichroeder & Company?

   a. Anthony Kennedy

   b. Michael Steinhardt

   c. George Soros

   d. Thomas Flattney

6. Michael Milken of Drexel Burnham Lambert was at one time a leader in which type of bond trading?

   a. Municipal

   b. International corporate

   c. Junk, or noninvestment-grade

   d. Convertible and placed

7. Alfred Jones was the first hedge fund manager to implement a 20 percent performance-incentive fee.

   a. True

   b. False

8. Approximately how much money is presently invested in hedge funds today?

   a. $150 billion

   b. $500 billion

   c. $1.4 trillion

   d. $5 trillion

9. Hedging risk first began in the nineteenth century when commodity producers and merchants began using _____ to lock in pricing and supply.

   a. Leverage agreements

   b. Forward contracts

   c. Supply/demand contracts

   d. Buy-sell arrangements

10. What was the profession of Alfred Winslow Jones prior to establishing his hedge fund company?

   a. Professor at Harvard

   b. Mutual fund manager

   c. Securities law attorney

   d. *Fortune* magazine writer

CHAPTER 3

Attractions and Merits

Making the Case for Hedge Funds

Thus far you have learned about the fundamentals and history of hedge funds and the broad reasons for investing in hedge funds. Many specific reasons behind using hedge funds support the idea that even a small portfolio allocation can generate solid results over time. But what are these more specific reasons? In general, hedge funds have outperformed most other asset classes over time. In addition, hedge funds offer capital protection, risk management, neutral-market correlation, low volatility, and they help to foster a properly allocated and diversified portfolio. The following are the important reasons why hedge funds can make a solid addition to your investment portfolio.

Potential for Positive Returns in All Market Conditions

One of the primary aims of hedge funds is to generate attractive positive returns regardless of how well or poorly the market is performing. Thus hedge fund managers strive for absolute returns rather than superior relative returns, the aim of nearly all traditional managers. This is important because the value of your portfolio can be protected with greater ease. Furthermore, this represents a significant consideration for investors who prefer earning controlled positive returns each year than earning more volatile returns from traditional managers that can either outperform or underperform hedge funds depending on the market. Hedge funds are uniquely positioned to deliver positive returns in any market regardless of bear or bull conditions because they can sell short securities. Thus, when the market falls, you will profit on any short positions you may hold. Without the freedom to sell short, money managers are very much at the will of the market and typically will experience declines during bear markets and gains in bull markets. This flexibility is a very important consideration for hedge funds because it helps you to weather any market condition.

Minimal Volatility Risk and Smoothed Returns

Nothing can devastate a portfolio like market crashes or prolonged market weakness. Over the history of the stock market, investors have experienced some crashes and numerous periods of prolonged weakness. At times, one investment will perform well, whereas at other times, another investment will perform well. Hedge funds provide you with yet another investment option. By allocating to multiple-asset classes–including hedge funds–which do not move in perfect lockstep with each other, your portfolio will be shielded to a degree from excessive portfolio volatility. Holding a portfolio of only fixed-income securities typically creates greater portfolio risk than a balanced portfolio of both fixed-income securities and hedge funds. This means that your portfolio will have lower volatility than if you did not invest in hedge funds, and as we have learned, lower volatility equates to lower portfolio risk and returns that are smoothed out over time. Most investors would agree that smoother returns from month to month are more ideal than returns that fluctuate greatly during the same time period.

Potential for Aggressive Returns

Hedge funds provide the means to generate aggressive portfolio returns given their ability and freedom to employ alternative investment strategies. This is not to be confused with the aim most hedge funds establish—that being to generate attractive absolute performance over time. But rather, this merit is about hedge funds that can deliver substantial performance in the short term, far outpacing that of the overall market. Most hedge funds are not organized to knock the cover off the baseball when it comes to performance; however, there are some hedge funds that target aggressive returns. Given the ability of hedge fund managers to take advantage of less efficient markets, their freedom to move quickly with portfolio transactions, and their freedom to highly leverage their positions, hedge funds provide the perfect means for investors looking to take excessive risk in the hope of receiving aggressive returns. For example, suppose that a hedge fund manager anticipates the Standard & Poor's (S&P) 500 Index earning a 12 percent return over the next year. To capitalize on this expectation and to generate superior returns, the hedge fund manager employs leverage and doubles the investment by making the fund 50 percent leveraged. As a result, if the S&P 500 earns the 12 percent as anticipated, the fund will generate a gross return before borrowing costs of 24 percent. A return such as this is surely considered superior and the hedge fund investors will be pleased. Of course, using leverage is also a liability and increases the risk of the hedge fund because both losses and gains are magnified. Nevertheless, hedge funds provide investors with the means to earn aggressive returns if desired.

Enhanced Portfolio Efficiency and Diversification

Each and every investor has tolerance for risk, as well as specific financial goals and needs. These goals are sometimes related to wealth accumulation, wealth preservation, or both. Once you identify your risk profile and specific financial goals and obligations, you are then able to design an optimal portfolio that can best achieve them. More specifically, you want to earn suitable portfolio performance over the long term. Why is this important? It is important because many portfolios are designed with little regard for risk profile or goals and needs. You should never design or hold a portfolio that does not align expected portfolio performance with what you want to accomplish. A portfolio that aligns your goals, obligations, and risk profile with expected portfolio performance provides you with your best opportunity for achieving them.

Hedge funds allow you to incorporate the assets that best suit your risk profile. By adding a hedge fund element to your portfolio, you will effectively create a more optimal portfolio. At the same time, given that hedge funds typically have more than one investment, portfolio diversification is also enhanced.

Exploits Inefficiencies and Underused Opportunities

There are many strategies for managing a portfolio. One way is to employ mutual funds or other traditional managers to do the job, and this may or may not be a good approach. The true downside of this approach is in their restrictions on which tools they are permitted to employ. Hedge funds do not have these same restrictions. As a result, your hedge fund manager is free to use many strategies and tools to take advantage of underused opportunities and profitable inefficiencies. Merger arbitrage and convertible arbitrage are two very good examples. For the most part, traditional managers cannot use these tools, whereas most investors have neither the knowledge nor the skill to execute these as well. Hedge fund managers provide the expertise and tools needed to take advantage of these opportunities. In addition, hedge fund managers not only have the freedom to take advantage of profitable inefficiencies and underused opportunities, but they also can employ leverage to magnify their returns. This can equate to enhanced returns in your portfolio.

Maximizes Risk-Adjusted Returns

Modern portfolio theory says that when an investor is faced with two investments with identical expected returns but different levels of risk, he or she should select the investment that has the lower risk. Said a different way, a rational investor will select the investment with the higher return when faced with two investments that have different expected returns but identical levels of risk. By combining fundamentally different investments with various expected returns and risk levels, investors build a portfolio that maximizes risk-adjusted returns. Allocating to hedge funds can do just this.

The aim of hedge funds is to deliver attractive positive returns, or what are called *absolute returns*. To accomplish this aim, hedge fund managers need to develop funds that have low or neutral correlations with the overall market. Thus, when the market is rising or falling, funds do not follow suit. This means that your level of portfolio risk will decline, and the potential for enhanced returns increases. In summary, the risk-adjusted return of an investor's portfolio will become more attractive with an allocation to hedge funds.

Enhanced Portfolio Risk Management

Protecting your portfolio and keeping risk under control are vitally important to becoming a successful hedge fund investor. Given the complexity and tools necessary to manage a portfolio using alternative strategies, investors will find it beneficial to leave this task to a professional. Hedge fund managers are well versed on the investing marketplace and how best to profit from it. At the same time, hedge fund managers are experts at assessing risk and minimizing that risk as much as possible. Most hedge funds are all about reducing portfolio risk rather than generating aggressive returns. One of the best ways to reduce risk is to incorporate investments that have neutral or, better yet, negative correlations with the total market. This is a specialty of many hedge fund managers. Hedge funds provide the ability and opportunity to reduce portfolio risk more than most other investments, given their emphasis and focus on risk management.

Managers Commit Their Own Capital

Most hedge funds are established when a hedge fund manager contributes his or her own capital as a way to seed the fund. Over time, as more people invest money in the hedge fund, the manager's need to invest a sizable amount of his or her wealth in the fund declines. However, it is very important for managers to invest most of their investable capital in their hedge funds. By doing so, they provide investors with a sense of comfort in knowing that the manager has a financial stake in the fund beyond simply earning fees. Moreover, their concerns for investment returns are very much the same. Suffice to say, hedge funds with substantial percentages of the managers' wealth provide comfort that the fund is being invested the right way and positioned to generate solid performance. If a hedge fund manager does not have a substantial amount of his or her wealth in the fund and instead invests outside the fund, then perhaps this is a signal of the manager's lack of confidence in the prospects of the fund.

Provides Access to the Top Money Managers

Lured by big paychecks and the prestige of the profession, many top money managers on Wall Street can be found managing hedge funds. Of course, this is good for hedge fund investors because they have the best and the brightest working to make them money. Think about this from the perspective of managers—if you were

considered among the top talent on Wall Street, would you continue to work on the traditional investment side, making good money (with the potential to earn even more), or would you transition to the hedge fund side with the potential to earn exceptional money for relatively comparable work? The answer is easy. As a result, to access the best on The Street, investors sometimes must branch out of traditional investing and invest in hedge funds.

Most hedge fund managers are very passionate about generating strong returns. They are generally not interested in the day-to-day administrative aspects of hedge funds, such as marketing and investor relations. Hedge fund managers are driven by the challenge of the markets and like to spend as much time managing money as they possibly can. However, most hedge fund managers recognize that they must do some administrative duties, but they prefer others to handle them if at all possible.

Restricts the Asset Size to Manageable Levels

One of the primary knocks against any investment fund–hedge funds, mutual funds, commodity pools, and others–is that over time, as more and more investors commit money, the fund will become too big to generate the returns they generated when they were smaller, more nimble, and could take advantage of investable opportunities—regardless of size—with relative ease. One of the best examples of this dilemma is the Magellan Fund from Fidelity Investments. Managed by legendary money manager Peter Lynch, this fund earned strong returns when assets were at a manageable level. Once investors began to see the strong returns, the fund experienced heavy capital inflows from people looking to get in on the action. Many financial experts say that these capital inflows were too much for the fund to handle, and the returns that investors were accustomed to earning were no longer being generated. Why does this occur? The reason is because funds get too large and cannot put the money to work in the same manner or under the same strategy they had used traditionally. This is not to say that the opportunities themselves disappeared completely; only that the opportunities are only so large, and even a modest investment from a titanic fund will exploit that opportunity fully.

Hedge funds clearly recognize this inherent issue, and most establish asset level limitations at which no new capital from new investors or perhaps no new money from even current investors is accepted. The result is a more manageable hedge fund that allows the hedge fund manager to continue to employ his or her set hedge fund strategy and to more fully take advantage of underused opportunities or market inefficiencies. This is a solid benefit for hedge fund investors that is not afforded to many traditional investors.

Performance Incentives Align Manager Goals with Investor Goals

Pay for performance is one of the underlying focal points of hedge funds. Hedge funds realize that if they do not generate profits for their investors, then they will not earn the performance-incentive fee, which is typically 20 percent of profits. In consequence, hedge funds will strive to generate returns, thereby enabling them to charge the fee. This provides hedge fund managers with an incentive to focus on generating profits in their respective funds. And profits are obviously good for investors as well. Paying a 20 percent fee is a good problem to have because it means that you made money. Performance-incentive fees all boil down to aligning the goals of the hedge fund manager with the goals of the hedge fund investor. Keep in mind that hedge funds have two provisions to safeguard investors in terms of paying performance-incentive fees—the high-water mark and the hurdle rate. Figure 3–1 illustrates the differences between mutual funds and hedge funds.

Figure 3-1. Differences between mutual funds and hedge funds

CATEGORY	MUTUAL FUND	HEDGE FUND
Liquidity	Daily Liquidity and Redemption	Liquidity Varies from Monthly to Annually
Performance Objective	Attractive Relative Return	Attractive Absolute Return
Regulation	SEC Regulated Investments	Nonregulated Private Investments
Investors	Unlimited	Highly Limited
Minimum Initial Investment	Typically Very Small, > $1,000	Typically Very High, > $1 Million
Availability	Open to All Investors	Open ONLY to Investors where net worth exceeds $1 million or individual income must have been in excess of $200,000, or joint income must have been in excess of $300,000 in the past two years. Plus investor must expect the same level of income in the subsequent year
Selling Short	Maximum of 30 percent of profits from selling short	Unlimited Freedom to Sell Short
Performance Incentive Fee	Typically No Performance Incentive Fee	Performance Incentive Fee of 20 Percent is Common
Investment Management Fee	Common Usage of 1-2 Percent	Common Usage of 1-2 Percent
Leverage	Practically No Use	Freedom to Use Extensively
Primary Sources of Risk and Return	Market, Strategy, and Skill	Strategy and Skill
Structure	Typically a Large Company	Typically a Small Company
Marketing and Promotions	Unlimited with Disclosure Requirements	Restricted to Only Accredited Investors
Offerings	Prospectus	Private Placement Memorandum
Manager Participation	Little to No Manager Participation	Substantial Capital from Manager Invested
Derivatives	Restricted from Trading	Free to Trade

Quiz for Chapter 3

1. One of the guiding principles of hedge funds is to generate positive returns in all market conditions. What is this called?

    a. Relative returns

    b. Performance guided

    c. Return-centric

    d. Absolute returns

2. Investors can expect to receive more erratic total portfolio returns when hedge funds are added to the mix.

    a. True

    b. False

3. Do hedge funds increase, decrease, or maintain portfolio volatility risk when added to a standard stock and bond portfolio?

    a. Increase

    b. Decrease

    c. Maintain

4. Hedge funds enhance total portfolio efficiency and improve overall diversification. This is so because

    a. they can generate superior total returns over time.

    b. they offer professional management from top managers.

    c. they add fundamentally different and low-correlated investments.

    d. they employ active management using alternative investment strategies.

5. Hedge funds _____ total portfolio risk-adjusted returns.

    a. reduce

    b. enhance

    c. do not affect

6. What practice by hedge fund managers can provide investors with a significant degree of confidence in the fund?

    a. Managing only one hedge fund

    b. Having a shifting investment strategy

   c. Charging lower performance-incentive fees

   d. Investing their own capital in the fund

7. The typical hedge fund avoids inefficient and underused opportunities and instead emphasizes exotic and very complex investments.

   a. True

   b. False

8. What is one of the benefits of hedge funds limiting the amount of assets in each fund?

   a. Less dilution of invested capital.

   b. Fewer SEC audits.

   c. Current strategies for generating returns can be maintained.

   d. No restrictions on pass-through of gains.

9. What is the benefit of performance-incentive fees to hedge fund investors?

   a. Aligns the hedge fund manager's interests with the investor's interests.

   b. Eliminates lockup provisions.

   c. Stipulates specific payback schedules.

   d. Guarantees provisional performance minimums.

10. Many of the top managers on The Street can only be accessed through investing in hedge funds.

   a. True

   b. False

CHAPTER

All About the Risks

Hedge Fund Hazards, Hurdles, and Hassles

As many investors know and the media never misses an opportunity to point out, there are many pitfalls with investing in hedge funds. Unfortunately, there are a number of risks, both fund-specific risks and industry-specific risks, investors need to be aware of and attempt to avoid. Both categories of risk play an important role in the preservation and growth of your hedge fund investment and should be understood before you make your initial investment contribution. I will begin the discovery of hedge fund risks with fund-specific risks and then transition to industry-specific risks (see Figure 4–1).

Fund-Specific Risks

As with any other investment, hedge funds pose different types of investment-specific risk. Each investment has general risks, such as market, industry, and political. However, hedge funds do have some unique risks unto themselves. These risks include operational risk, fraud risk, regulatory risk, transfer risk, settlement risk,

Figure 4-1. Hedge fund risks

1. Operational Risk
2. Pricing and Valuation Risk
3. Fraud and Fiduciary Risk
4. Transfer Risk
5. Settlement Risk
6. Credit Risk
7. Legal Risk
8. Transparency Risk
9. Liquidity Risk
10. Model Risk
11. Manager-Specific Risk
12. Investment-Specific Risk
13. Leverage Risk
14. Systematic Risk
15. Fee Risk
16. Conflict-of-Interest Risk
17. Reserve Risk
18. Style-Drift Risk
19. Market Risk
20. Regulatory Risk
21. Strategy-Specific Risk

credit risk, legal risk, and liquidity risk. Depending on the hedge fund and the type of strategy used, an investor may be confronted with a couple of these risks or many of them. Moreover, the degree of risk also can differ from hedge fund to hedge fund. Each of these risks is explored below.

OPERATIONAL RISK

Operational risk refers to the hedge fund company and the risks associated with not being able to manage the hedge fund properly. This risk is not related to the risk of market value loss or to losses arising from credit or counterparty risks. Operational risk, on the other hand, refers to risk owing to human error or risk due to an inadequate administrative system. For example, a hedge fund may accept newly invested capital and then fail to deposit the capital in a timely fashion owing to poor recordkeeping or outright human error. Another example of operational risk is the uncertainty of completing a performance composite and thus having nothing to provide prospects and clients on how well the fund did in the recent calendar year. Operational risk also includes the risk that hedge fund managers may leave the fund to pursue greener pastures with other hedge funds or even to start their own hedge fund. Another significant operational risk relates to technology and systems of a particular hedge fund. For newly established hedge funds, Microsoft Excel and Access are the software applications of choice, driven mostly by necessity. And this is fine, given their relatively small size. However, as a hedge fund grows, the need for more sophisticated software also grows. Without this software, a hedge fund may experience "growing pains." In summary, this risk is very manageable and should not be a big burden when hedge funds do their jobs properly.

PRICING AND VALUATION RISK

Risk and accounting professionals are typically the people at hedge funds charged with the role of valuing the positions held by the hedge fund and identifying accurate pricing. Making inaccurate valuations is commonplace with money managers for a number of reasons. Most valuation errors are immaterial and "true up," or self-correct, the very next day when accurate data are used. Errors in valuation can arise from price upload problems, system configuration issues, mismanagement of spreadsheets, deal modeling errors, or simply receiving the wrong prices or no prices. Beyond the more common process-oriented errors, problems with valuation methodology can have a great impact on overall results. There are many moving parts in hedge fund valuation and therefore many pitfalls for error.

FRAUD AND FIDUCIARY RISK

Fraud is perhaps the most serious of all types of hedge fund risk. When investors place their trust in hedge fund managers and invest their capital, they are expecting managers to conduct themselves with integrity. Fraud can bring down an entire hedge fund and hedge fund company. When a hedge fund manager or any other investment manager, for that matter, does not act with integrity, then everyone loses. Chapter 5 on colossal collapses mentions some hedge funds that were victims of fraud and eventually failed after losing millions for investors.

TRANSFER RISK

Transfer risk refers to the restriction of transferring ownership interest from one hedge fund investor to another. Most hedge fund investors are required to liquidate their hedge fund investment directly with the fund itself rather than selling to an existing investor or outside party. Although this risk is marginal, to some investors looking for greater liquidity, it can be quite important.

SETTLEMENT RISK

Settlement risk is the risk that a hedge fund will be unable to finalize a transaction at the terms of the contract agreed to on the purchase trade date. This risk is mini-mized for exchange-traded instruments but exists with off-exchange instruments. Not settling at agreed-on terms can be costly, create delays, and perhaps require legal or arbitrary means to resolve the issue.

CREDIT RISK

Credit risk refers to the risk inherent in companies in which a hedge fund has an ownership interest. These companies may declare bankruptcy or cease paying bond interest payments owing to challenging financial positions. Since some hedge funds invest in fixed-income securities, there is always the risk that they could default on payments. If this were to happen, then the hedge fund could experience perfor-mance challenges. Counterparty credit risk is also grouped under this type of risk. Hedge funds that employ derivative instruments such as swaps will assume greater risk because some counterparties may default on their obligation or challenge the terms of the agreement. For example, two hedge funds enter into a plain-vanilla swap in which one party pays a floating rate of interest, and the counterparty pays a fixed rate of interest. At contract expiration, the floating rate hedge fund party finds itself in the unfortunate position of having to make payment to the fixed-rate party. If this hedge fund were unable or unwilling to meet its obligation to make payment, then the fixed-rate party would lose out. Of course, the fixed-rate party will pursue payment but will incur costs and waste time when the counterparty should have fulfilled the agreement.

LEGAL RISK

Legal risk refers to the risk that a hedge fund will face legal challenges that need the attention of the management team. This risk should not be confused with regulatory risk, which is entirely different. Given the heightened risk with hedge funds, having an investor pursue legal remedies as a result of poor performance is not uncommon. Incurring costs to address nonregulatory legal issues is at the center of this hedge fund risk.

TRANSPARENCY RISK

Over the last few years, hedge funds have greatly improved their overall transparency with regard to asset positions, strategies employed, and performance results. Unfortunately, this was motivated by the need to calm investors during times of substantial financial losses and fund failures. Regulators became more involved and have mandated ever-increasing ways for hedge funds to enhance their transparency. Prior to this time, only select key people knew exactly what was happening with their hedge fund. When hedge funds do not provide adequate transparency, investors make less than optimal decisions, and the consequences can be disastrous. Over time, this risk should abate as more and more hedge funds enhance their transparency to avoid regulatory issues and to attract much desired institutional capital.

LIQUIDITY RISK

Liquidity risk can refer to two things. First, it can refer to the risk where a hedge fund is unable to liquidate an investment at a price close to the present market value. Larger investment positions needing to be sold can be especially challenging. In addition, since some hedge funds invest in relatively illiquid assets, selling those positions could take significant time and effort. Second, *liquidity risk* can refer to restrictions on withdrawing money from the hedge fund. Most hedge funds have restrictions on when money can be withdrawn, primarily only quarterly and not at all in the first year of the investment. This is an inconvenient provision to some hedge fund investors.

MODEL RISK

Much of risk management begins with what is called *value-at-risk,* or *VaR* for short. VaR is a model used to capture and quantify the risks inherent in a business enterprise. Hedge funds use VaR in an attempt to improve their risk-management functions and better operate their hedge funds. VaR, as with any financial model, is susceptible to its inputs. We have all heard of the expression, "Garbage in, garbage out." Depending on the inputs to VaR, the model may report a risk level that is lower than in actuality, creating a scenario in which the hedge fund manager assumes more risk because he or she believes that there is remaining risk capacity within established risk thresholds. VaR is not the only model that can break down. Many asset-valuation models also can self-destruct with severe consequences. The collapse of the hedge fund Long Term Capital Management can be attributed to model failure precipitated by human error related to the inputs of the model.

MANAGER-SPECIFIC RISK

Similar to model risk, *manager-specific risk* arises from the decisions of the manager with regard to selecting an investment strategy, when and how that strategy is implemented, and when to tweak a strategy that is clearly not working or not a competitive advantage owing to lack of knowledge or resources. Both traditional and hedge fund portfolios have inherent manager-specific risk; however, hedge funds have far greater manager-specific risk primarily attributed to their aim of minimizing or neutralizing market risk. When this is accomplished, most of the remaining risk is manager-specific risk and investment-specific risk. The more any one risk is hedged, the more prominent a role the remaining risks play in the hedge fund. What does this mean to hedge fund investors? It means that there should be greater scrutiny of the investment decisions of the hedge fund manager given that the results are driven by the manager's investment choices rather than being driven by the market.

INVESTMENT-SPECIFIC RISK

Investment-specific risk refers to the risk inherent in the asset positions held by the hedge fund. These risks include poor company management, product obsolescence, government intervention, changing consumer tastes, and even unforeseen catastrophic events that affect companies—think Hurricane Katrina and homeowners' insurance companies. The result of any negative event could be detrimental to an investment, and hedge funds are not immune to this type of risk, nor are traditional investment managers. The more diversified a hedge fund portfolio, the lower probability there is that a drastic loss will occur and the lower probability there is that a large dollar loss will occur. With mutual funds, investment-specific risk typically is diversified away, given the significant number of investments such funds hold. This may or may not be the case with hedge funds. Most hedge funds will hold a significant number of investments, but some hedge funds recognize that diversification not only offers protection from large losses but also dilutes potential strong returns earned by the individual investments held. If a fund were not diversified well, then the effect of a gain or loss attributed to a single investment would be higher. Some hedge funds prefer this and build their funds in such a manner as to take advantage of this impact, whether gains or losses. Most research clearly articulates that a diversified portfolio can be achieved with 15 to 20 similar investments.

LEVERAGE RISK

Perhaps the biggest risk a hedge fund can assume is that of *leverage risk*. Leverage can be both villain and hero depending on how the investments held in the fund are performing. When a highly leveraged hedge fund is doing well, leverage will enhance the gains. In contrast, however, when a highly leveraged hedge fund is doing poorly, the losses will be exaggerated. The positive aspect of leverage risk is that it can be controlled because hedge fund managers have discretion over the amount of leverage they wish to employ. If no leverage is employed, then there exists no leverage risk in the hedge fund. Some hedge fund strategies specifically call for leverage—most notably the arbitrage strategies. Under best-case scenarios, arbitrage offers only modest returns on a per-investment or per-opportunity basis. Of consequence, hedge fund managers typically will employ leverage to turn what would have been a modest gain into a higher gain. This is the good side of leverage. What can leverage do to a hedge fund? Long Term Capital Management employed significant leverage that ultimately brought down the fund even though two of its partners were Noble Laureates. Remember, when there is leverage, your losses hurt more.

SYSTEMATIC RISK

Systematic risk refers to the risk hedge funds face in the light of other more macro-events occurring. This type of risk is very common with traditional investing as well. For example, suppose that the hedge fund you invested in targets foreign emerging-markets debt. If the largest single issuer of this type of debt were to default on its debt, there would be a ripple effect throughout the industry. Regardless of whether or not your hedge fund manager invested in the debt of this nation, the hedge fund probably will experience a loss in the short term for no other reason than sympathy declines. This means that hedge funds can suffer losses as a result of being caught up in the crowd so-to-speak. Unfortunately, research has shown that this type of risk is rising in the investment marketplace.

FEE RISK

The typical hedge fund will charge two types of fees—a performance-incentive fee and an investment-management fee—with some charging special fees such as a redemption fee. For investors, paying these fees is more or less acceptable when the portfolio is experiencing good performance. However, when performance is poor, investors will not be extremely pleased with paying the annual investment-management fee. The performance-incentive fee, of course, is not applicable when a fund loses money. Regardless of portfolio performance, many hedge funds will charge 1 percent of the portfolio asset value for the annual investment-management fee. Some even charge more than the common 1 percent, but some charge less. Losing money and paying fees on top of that is a risk hedge fund investors face. Investors in mutual funds and investors using private money managers face the same risk as well. This risk is standard across the entire money management trade.

CONFLICT-OF-INTEREST RISK

Performance-incentive fees are a great way for hedge fund managers to align their interests with those of their investors. When investors make money, so too do hedge fund managers in the form of fees on the gains generated. Unfortunately, this can create scenarios where the hedge fund manager assumes greater risk than appropriate with the aim of generating higher fees. If the added risk works as anticipated, then the hedge fund investor will benefit in the form of higher performance. However, the added risk can backfire and cause significant losses. Hedge fund investors therefore need to conduct proper due diligence when searching for suitable hedge fund managers. By looking at performance composites, investors can gain a good perspective on the levels of risk the hedge fund manager has assumed in the past. This may provide comfort in knowing that the same hedge fund manager will adhere to such a policy going forward.

RESERVE RISK

Many hedge funds will reserve a portion of their gains rather than report the full profit from special transactions. Typically, this is done when a hedge fund holds low liquidity assets, invests in companies with less than ideal credit strength, or perhaps enters what are called *structured deals*. Given the uncertainty in these situations, hedge funds believe it prudent to reserve some of the profits in the event that they are not able to earn the fully anticipated gains when the asset position is sold or closed. How does this affect investors, you might ask? Investors who remain invested in the hedge fund until the asset position is sold will earn the full profit, which consists of the reported gain and the reserved gain. However, investors who withdraw their invested capital prior to the asset positions being sold will forgo the amount held in reserve. The amount is not especially significant, nor is the frequency of posting reserves especially high. However, there may come times when an investor can terminate the relationship and not receive the full and complete gains that perhaps he or she should.

STYLE-DRIFT RISK

Style-drift risk refers to the uncertainty of hedge funds keeping true to their stated core strategy or strategies without changing or drifting to a new strategy where they have little to no expertise. During times when the market is strong, style drift may go unnoticed because performance is solid. However, during periods of poor performance, style drift can become a big problem and cause significant losses to occur in the hedge fund. Regardless of whether or not hedge funds gain or lose from style drift, there is the question of professional integrity and following through on the stated plan. Most hedge fund investors probably would not be too thrilled if a hedge fund manager said that he or she employs no leverage in his or her hedge fund and then employs some leverage not long into the engagement.

This is a common risk not only with hedge fund investing but also with traditional investing. Other examples of style drift include using derivatives against stated policies, buying growth stocks when the fund presents itself as a value fund, and having a long-bias in a short-bias fund.

Industry-Specific Risks

As with mutual funds and more traditional investing, hedge funds also face risks associated with the overall hedge fund trade. Hedge funds do have some flexibility in being able to minimize these *industry-specific risks;* however, hedge funds can never really avoid these risks completely. It is simply the nature of the business and therefore must be addressed accordingly by each hedge fund in its own way. The three primary industry-specific risks include market risk, regulatory risk, and strategy-specific risk.

MARKET RISK

Market risk refers to outside factors that can cause hedge fund investment losses. Some of these outside factors include foreign exchange rates, interest rates, and commodities prices. However, there are numerous other factors as well. Given their specialized knowledge, hedge fund managers are keen to these risk factors and make every effort to avoid potential losses. Nevertheless, hedge funds will have to face this risk from time to time depending on the strategy employed. For example, macrocentric hedge funds are most vulnerable to foreign exchange risk because they target the global marketplace with their investments. Many of these funds even make a living out of placing bets on the direction of future foreign exchange rate movements. Other hedge funds will invest directly in some segment of the global market, and this means that adverse foreign exchange movements will either reduce gains or cause losses. The use of derivatives can help to minimize or eliminate external market risk.

Another aspect relating to market risk is the issue of underperforming the equity market when that market is advancing. Since the most important aim of most hedge fund managers is to generate attractive absolute returns, hedge funds are not always positioned to take complete advantage of market moves upward. This is attributed to the offsetting effect of short positions that experience losses when the market is advancing. Nevertheless, hedge fund managers strive to deliver positive performance in all market conditions but may lag when the market is advancing. This is the ultimate trade-off with hedge funds that target absolute returns.

REGULATORY RISK

Regulatory risk refers to the current and future restraints imposed on hedge funds that cause hedge funds to incur extra financial costs or impede investment strategy and potentially reduce fund performance. These restraints include margin requirements, disclosure of information, registration of hedge funds, and restrictions on the number and type of investors permitted to invest with hedge funds. As recently as 2007, the Securities and Exchange Commission (SEC) toughened the requirements for individuals to qualify for "accredited investor" status and thus be eligible to invest with hedge funds. An example of how regulators can affect hedge funds is changes in the margin requirement by the Federal Reserve. If the Fed were to require hedge funds—including other investment managers—to post additional margin, thus reducing leverage, some hedge funds would need to alter their strategies with potential implications for generating gains. Hedge funds that employ significant leverage, such as the arbitrage-style funds, would be most affected by this change in margin requirement.

STRATEGY-SPECIFIC RISK

Strategy-specific risk refers to the risk embedded in the strategies employed by hedge fund managers. This includes the trading styles employed, the investment markets and industries the hedge fund targets, and the specific investments selected and held in the hedge fund. As long as opportunities continue to present themselves, hedge funds will be able to generate profits from taking advantage of them. However, there may arise times when certain opportunities do not exist or exist in such small amounts that hedge funds are left with nothing to invest in to make money. Let's look at an example that illustrates the supply side of hedge fund opportunities. If corporate merger activity dries up, then arbitrage hedge funds that target these opportunities will be negatively affected. This basically means that the supply side, or the opportunities, for hedge funds to invest is no longer robust. Now let's look at the demand side. Suppose that corporate merger activity remains the same, but the number of hedge funds interested in capitalizing on arbitrage strategies rises dramatically. Under this scenario, the opportunities still exist but are now chased by far greater numbers of hedge funds. This means that there will be fewer gains to go around. Macrofactors can have a serious negative impact on hedge funds regardless of the actions of the hedge fund manager. Figure 4–2 lists the advantages and disadvantages of hedge funds.

Figure 4-2.   Hedge fund advantages and disadvantages

CATEGORY	ADVANTAGES	DISADVANTAGES
Absolute Return	Potential to outperform in bear markets	Probability of underperforming in bull markets
Alternative Strategies	Extensive Manager Freedom	Shifts risk from market to manager-specific
Structure	Quick-and-easy decisions	Fewer thoughts on the issue at hand
Fee Charged	Promotes performance over growth of assets	Incentive to take extra risk on occasion
Liquidity	Fewer daily or weekly burdens	Turn-off potential clients

Quiz for Chapter 4

1. Mispricing the investments held by a hedge fund is an example of which type of risk?

   a. Transfer

   b. Valuation

    c. Settlement

    d. Credit

2. Fund-specific risks are risks that are unique to a particular hedge fund.

    a. True

    b. False

3. Stealing of hedge fund assets by the manager or other key persons is an example of which type of risk?

    a. Settlement

    b. Valuation

    c. Model

    d. Fraud

4. When an investor is restricted from selling his or her hedge fund interest to another investor, this is an example of which type of risk?

    a. Credit

    b. Model

    c. Fraud

    d. Transfer

5. When a hedge fund is unable to finalize a transaction at agreed-on terms, this is an example of which type of risk?

    a. Settlement

    b. Credit

    c. Fraud

    d. Transfer

6. When investors are unable to obtain sufficient information from hedge fund management, this is an example of which type of risk?

    a. Legal

    b. Regulatory

    c. Transparency

    d. Transfer

7. Liquidity risk refers to hedge funds being unable to meet required margin calls.

    a. True

    b. False

8. When a hedge fund changes its investment focus without adequate rationale, this is an example of which type of risk?

   a. Legal

   b. Style-drift

   c. Regulatory

   d. Model

9. Which risk metric is used to measure and quantify in dollars the risk of loss?

   a. Systematic risk

   b. Beta

   c. Value-at-risk

   d. Treynor ratio

10. Failure to implement strategy is best defined by which risk category?

    a. Manager-specific

    b. Credit

    c. Liquidity

    d. Transparency

CHAPTER 5

Colossal Collapses and Crashes

Hedge Funds Gone Wild

Hedge Funds: Heroes or Villains?

Depending on whom you ask, hedge funds can be heroes and hedge funds can be villains. Some people will say that hedge funds provide a necessary function within the investing field and that hedge funds provide opportunity and have demonstrated solid success over the years. Given the safeguards put in place by hedge funds, related brokerage firms, and the regulatory agencies, hedge funds can only help rather than hurt. However, there are some people who believe that hedge funds are not heroes but rather villains. They point to well-publicized hedge fund meltdowns as evidence. Some of the headline-grabbing hedge fund collapses of the recent past are presented in this chapter. Please note that not every well-known hedge fund collapse is included here, although most are. Nevertheless, the details on the ones included will give you a solid introduction to how many of the hedge funds got themselves into big trouble and lost millions and sometimes billions of dollars of investor wealth (see Figure 5–1).

Figure 5-1. Largest Global Hedge Fund Failures in History

1	Manhattan Fund
2	Bailey Coates Cromwell Fund
3	Eifuku Master Fund
4	Marin Capital
5	Granite Fund
6	Beacon Hill Asset Management
7	Tiger Funds
8	Aman Capital
9	Princeton Economics
10	Maricopa Fund
11	Ellington and MKP
12	Lancer Offshore Fund
13	Brown Simpson
14	Lipper Convertible Fund
15	Askin Capital
16	Orca Funds
17	Long-Term Capital Management
18	Amaranth Advisors

MANHATTAN FUND

Failure Attributed to Fraud from Hidden Losses

Run by hedge fund manager Michael Berger, the Manhattan Fund sold short technology stocks during the period of 1996 to 2000. This was the very same period when technology stocks experienced a significant runup in price and created a technology bubble that finally burst in the early 2000s. Berger saw this technology bubble and took short positions in the hopes of capturing profits when the bubble finally burst. Unfortunately for him and his investors, his timing was slightly off, and the stocks sold short continued to appreciate in value. This precipitated massive losses that Berger covered up by falsifying monthly investor statements by showing gains of between 12 to 27 percent. These falsified gains attracted new investors who contributed substantial capital to the losing fund. Berger used the new capital to cover his frequent and rising margin calls attributed to the losses. During the summer of 1999, Berger claimed to manage $436 million in fund assets, whereas the fund really only had $28 million. Due to the mounting losses, the fund was unable to meet growing margins calls by early 2000 and was forced to close. Berger was promptly arrested and pleaded guilty to securities fraud in 2000. He later attempted to reverse his plea but instead skipped bail and is today on the run. The end result—investors lost $400 million, and Berger was named to the FBI's Most Wanted list.

BAILEY COATES CROMWELL FUND

Failure Attributed to Mismanagement

Although this London-based hedge fund was named "Best New Equity Fund" by Eurohedge in 2004, mismanagement and bad investments established to capture profits from the movements of U.S. stocks caused the fund to lose 20 percent of its $1.3 billion in assets. Soon thereafter, investors redeemed their capital, and the fund closed by the middle of 2005.

EIFUKU MASTER FUND

Failure Attributed to Leverage and Concentration

Operated by John Koonmen, this Tokyo-based hedge fund lost approximately $300 million, or nearly all its capital, over a one-week period in 2002 when highly leveraged, concentrated, tactical (directional) positions moved against the fund.

MARIN CAPITAL

Failure Attributed to Mismanagement

Operated in California, this hedge fund once managed nearly $2 billion in capital using credit arbitrage and convertible arbitrage strategies. The hedge fund manager decided to take a chance on General Motors using a convertible arbitrage strategy. The aim was to purchase the convertible debt of General Motors, redeem it for shares of common stock, and then sell short the common stock. The hope was to make money when the wider than normal spread began to narrow. However, the price of General Motors stock not only declined, it tumbled. At the same time, the convertible debt that the hedge fund held was downgraded to non-investment-grade, or junk, status. Consequently, the hedge fund experienced substantial losses and informed its shareholders by letter on June 16, 2005, that the fund would be closed due to "lack of suitable investment opportunities."

GRANITE FUND

Failure Attributed to Excessive Leverage

Run by David Askin, this hedge fund lost nearly all of its $600 million in capital in early 1994. This was the result of massive losses in the fund's leveraged collateralized mortgage obligation (CMO) positions triggered when the Federal Reserve raised interest rates. The losses were finally revealed to investors when the prime broker for the hedge fund terminated the fund's extension of margin. Both Granite and the prime broker were sued by investors for the massive loss of capital.

BEACON HILL ASSET MANAGEMENT

Failure Attributed to Mispricing

Primarily run by fund manager John Barry, this hedge fund held highly leveraged mortgaged-backed securities positions and suffered severe losses when hedging strategies relating to derivatives arbitrage failed. During 2002, Barry and other members of the management team falsified reports by mispricing the securities held in the fund to show gains. In addition, the fund also defrauded its investors by booking trades between the fund and other portfolios the team managed at off-market prices. In other words, the team transacted at prices that allowed principals to manipulate the value of the fund. They were able to get away with this because they managed the counter portfolio as well. In reality, the hedge fund had lost nearly 54 percent of its value in late 2002. John Barry and the other principals in the firm settled with the Securities and Exchange Commission (SEC) for $4.4 million, an amount that was distributed to investors who were victims of the mispricing scheme. As part of the settlement, Barry was forever banned from working as a money manager in the securities industry by the SEC.

TIGER FUNDS

Failure Attributed to Mismanagement

Run by legendary hedge fund manager Julian Robertson, this fund placed large investments in value securities and sold short growth securities during the bull market of the early 2000s. Although his strategy was accurate, short-term buying momentum kept prices high and fund losses huge. Unable to sustain these losses, the fund closed shortly thereafter.

AMAN CAPITAL

Failure Attributed to Mismanagement

Established in 2003 by former derivatives traders from UBS, Aman Capital set out to become the flagship hedge fund of Singapore. Unfortunately, the fund's bets in leveraged credit derivates did not go as planned, and the hedge fund lost hundreds of millions of dollars over a short time period. Panicked by the losses, investors in the hedge fund began redeeming their investments, and by March 2005, the hedge fund managed less than $250 million. Not too long thereafter the fund issued a statement published in the *Financial Times* saying, "The fund is no longer trading." The fund closed in June of that year, and the remaining capital was distributed to the few investors left.

PRINCETON ECONOMICS

Failure Attributed to Fraud

Based in Princeton, New Jersey, Princeton Economics was established by technical analyst and newsletter publisher Michael Armstrong. In 1999, authorities filed documents in the U.S. District Court of Manhattan that detailed a scheme in which Armstrong attempted to cover up hundreds of millions of dollars in losses caused from high-risk trading. His trading was in contrast to the conservative strategy he claimed to employ. Armstrong may have received the help of Republic New York Securities Corp., a unit of Republic New York Corp., in defrauding investors, principally the firm's Japanese investors. Armstrong targeted sizable institutional Japanese investors and sold them "Princeton Notes" through his Princeton Global Management Limited company. The investigation into the defrauding scheme involved the Financial Supervisory Agency of Japan (FSA) as well as the Philadelphia branch of Republic. Republic was not charged with wrongdoing, and the hedge fund finally was seized by American authorities with less than $50 million in assets remaining.

MARICOPA FUND

Failure Attributed to Theft

Run by "fund manager" David Mobley, Maricopa lost significant assets as a result of withdrawals used not only to finance private businesses established by Mobley but also to fund his extravagant lifestyle. Mobley reported to his investors annualized returns of nearly 50 percent net of his 30 percent performance-incentive fee. By 2000, most of his private businesses financed by the fund had failed. At the same time, Maricopa held only $33 million in assets, even though Mobley claimed to be managing $450 million. Soon thereafter, his outright thievery was discovered, and Mobley was arrested. His luxurious lifestyle was over.

ELLINGTON AND MKP

Failure Attributed to Prime Broker Dispute

During 1998, the Ellington and MKP hedge funds ran into issues with their prime broker over pricing of securities held in the funds. The year 1998 was a challenging period in the global financial markets owing to the Russian financial crisis. This dispute with the prime broker happened during this period of financial instability. Given its decision on pricing, the prime broker required the hedge funds to post additional margin to cover losses from the market. The funds basically had no choice and had to liquidate some of their positions at unfavorable prices to meet the margin calls. The prime broker took significant flack over the event from industry insiders, and not too long afterward, the hedge funds sued the prime broker, accusing it of wrongdoing.

LANCER OFFSHORE FUND

Failure Attributed to Mismanagement and Fraud

Operated by Michael Lauer, the Lancer Offshore Fund sought to profit from distressed small-cap stocks. This strategy was successful at the beginning; however, losses began

to mount during the period of 2000 to 2003 when small-cap stocks went into decline and experienced a prolonged bear market. In an attempt to hide losses, Lauer committed fraud by reporting gains to investors. The fund lost nearly $600 million.

BROWN SIMPSON

Failure Attributed to Reg D Collapse

The Brown Simpson Fund experienced sizable gains from the technology runup during the late 1990s and early 2000s. Specifically, the value of warrants held in the fund rose sharply. This runup ended when the technology bubble burst. Frantic investors tried desperately to withdraw their invested capital but were unable to do so given the underlying Reg D and the highly illiquid positions.

LIPPER CONVERTIBLE FUND

Failure Attributed to Gross Mispricing

Lipper was established by Ken Lipper, a former Salomon Brothers executive and even cowriter of the popular movie *Wall Street,* starring Michael Douglas as Gordon Gecko. Given Ken Lipper's exposure to Hollywood, his hedge fund managed money for many celebrities, including Julia Roberts. Managed by Edward Strafaci, director of fixed income and chief compliance officer, the Lipper Convertible Fund experienced significant losses during the period 1996 to 2002. In an attempt to cover up the decline in fund value, Strafaci falsified returns by grossly exaggerating the prices of investments held in the fund during the period. For the year 2001 alone, Strafaci reported to investors that the fund generated a return of 7.7 percent, when, in actuality, it lost nearly 40 percent. In 2004, he pleaded guilty to securities fraud and was sentenced to prison. Ken Lipper was not brought to trail and voluntarily returned millions of dollars earned in investor fees from the fraudulent work of Strafaci.

ASKIN CAPITAL

Failure Attributed to Hedging Policy

The troubles all began for Askin Capital when the Federal Reserve raised interest rates in 1994. Unfortunately, the manager was not properly hedged against this level of interest-rate hikes, and the losses began to build. At the same time, the counterparties began to withdraw their capital used by the fund to create leverage. This triggered liquidation of the hedge fund at less than ideal exit points and brought about its ultimate demise.

ORCA FUNDS

Failure Attributed to Theft

Operated by professional manager turned professional gambler Donald O'Neill, Orca invested primarily in foreign currency futures contracts. However, rather than invest capital from new investors in the fund, O'Neill took the money and gambled it away in Las Vegas. One such story has him losing $800,000 in one outing. He disappeared for a time but was later arrested in Italy and brought back to the United States to stand trial. He was convicted of mail and wire fraud and sentenced to a South Carolina prison.

TRADEWINDS INTERNATIONAL AND ASHBURY CAPITAL PARTNERS

The last two hedge fund failures in this section are relatively modest in comparison with the substantial failures mentioned previously. Ashbury Capital Partners was essentially a bogus hedge fund established by Mark Yagalla with the sole purpose of swindling money from people and using that money to finance Yagalla's extravagant lifestyle—a mansion in Las Vegas, expensive cars, and gifts for his Playboy bunny girlfriend, Sandy Bentley. Bentley broke up with Yagalla when the FBI arrested him for securities fraud, a charge he pleaded guilty to in 2003. With Tradewinds International, hedge fund manager Charles Harris reported sizable gains when in fact he had lost most of the assets in the fund. As a result of the losses, Harris created and mailed DVDs to each investor communicating his tearful confession and even mentioned that he intended to make back the losses from his undisclosed foreign location. Fortunately for all, his conscience ate away at him, and he turned himself in for prosecution.

The Big Two Monumental Fund Failures

LONG-TERM CAPITAL MANAGEMENT

Founded in Greenwich, Connecticut, in 1994, Long-Term Capital Management (LTCM) was a hedge fund established by John Meriwether, the former vice chairman and head of bond trading at Salomon Brothers. In addition to Meriwether, other founders included two 1997 Nobel Prize–winning economists, Myron Scholes and Robert C. Merton. Scholes and Merton, together with the late Fischer Black, developed the Black-Scholes formula for option pricing. Also part of the team was

David Mullins, a former vice chairman of the Board of Governors of the Federal Reserve System. Rounding out the team were many talented arbitrage analysts from Salomon Brothers. The group was definitely very elite.

The minimum investment was originally set at $10 million, with Merrill Lynch coordinating the financing. The legal structure involved the establishment of two partnerships, Long-Term Capital Portfolio in the Cayman Islands (the owner of record for the securities held) and Long-Term Capital Management (a Delaware company) managed in Connecticut. Contrary to the typical hedge fund, LTCM charged a performance-incentive fee of 25 percent (rather than 20 percent), assessed a 2 percent investment-management fee (rather than 1 percent), and implemented a three-year lockup period (rather than one year). All not exactly investor-friendly provisions.

On February 24, 1994, LTCM began trading with an asset base of just over $1 billion. The strategy of the hedge fund was to hunt for and identify arbitrage opportunities in markets using computers, massive databases, and the forecasts of top-level analysts. More specifically, LTCM had developed sophisticated and complex mathematical models with the aim of taking advantage of fixed-income arbitrage opportunities (termed *convergence trades*) typically found with American, European, and Japanese government bonds. In essence, the thought was that over time, the value of different long-dated government bonds, issued together around the same date, would be approximately the same. Given the liquidity and heavy trading activity, U.S. Treasury bonds could approach the long-term price more quickly than the otherwise less heavily traded and less liquid government bonds from Europe and Japan. In hedge fund speak: this amounted to buying the cheaper "off-the-run" bond and selling short the more expensive but more liquid "on-the-run" bond.

The ideal opportunities came from markets that deviated from normal patterns and were likely to readjust to normal patterns over time. By establishing hedged positions, the risks inherent in the market would be minimized to the lowest possible levels. This was the major flaw in the model developed by Robert C. Merton. Although the model assumed very low risk levels, in practice, some of the vital model inputs and assumptions did not hold as anticipated. As a result, the risk of the fund was not really zero, as subsequent events unfortunately proved out. Myron Scholes was known for expressing the goal of the hedge fund as a giant vacuum cleaner sucking up nickels that everyone else had overlooked or deemed immaterial. LTCM became an overnight success.

In 1996, the firm generated a mind-boggling $2.1 billion profit. The secret wasn't that its investments highly appreciated in value. Rather, it was the staggering amounts of leverage that it employed. The firm earned a meek 1 to 2 percent return on its bets, but given the significant leverage, it turned the pity profits into substantial profits. At its peak, LTCM had equity of $4.72 billion, borrowed funds of over $124.5 billion, and asset positions of $129 billion. In addition, LTCM held

off-balance-sheet derivative positions totaling $1.25 trillion, the majority of which included interest-rate derivatives. This asset level made the fund two and a half times the size of Fidelity Magellan, one of the largest mutual funds at that time.

Everything stopped in 1998 when the Russian government defaulted on its government bonds (GKOs) in August and September. Nervous global investors sold their Japanese and European bonds and purchased U.S. Treasury bonds, a flight to liquidity. The profits that LTCM expected as the value of these bonds converged became huge losses as the value of the bonds diverged. This flight to liquidity led to a global repricing of all risk. Rather quickly, the correlation of LTCM's positions increased, and the diversified aspect of the fund vanished with large resulting losses. By the end of August, the hedge fund had lost a whopping $1.85 billion in capital and was in danger of defaulting on its loans. Given the size of the loss, it was extremely difficult for the fund to cut its losses by executing offsetting transactions in the marketplace. This is understandable because LTCM held huge positions—roughly 5 percent of the total global fixed-income market.

With substantial losses of capital by LTCM racking up, the banks that had provided the borrowed money for it to leverage with became worried about the security of their loans. With LTCM on the brink of total failure and collapse, the Federal Reserve Bank of New York stepped in and brokered a bailout of the hedge fund. Fourteen major banks contributed nearly $300 million each to establish a $3.625 billion bailout loan fund. This bailout fund, together with the remaining assets held by the hedge fund, allowed it to make it through the 1998 global financial crisis. This group of banks and the Fed reorganized LTCM and allowed it to operate for the single purpose of liquidating positions.

The hedge fund repaid all creditor banks and completely liquidated in early 2000. In total, LTCM generated losses of about $4.6 billion, a feat done in less than four months. The losses included the following:

- $1,600 million in swaps
- $1,300 million in equity volatility
- $430 million in Russian and other emerging-market debt
- $371 million in directional trades in developed countries
- $215 million in yield-curve arbitrage
- $203 million in Standard & Poor's (S&P) 500 Index equities
- $100 million in junk bond arbitrage

If LTCM had gone into default, a more intense global financial crisis may have occurred, leading to a chain reaction as the company liquidated its securities to cover its debt. For the sake of the financial markets, the situation was addressed quickly and resolved. Believe it or not, John Meriwether and his team recently launched a

new hedge fund called JWM Partners. The initial funding was approximately $250 million, pooled from former investors of LTCM. Strange twist of fate.

AMARANTH ADVISORS

Which hedge fund company claimed on its Web site to manage capital "in a highly disciplined, risk-controlled manner"? That's correct, Amaranth Advisors, the largest hedge fund to collapse in U.S. history.

In the fall of 2006, the hedge fund trade was hit with another massive failure of epic proportions. This time the victim or, should I say, the villain was Amaranth Advisors of Greenwich, Connecticut (both Amaranth and LTCM were based out of the same city). What was so ironic about the loss was that only one week prior to the disclosure, Charles H. Winkler, the chief operating officer at Amaranth, announced that the hedge fund was up 25 percent on the year. The truth soon followed.

Amaranth made close to $1 billion in profits during the one year prior to its demise, all attributed to sharply higher energy prices. People on The Street said that Amaranth's big gains came in September 2005 when the natural gas trades placed earlier in the year made $1 billion after hurricanes Katrina and Rita hit and prices skyrocketed. Given the highly volatile natural gas market—some five times more volatile than oil given the difficulty with storage—Amaranth was well positioned to take full advantage of this opportunity.

Rumors were circulating that Amaranth was losing massive amounts of money on one of its natural gas bets, the same trade that had generated the substantial profits over the last couple of years. Amaranth initially announced that it had lost more than $3 billion as a result of falling natural gas prices that wrecked havoc on its derivative positions. Soon thereafter, the situation began to snowball, and the hedge fund began to wrack up even more losses. During one week in September alone, the hedge fund lost about $4.6 billion, and by the end of the month, the fund reported losses amounting to $6.6 billion, or 70 percent of Amaranth's total assets.

Amaranth was once a popular investing destination for many institutional players, including pension funds, endowments, insurance companies, funds of funds, brokerage firms, and even banks. In its heyday, Amaranth managed over $9 billion in assets, employed over 100 hedge fund professionals, and boasted offices in New York, Calgary, Houston, London, Singapore, and Toronto. The hedge fund was founded by Nicholas Maounis, a former convertible bond trader at Paloma Brothers, in September 2000 with $600 million in assets. The original aim was to profit from opportunities related to merger arbitrage, distressed debt, and stocks. The result was a 15 percent annualized return since inception. A return of 15 percent may not appear exciting, but when compared with other multistrategy funds during the same period, Amaranth's performance was nearly double the average return.

In April of 2004, Maounis hired the mastermind behind the rise and fall of the hedge fund, Brian Hunter. Prior to joining Amaranth, Hunter held similar energy-trading positions with TransCanada and Deutsche Bank in New York. It was Deutsche Bank that Hunter claimed owed him $69 million in compensation that was never paid. To capitalize on his expertise in the energy markets, Maounis initially named Hunter cohead of the energy desk—with control of trading on more than half the firm's assets. When Brian Hunter was offered a $1 million bonus to join rival energy-trading firm SAC Capital Advisors, Maounis granted him even more authority over the trading operations. Near the end of 2005, Hunter was earning close to $75 million, making him the highest-paid trader at Amaranth and among the 30 most highly paid traders in the world, as reported by *Trader Monthly* magazine.

Not long after, Hunter and his family moved to his native Canada to open an office in Alberta with eight other traders. There, Hunter placed the trades that would lead to his and Amaranth's demise. Believing the price difference of natural gas between the winter months and summer months would widen, he placed highly leveraged trades at an 8:1 ratio of assets to equity with durations extending to 2012. He also anticipated that natural gas prices overall would rise but that heating oil and other fuels would remain flat or fall slightly. This was the perfect opportunity to capture profits, he thought. Unfortunately, the price spreads between October and January contracts narrowed, and the spreads between March and April contracts also narrowed. The fund started to hemorrhage money.

Once word hit The Street that Amaranth was in big trouble, it was like blood in the water, and the sharks attacked. Amaranth attempted to get out of trouble by liquidating its positions, but no one on The Street would bite. As a result, the pricing continued to drop, and the losses continued to stack up for Amaranth.

Amaranth became desperate and needed to find an immediate way out. To the rescue came three firms. After long and grueling negotiations, Amaranth was able to convince Merrill Lynch and J. P. Morgan to take possession of all Amaranth asset positions. It took an all-night negotiating session signed at 5:30 A.M. for the deal to get done. Amaranth had to make large payments to these firms to accept the deal. J. P. Morgan quickly sold some of the deals to Citadel and netted close to $800 million. In all, Amaranth lost approximately $6.6 billion owing to market losses and the fees associated with selling the asset positions.

Quiz for Chapter 5

1. Name the fund considered the biggest hedge fund collapse of all time.

   a. Marin Capital

   b. Manhattan Fund

    c. Long-Term Capital Management

    d. Amaranth Advisors

2. Long-Term Capital Management boasted two Nobel Laureates as founders.

    a. True

    b. False

3. Approximately how much did Long-Term Capital Management lose?

    a. $1.6 billion

    b. $4.6 billion

    c. $7.6 billion

    d. $11.6 billion

4. Which of the following funds was brought down by investments in General Motors?

    a. Marin Capital

    b. Eifuku Master Fund

    c. Bailey Coates Cromwell Fund

    d. Beacon Hill Asset Management

5. The Lancer Offshore Fund made bad bets—leading to its downfall—in which class of stocks?

    a. Emerging markets

    b. Convertible preferreds

    c. Small caps

    d. Exchange-traded funds

6. Which hedge fund was run by Donald O'Neill, the manager who took fund assets and lost them gambling in Las Vegas?

    a. Askin Capital

    b. Tradewinds International

    c. Orca Funds

    d. Brown Simpson

7. The Brown Simpson Fund was the first massive hedge fund failure in global history.

    a. True

    b. False

8. Amaranth Advisors targeted what type of trading?

    a. Foreign exchange futures

    b. Natures gas futures

    c. Coal emission allowances

    d. Synfuel credits

9. Who was the head trader at Amaranth Advisors and most responsible for the fund's collapse?

    a. Julian Robertson

    b. Robert C. Merton

    c. Mark Yagalla

    d. Brian Hunter

10. What did Amaranth Advisors do to get out of its mess?

    a. Offset losing positions with gains in oil derivatives

    b. Sold all positions to other trading firms

    c. Received a bailout from a Federal Reserve–led bank group

    d. Defaulted on nearly all losing positions

CHAPTER 6

Revealing the Key Players

The Who's Who of Hedge Funds

Given the way the media portrays hedge funds, many people may have the misconception that hedge fund managers and other key people are somewhat exotic and mysterious. In reality, this is not the case at all. Are you ready to pull back the curtain and see the real who's who of hedge funds? This chapter will do just that.

There are many key players that participate in the hedge fund trade, and they can be classified into three distinct groups. The first group of key players is the clients or investors of hedge funds. These people are the limited partners, which means that they are only liable to the extent of their invested capital. The second group of key players consists of the insiders, or those who establish and operate hedge funds. These people are the decision makers of the hedge funds and are solely responsible for how well they perform. Lastly, the third group of key players is made up of the external professionals who either support or provide oversight to the hedge fund trade. Let's explore each one of the three distinct groups in greater detail.

Investors: The Limited Partners

The first group of key participants with hedge funds consists of the investors, or what are commonly referred to as the *limited partners.* When people think of hedge fund investors, they typically think of high-net-worth individuals and families. Given the high hurdles that must be met to invest in hedge funds, it is no wonder that most individuals who invest in hedge funds are wealthy. However, hedge funds are not just the investment domain of high-net-worth investors because many institutions are entering the hedge fund marketplace with serious momentum. Following is a list of the major investors who contribute to stand-alone hedge funds. The reason I say *stand-alone* hedge funds is that one of the most important sources of new money flowing into hedge funds is actually coming from funds of funds. With this type of fund, individuals invest directly in a fund of funds, and that fund turns around and invests the money in any number of stand-alone hedge funds. This trend is expected not only to continue but also to gain traction over time as more individual and institutional investors look to hedge funds, but more specifically to funds of funds, for investment alternatives.

HIGH-NET-WORTH INDIVIDUALS

High-net-worth investors have been the traditional backbone of hedge fund investors, and the very first hedge funds targeted this type of investor from the outset. The Securities and Exchange Commission (SEC) places very restrictive provisions on who can and cannot invest in hedge funds, and this has a direct impact on individual investors. These restrictions are based on the wealth of the individual and the income that he or she is earning now and expects to earn in the near future. Individual high-net-worth investors provide roughly half the total capital invested in hedge funds. Furthermore, according to data from Watson Wyatt Worldwide consulting analysts, as published in *Global Alternatives* (June 2005), high-net-worth investors allocate 56 percent of their investments in alternative assets to hedge funds.

PENSION FUNDS

One of the largest institutional players targeting hedge funds for investment is pension funds. Decision makers of these sometimes mammoth-sized portfolios are always on the hunt for top managers, and their search often leads them to hedge funds. Of course, pension funds consist of assets from individual investors, but the decision making is done on the institutional level. Pension funds have substantial assets and therefore are one of the top nonindividual hedge fund investors. Pension funds present golden opportunities for hedge fund managers but also bring added burdens. They are typically much more discerning than high-net-worth individuals and demand more transparency from hedge fund management as well. This has caused the hedge fund industry to create a more transparent culture, and this is good not only for pension funds but also for all investors.

INSURANCE COMPANIES

A second institutional investor in hedge funds is insurance companies. Although insurance companies generally take a conservative approach to investing to ensure that capital is available to pay claims in the future, they also know the importance of proper asset allocation and therefore seek out return-enhancing and risk-reducing opportunities. Their search often leads them to hedge funds to manage small allocations of their overall pool of capital, or the insurance premiums paid by people. They too are more selective in their hedge fund managers and help to promote investor-friendly provisions for all hedge fund investors.

ENDOWMENTS AND FOUNDATIONS

Although foundations and endowments traditionally have invested conservatively, they recognize the benefits of allocating even small portions of their portfolios to alternative assets, notably hedge funds. By investing in hedge funds, endowments and foundations are able to build more optimal portfolios and enhance the risk-adjusted returns of their portfolios. Many, but not all, endowments and foundations will hire a consultant to develop an optimal asset allocation plan for them and then work to hire the investment managers, including hedge fund managers, to build out the portfolio.

MONEY-CENTER BANKS

The fourth type of institutional investor is money-center banks and related financial institutions. These institutions are now becoming a bigger force in hedge funds and will continue to gain traction in this trade over the next few years. Some are establishing their own stand-alone hedge funds, whereas others are selecting, and starting funds of funds as their hedge fund of choice.

BROKER-DEALERS

Broker-dealers, also referred to as brokerage firms, are involved with hedge funds for two primary reasons. First, broker-dealers serve as the first point of entry to hedge

funds for many individual investors. Here, individual investors rely on the expertise of their broker-dealer to suggest appropriate hedge funds, whether in-house or external. This brings us to the second reason why broker-dealers are involved with hedge funds—that being the establishment of both stand-alone hedge funds and funds of funds. The aim of broker-dealers is to offer investment alternatives to their clients to keep all invested capital in-house rather than seeing that money leave the firm and go to outside managers. In addition, many broker-dealers establish hedge funds to hedge their own financial risks related to business operations.

LARGE CORPORATIONS

Many corporations are central figures in hedge funds. This is not a big source of funds for hedge funds, but corporations do provide adequate funding. As with banks and other financial institutions, corporate interest in hedge funds will continue to rise. Corporations view hedge funds as a way to invest excess capital while reducing the volatility of not only their investment portfolio but also their own sales cycle. Imagine a copper mining company establishing a hedge fund to sell short copper to help offset the impact of any decline in copper prices. Although many corporate treasury departments already serve this role, hedge funds help to shelter such companies and to differentiate the entity from core operations.

FUNDS OF FUNDS

As mentioned previously, one of the biggest single sources of capital for stand-alone hedge funds is funds of funds. Yes, this type of fund is technically a hedge fund itself, but as far as where new assets originate and flow into stand-alone hedge funds, funds of funds are a major force. More important, funds of funds are growing quickly, and this means that this source of capital should continue to supply a great amount of assets to hedge funds in the near future. Funds of funds also have wide appeal to both individual investors and institutional investors. Many financial institutions prefer this route when entering the hedge fund trade because they are not required to start an entire stand-alone hedge fund from scratch, and they limit their risk exposure given the diversification benefits inherent in funds of funds.

Hedge Fund Insiders: The General Partners

The second group of key participants in hedge funds is made up of the hedge fund insiders, or those most responsible for the operation of hedge funds. This section presents key professionals that are typically found working for a hedge fund management company. These insiders are generally considered general partners, or those on the hook for financial liability beyond their initial investment. Most medium to large firms have staff that fits one of the following roles. However, for the smaller hedge funds, any one person may be required to wear many hats and serve in multiple capacities. This means that a hedge fund manager may conduct the roles of analyst, trader, and hedge fund manager. Likewise, an accountant may need to serve the roles of risk manager and general support staff. Many of the general partners have a significant amount of their own assets invested in the hedge fund, typically considered seed money. Note that many firms will have positions not mentioned here, but for the most part, these positions comprise those generally seen from hedge fund to hedge fund.

MANAGERS

Hedge fund managers are the lifeblood of a hedge fund and hedge fund company. Hedge fund managers are typically the people who took the initiative to establish the hedge fund and often have a vested interest in how well it does, given that most have a substantial amount of their own wealth invested in the hedge fund they manage. Hedge fund managers are first and foremost responsible for the investment decisions of the hedge fund. They make the buy and sell decisions and sometimes execute the trades in smaller firms. The vast majority of managers are actively involved in researching opportunities and deciding which strategies and tools of the trade to employ. Obviously, this is the most important and most celebrated key player participating in hedge funds.

ANALYSTS

The typical role of an analyst is to research investment alternatives and provide recommendations to hedge fund managers. Analysts can either recommend to buy a certain investment or perhaps even recommend that a hedge fund to sell an existing investment. Of course, this process is reversed for selling short rather than going long. Analysts typically target one or more industries and drill down into the details that can affect valuation. Some analysts use a top-down methodology, whereas others use a bottom-up methodology. They pour over financial statements and ask company executives numerous questions, all in the hope of gaining better insight and making smarter investing decisions.

RISK MANAGERS

Risk managers are charged with the responsibility of performing compliance-related tasks. Their first task is to identify hedge fund positions, performance, valuations, and levels of risk. Once this is complete, they report this information to hedge fund executives for their due-diligence activities. Another vital role risk managers play is to implement control and restrictions on the hedge fund once certain risk parameters are breached. For example, if a certain hedge fund breached their value-at-risk (VaR) metric, then a risk manager may force the hedge fund manager to sell some of the fund's positions that are considered too risky. Risk managers play an important role when they do their job the right way. Risk managers also are charged with the responsibility of helping to draft risk and performance reports for interested potential clients. Can you think of risk managers who didn't do their jobs? Think of Long-Term Capital Management and Enron.

TRADERS

Traders are the people who make the financial transactions happen. These people typically are glued to a computer screen or, more likely, multiple computer screens. I can personally attest to seeing some traders with eight computer screens all feeding relevant and useful information. Traders execute transactions as instructed from hedge fund managers. Transactions, or deals, are executed with other traders, who can be located anywhere across the globe. Traders need to react quickly to execute orders, and they generally fight hard for pennies on the dollar.

ACCOUNTANTS

Hedge fund accountants can serve in many different roles. The two leading roles include the valuation and pricing of hedge funds and the daily transaction reporting for not only the hedge fund but also the company as a whole. Serving as an accountant also can be a stepping stone to hedge fund management once exposure and experience are gained. Who better is there to move into a junior hedge fund management role than someone who knows the fund inside and out? Finally, accountants also work closely with outside auditors to generate compliance and regulatory disclosures.

ATTORNEYS

Attorneys play two prominent roles in hedge funds. First, they help hedge funds to draft their offering documents and ensure that the funds are complying fully with all regulations—SEC, Internal Revenue Service (IRS), Federal Reserve, etc. The second prominent role they play is to help investors understand and evaluate the offering and partnership documents of the hedge fund they wish to buy. Attorneys can either work internally for the hedge fund or be a hired outside attorney who works in coordination with the hedge fund compliance department.

SUPPORT STAFF

This group of insiders typically includes those not listed previously, specifically administrative professionals, information technology technicians, customer-service representatives, professional assistants, and anyone else who supports any of the primary roles within a hedge fund.

External Professionals: No Partnership

The final group of key participants in hedge funds consists of external professionals. These professionals do not work for hedge funds, but rather, they provide any number of services that are essential to the continued success of hedge funds. Note that some external professionals are not presented here, but this list captures the key players.

PRIME BROKERS

Prime brokers are the investment banks and financial institutions that serve as custodians for hedge fund assets. In addition, prime brokers also provide loan sourcing and securities to borrow for hedge funds that sell short. This service is not free, however, and prime brokers will charge hedge funds for their services. Most of the global investment banks compete in this space, given the explosive growth in both the number of hedge funds and the assets they manage.

SPONSORS

In the past, some hedge funds were established through the seed capital of another fund management company. This external company would partner with the hedge fund manager and offer the fund under its own name and market it to their own clients. This arrangement provided a quick and easy way for some hedge fund managers to get involved in the hedge fund trade. This type of an arrangement is much less common today than in the past.

CONSULTANTS

Some of the most prominent hedge fund investors will seek out the help of consultants. These consultants will assist investors with finding and selecting appropriate hedge funds. For this work, the investor or hedge fund manager typically will pay the consultant a "finder's fee." Consultants also work exclusively on marketing

hedge funds to accredited investors and receive fees as compensation for clients placed with hedge funds.

FINANCIAL ADVISORS

Financial advisors play an important role in hedge funds in that they are typically the first people to expose many investors to all things related to hedge funds. Financial advisors will emphasize their company's sponsored hedge funds, but this is not always the case. Financial advisors often have the trust and confidence of their clients and become the natural connection and source of education on hedge funds. They typically provide excellent ways for investors to discuss hedge funds and how best to incorporate them into their portfolios and current asset allocation.

MARKETING SPECIALISTS

Marketing specialists are focused on presenting a partnered hedge fund in the best possible light to prospective investors. They will attempt to paint the best picture possible and, in turn, become a solid resource for investors looking to gain a foothold in hedge funds. Marketing specialists do much of the legwork that managers otherwise would have to do to grow their assets under management. This frees up the manager to focus on what he or she does best, manage money.

ACCOUNTANTS AND AUDITORS

Accountants and auditors accomplish much of the grunt work of hedge funds from a financial operations standpoint. They are focused primarily on auditing the performance of the hedge fund and provide confidence to potential investors in knowing that the stated performance was reviewed and approved by an external auditor. Without an external auditor or accountant providing such an assurance, many investors—particularly institutional investors—simply would be too skeptical about the stated performance and would decline to invest in that hedge fund.

REGULATORS

Regulators are the watchdogs of the hedge fund industry. There are many such regulating agencies such as the SEC, the Commodity Futures Trading Commission (CFTC), the Federal Reserve, and the U.S. Treasury Department. The primary aims of these regulators are to ensure that the laws of the land are upheld, that there is full disclosure of the risks of hedge funds to the investing public, and that the chances of hedge fund failures and their subsequent negative effects on the domestic and global financial systems are minimized.

RATING AGENCIES AND DATA SOURCES

The final external players participate in the job of collecting, evaluating, reporting, and sometimes rating hedge fund performance. Data sources are actively involved in collecting hedge fund performance data and reporting those data in the form of an index. Standard & Poor's is one such data source. Other organizations, such as Morningstar of Chicago, collect hedge fund performance data and issue ratings and commentary on how well the hedge fund is doing and how well it stacks up against other hedge funds. There is significant growth potential in this group as more and more people invest in hedge funds and require unbiased information for making decisions. Figure 6–1 provides a who's who of hedge funds

Quiz for Chapter 6

1. The founders of a hedge fund are considered what type of partners?

    a. Associated

    b. Limited

    c. General

    d. Unlimited

2. Most hedge fund managers avoid investing their own money in the funds they manage.

    a. True

    b. False

3. All the following are considered investors in hedge funds, *except*

    a. high-net-worth individuals.

    b. pension funds.

    c. rating agencies and data sources.

    d. insurance companies.

4. Of the total amount high-net-worth investors allocate to alternative assets, approximately what percent is allocated to hedge funds?

    a. 36 percent

    b. 56 percent

    c. 76 percent

    d. 96 percent

Figure 6-1. The who's who of hedge funds

Investors: The Limited Partners

1. High Net-Worth Individuals
2. Pension Funds
3. Insurance Companies
4. Endowments and Foundations
5. Money-Center Banks
6. Broker-Dealers
7. Large Corporations
8. Funds of Funds

Hedge Fund Insiders: The General Partners

1. Managers
2. Analysts
3. Risk Managers
4. Traders
5. Accountants
6. Attorneys
7. Support Staff

External Professionals: No Partnership

1. Prime Brokers
2. Sponsors
3. Consultants
4. Financial Advisors
5. Marketing Specialists
6. Accountants and Auditors
7. Regulators
8. Rating Agencies and Data Sources

5. As investors in stand-alone hedge funds, are funds of funds considered general partners or limited partners?

    a. General partners

    b. Limited partners

6. All the following are considered general partners *except*

    a. managers.

    b. analysts.

    c. risk professionals.

    d. regulators.

7. Risk management professionals are charged with the responsibility of hedge fund compliance.

    a. True

    b. False

8. Which external professional is responsible for the custody of hedge fund assets?

    a. Prime brokers

    b. Sponsors

    c. Consultants

    d. Financial advisors

9. Standard & Poor's is an example of what type of external professional?

    a. Marketing specialist

    b. Rating agency and data source

    c. Consultant

    d. Sponsor

10. Which of the following external professional is rarely used today with the startup of hedge funds?

    a. Consultant

    b. Financial advisor

    c. Marketing specialist

    d. Sponsor

Risk, Return, and Market Dynamics

Framework for Hedge Fund Investing

No one particularly likes risk. Furthermore, no one particularly likes risk when risk becomes reality and misfortune occurs. Avoiding risk is therefore ideal. However, doing so is not entirely feasible in the world of investing because there is a clear and profound relationship between risk and return. Risk is an inherent part of any investment undertaking, making it critical to understand this inescapable trade-off. Getting blindsided by the realization of risk needs to be evaluated when making investment decisions. So too does the potential for strong returns.

Unfortunately, we hear the very opposite practically every day in nearly all places—that reward can be earned with little to no risk. Reward without risk does not exist in the investment marketplace. Don't let anyone tell you otherwise. Abnormally high returns are not uncommon, but they are neither predictable nor consistent over time. Consequently, if you desire a return that outpaces both inflation and taxes, then you must be prepared to assume some level of risk. You get what you pay for and earn what you invest in. As you know, you do not get something for nothing.

Two of the most important concepts an investor should learn and fully understand are investment return and investment risk. These two concepts and how they work together are the foundations of asset allocation and its application to building an optimal portfolio including the use of hedge funds. Depending on your objectives and constraints, you may invest in assets that exhibit low risk and therefore the potential for low but stable returns, or you may invest in assets that exhibit high risk and therefore the potential for high but often volatile returns. In basic asset allocation theory, the higher the potential risk you take, the higher is the potential return you should earn. Moreover, rational investors will not assume a higher level of risk in the hope of earning a return that another investment may earn, but with a lower level of risk.

The million-dollar question is how to enhance your returns and still avoid risk. Although risk cannot be eliminated entirely from a portfolio, it can be controlled and managed with a proper asset allocation policy. A portfolio that is optimally designed, built, and managed will exhibit a higher risk-adjusted return than a portfolio that does not subscribe to proper asset allocation regardless of whether high-return investments are part of that portfolio.

Investment Return

Investment return is of primary importance. Why would you invest otherwise? Without appropriate compensation in the form of returns, people would not invest their hard-earned money. Earning the highest return for the least amount of risk assumed is at the core of asset allocation. Return can come in many different ways. Although I will be discussing quantitative measures of return, do not forget that return often has qualitative rewards. Qualitative rewards include comfort, piece of mind, security, simplicity, and a feeling of control over one's life.

It is vitally important that you consider the return you wish to receive and what risk you must assume to obtain that return. Moreover, investing more money in a higher-return asset class does not mean that your return will be any higher than someone who invested less in that same asset class. The individual investments that make up your portfolio are not so important; rather, it is the portfolio as a whole that is most important. For this reason, it is wise to build a portfolio of multiple asset classes rather than allocating to only the current high-return-potential asset class. Generally speaking, a higher probability of return also means a higher probability of losing some or all of an investment. Some people are willing to assume this risk, whereas

others are not. This is what makes asset allocation and portfolio construction so unique from person to person.

The profit or loss from an investment consists of both appreciation or depreciation in market value over the holding period and the dividends or interest received during the same holding period. Summing the two profit or loss components and dividing by the market value of the investment at the beginning of the period will give what is referred to as *total return*. This measure takes into account both the change in price of the security and any cash flows received during the holding period. It is commonplace in the investment field to measure return using the total return calculation. An example of calculating total return follows.

Example

The Smith Foundation purchased 1,000 shares of Deere & Co. at $40 a share. One year later the Jones Foundation sold the investment for $44 a share. During the one-year period, Deere & Co. paid a $1 per share dividend. The total return of the investment, not including transaction costs, is 12.5 percent, $4 appreciation plus $1 dividend divided by $40 cost. Thus, to calculate total return, sum the appreciation (ending value – beginning value) and all interest and dividends received during the period, and divide by the beginning value.

The concept of return can be divided into two distinctions, actual return and expected return. *Actual return* is the return you have realized, or one that has occurred in a past holding period. Conversely, *expected return* is an estimate of what you will earn, both appreciation and income (dividends and interest), in a future holding period. Both actual and expected returns are commonly expressed as annualized percentages. The process of forecasting expected returns is especially difficult. However, the following basic steps will provide you with a cursory understanding:

1. Forecast all possible material outcomes that may occur.
2. Assign probabilities of occurrence to each outcome.
3. Forecast the return for each specific material outcome.
4. Multiply the probabilities with their related forecasted return.
5. Add the results for each possible outcome.

Example

An analyst estimates that the Smith Company has a 50 percent probability of returning 12 percent, a 25 percent probability of returning 5 percent, a 15 percent probability of returning 0 percent, and a 10 percent probability of returning –5 percent. Thus the estimated return is

$$(0.50 \times 0.12) + (0.25 \times 0.05) + (0.15 \times 0) + [0.10 \times (-0.05)] = 6.75 \text{ percent}$$

Potential outcomes are usually based on estimates of how well the economy will perform in the future holding period. The resulting return is simply an estimate given each economic scenario.

Investment Risk

Investment risk can be defined in many different ways, and some investors view risk differently than other investors. Some investors define risk as losing money, whereas others define risk as unfamiliar investments. Still others define risk as contrarian risk, or the risk that investors feel when they are not "following the crowd." If you were to toss out all the subjective definitions, risk is defined more objectively as uncertainty, or the uncertainty that actual investment returns will equal expected returns. Pension funds and insurance companies view risk as the uncertainty that they can meet future benefit obligations, whereas mutual funds view risk as under-performing peer mutual funds and/or an industry benchmark, such as the Standard & Poor's (S&P) 500 Index. As for individual investors, they tend to view risk as losing money in their portfolios, whether that loss is temporary or permanent. This may not be the best way to view risk, but it is the most understood and most applied by individual investors.

In aggregate, most investment experts define risk quite rigidly as the volatility of returns over a specific time period. Most risk measurements are accomplished using monthly price movements for individual securities, whether those movements are up or down. The greater the monthly movement, regardless of direction, the larger is the volatility measure, and therefore, the greater is the risk. Volatility also affects total performance. Portfolios with more volatility will exhibit lower long-term com-pounded growth rates of return. Thus it is essential to minimize volatility in your portfolio for maximum appreciation over time.

Risk management and proper asset allocation reduce both the frequency and the amount of portfolio losses. Since you rely on estimates of future returns to design your optimal portfolio, it is critically important that actual returns come close to matching expected returns. Investments with more predictable returns are considered lower risk. Conversely, investments with less predictable returns are considered higher risk. Risk in one word can be called *uncertainty*—more specifically, the uncertainty that actual returns will match expected returns.

SOURCES OF INVESTMENT RISK

There are two primary sources of risk. The first is called *systematic risk,* or risk attributed to relatively uncontrollable external factors. The second is called *unsys-tematic risk,* or risk attributed directly to the underlying investment.

Systematic Risk

Systematic risk results from conditions, events, and trends occurring outside the scope of the investment. At any one point there are different degrees of each risk occurring. These risks will cause the demand for a particular investment to rise or fall, thus affecting actual returns. The four principal types of systematic risk are

- *Exchange-rate risk.* The risk that an investment's value will be affected by changes in the foreign currency market.

- *Interest-rate risk.* The risk attributed to a loss in market value owing to an increase in the general level of interest rates.

- *Market risk.* The risk attributed to a loss in market value owing to a declining movement of the entire market portfolio.

- *Purchasing-power risk.* The risk attributed to inflation and how it erodes the real value of an investment over time.

Unsystematic Risk

Unlike systematic risk, unsystematic risk is not attributed to external factors. This source of risk is unique to an investment, such as how much debt a company possesses, what actions a company's management takes and what industry it operates in. The principal types of unsystematic risk are

- *Business risk.* The risk attributed to a company's operations, particularly those involving sales and income.

- *Financial risk.* The risk attributed to a company's financial stability and structure, namely, the company's use of debt to leverage earnings.

- *Industry risk.* The risk attributed to a group of companies within a particular industry. Investments tend to rise and fall based on what one's peers are doing.

- *Liquidity risk.* The risk that an investment cannot be purchased or sold at a price at or near market prices.

- *Call risk.* The risk attributed to an event in which an investment may be called, or forced to sell, prior to maturity.

- *Regulation risk.* The risk that new laws and regulations will have a negative impact on the market value of an investment.

Summing systematic and unsystematic risk gives total risk. Since the goal of asset allocation is to create a well-diversified portfolio, unsystematic risk is considered unimportant because it should be eliminated with proper diversification.

Therefore, an optimal portfolio should only possess systematic risk, or risk resulting from market and other uncontrollable external factors.

MEASURING INVESTMENT RISK

Since different investments have both different types of risk and different degrees of risk, it is essential to quantify risk in order to make comparisons across the broad range of asset classes. As mentioned earlier, *risk* can be defined as the uncertainty that actual returns will not match expected returns. Intuitively, one can see that the greater the difference between actual and expected returns, the less predictable and more uncertain that investment is considered. This translates into greater risk.

Using historical return data, one can define risk more accurately. Historical volatility data can be obtained using numerous intervals of time—days, weeks, months, and years. Monthly volatility generally is used in practice. In simple analyses, averaging the degrees of difference between actual and expected returns for a given investment gives us the statistical measure called *standard deviation*. A higher standard deviation means higher risk.

One important note to remember is that standard deviations for investments or asset classes are not static. They will change over time. Some asset classes will change more frequently and to a greater degree than other asset classes. Historically, small-cap stocks have exhibited the greatest amount of variability with regard to standard deviation. Large-cap stocks follow right behind.

Volatility has been shown to rise during periods of falling prices and moderate during periods of advancing prices. Even with changes to asset-class volatility in the short-term, the range of asset-class volatility has remained relatively stable over the long term. That is good for investment planning. Standard deviation is a statistical measure of the degree to which actual returns are spread around the mean actual return. Expressed as a percentage, standard deviation is considered to be the best measure of risk.

Since actual returns are affected by both systematic and unsystematic risks, standard deviation is a measure of total risk. As a result, standard deviation gives an investor a way to evaluate both the risk and return elements of an individual investment. Although standard deviation is one of the best measures of risk, it is by far not without issues. Depending on the holding periods selected for comparison, standard deviation may vary from analysis to analysis.

Risk and Return Trade-off

The relationship between risk and return is central to the investing decision framework. This relationship essentially says that to earn higher level of returns, investors need to assume higher levels of risk. There is simply no other way to accomplish this aim. In addition, investors looking to assume low levels of risk will in aggregate earn lower returns. Asset allocation is very much related to risk and return and the part they play in portfolio construction. Hedge funds should not be approached as a stand-alone single investment. Rather, they should be approached as part of the overall picture, a component of asset allocation. It is for this reason that I dedicate this chapter to learning asset allocation, including risk and return. For a more detailed discussion of asset allocation, please pick up a copy of my book *Understanding Asset Allocation*, also published by McGraw-Hill.

Asset allocation is founded on two celebrated and highly influential investment theories. These two theories are the *modern portfolio theory* (MPT) and the *efficient market hypothesis* (EMH), which is essentially a refinement of MPT. These two theories are the most discussed and most widely used theories in all of investment management. You cannot pick up a book on hedge funds without finding a discussion of the risk-return profile of individual hedge fund strategies. This discussion provides charts and graphs and typically incorporates Sharpe ratios. All these are directly related to both the aforementioned theories.

MPT says that investors and portfolio managers should not evaluate each investment on a stand-alone basis. Rather, each investment should be evaluated based on its ability to enhance the overall risk-return profile of a portfolio. When faced with two investments with identical expected returns but different levels of risk, investors should select the investment that has the lower risk, according to MPT. In other words, a rational investor will select the investment with the higher return when faced with two investments that have different expected returns but identical levels of risk (see Figure 7–1).

Figure 7-1. Investment alternatives and rational decisions

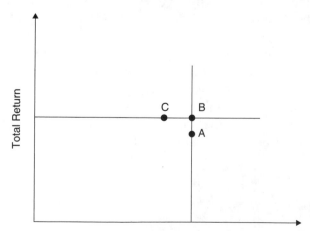

When faced with investments A and B, a rational investor will select investment B over investment A because the total return of investment B is higher, with both having the same level of risk. Moreover, when faced with investments B and C, a rational investor will select investment C over investment B because the total risk of investment C is lower, with both having the same total return. This is pretty simple stuff, but it was revolutionary when it was first put forth.

Lastly, MPT introduces the concept of correlation and stresses how it enhances the risk-return profile of a portfolio. The Employee Retirement Income Security Act of 1974, which governs the management of pension funds, emphasizes this point, thus essentially endorsing MPT. Harry M. Markowitz, who was awarded the Noble Prize in economics in 1990, is considered the "father of modern portfolio theory" for this work.

Understanding Asset Classes

An *asset class* is a group of securities that share similar underlying characteristics as well as very similar risk-return trade-off profiles. As a result of their similarities, the market prices of securities within each asset class tend to move together. The market price for each security within an asset class is highly influenced by events involving other securities within the asset class or the asset class as a whole. Whether justified or not, even one security can greatly influence the prices for the other securities within an asset class. Asset classes are sometimes referred to as *investment classes*. The four primary asset classes are

- Equity assets
- Fixed-income assets
- Cash and equivalents assets
- Alternative assets

Each asset class can be divided into asset subclasses, such as large- and small-market-capitalization equity securities and taxable and tax-exempt fixed-income securities. *Market capitalization* is defined as the total market value of a publicly traded company, whereby the number of shares outstanding is multiplied by the market price per share.

As with the primary asset classes, each asset subclass is distinguished by its own unique risk and return characteristics. The benefit of asset subclasses is their less than perfect correlations with other asset classes but more specifically with other asset subclasses. Thus you can add different asset subclasses to your portfolio to

enhance your portfolio's risk-return trade-off profile. For instance, a portfolio with both international and U.S. large-cap equity securities will exhibit a more ideal risk-return trade-off profile than a portfolio consisting of only international large-cap equity securities. Asset subclasses can be thought of as providing enhanced asset allocation or asset allocation within the primary asset classes.

Different Asset Classes

As mentioned previously, securities within each asset class share similar underlying characteristics. Each characteristic allows for portfolio customization. This is beneficial because different investors have different needs. But what are the underlying characteristics within each asset class? The most important underlying characteristics include

- Total return potential
- Price volatility
- Correlation with other asset classes and asset subclasses
- Growth versus income trade-off
- Liquidity
- Market efficiency
- Factors that influence their market value
- Type of underlying entity (corporation, government, etc.)

EQUITY ASSETS

Equity assets represent an ownership interest in a corporation and signify a claim to a corporation's assets. In order to fund business operations, corporations first raise capital by issuing equity securities. Each share of stock owned gives an investor a proportional share of the corporation's profits, which are usually distributed in the form of dividends. In addition, owners of most equity securities are given voting rights. Voting rights allow you, for instance, to vote for a corporation's board of directors, approve or disapprove of employee stock option programs, and vote for or against acquisitions. From my experience, individual investors foolishly do not exercise their right to vote. In response, more power shifts to corporate management shareholders and to large institutions. Each has its own agenda, which typically isn't always on the same page as individual investors. Remember to always exercise your right to vote. There are essentially two types of equity securities: preferred stock and common stock.

Preferred Stock

Preferred stock represents ownership of a corporation but is slightly different from common stock. Preferred stock shareholders do not have voting rights. In exchange, shareholders receive a higher priority on the assets of the corporation in the event of liquidation owing to bankruptcy. Furthermore, it is commonplace for shareholders of preferred stock to receive not only a higher-yielding dividend but also priority in receiving dividends over common stock shareholders. For example, if a corporation is having difficulty in meeting its dividend payments to both preferred and common stock shareholders, the corporation must make dividend payments to the preferred stock shareholders first. Afterwards, provided that enough cash remains, common stock shareholders will receive their dividend payments.

Many corporations issue what is called *convertible preferred stock*. This type of preferred stock is very similar to nonconvertible preferred stock with one significant difference: Convertible preferred stock gives the owner the option to convert, or exchange, his or her preferred shares into a fixed number of common stock shares after a predetermined date. The market value of this type of preferred stock is more volatile because its value is influenced by the market value of the related common stock.

Common Stock

Common stock is the most widely used form of equity ownership. Common stock shareholders have voting rights and often participate in receiving profits in the form of dividends. However, not all corporations distribute profits in the form of dividends. Rather, some reinvest the dividends back into the company in order to fund existing and planned operations.

Two of the most common asset subclasses are growth and value stocks. A *growth stock* is common stock that produces higher rates of return than the stocks of its industry peers, whereas a *value stock* is common stock that is considered undervalued given its expected rate of return and present stock price. Again, each possesses its own unique risk-return trade-off profile. Both these asset subclasses have similar characteristics because they both are equity securities; however, they also have very important differences. As a result, growth and value stocks tend to have a low correlation with each other, a risk-reducing and return-enhancing benefit.

FIXED-INCOME ASSETS

Fixed-income assets represent a loan to a corporation or governmental entity that wishes to raise capital. Fixed-income assets are commonly referred to as *debt* in the investment community. In most cases, assets of the issuer back each fixed-income security, thus providing the purchaser with some protection in the case of default. These assets, or *debt instruments,* hold the issuer to a contractual obligation to make periodic interest payments to the purchaser on predetermined dates in prede- termined amounts until the security reaches maturity or is called by the issuer. *Maturity* is defined as the date on which an issuer is obligated to pay the principal of a fixed-income security to the purchaser. The *call date,* then, is the date on which a fixed-income security is redeemed by the issuer prior to maturity. Typically, the longer the time to maturity for a fixed-income security, the higher its yield tends to be. Thus short-term securities typically have lower yields than do long-term securi- ties. Yield is best described as an annual rate of return determined by dividing the annual interest payments by the purchase price or market value (depending on when and how you are evaluating the security).

For a real world example, simply look at cash and equivalents. Cash and equiva- lents do have many similarities with fixed-income securities; however, the one char- acteristic that defines them as cash and equivalents rather than fixed-income securities is their short-term maturity. But why do securities with longer maturities have higher yields? The principal and most accepted theory (since there are other theories) says that investors demand higher rates of return for each progressively longer period of time because they must forego current consumption of the money they invest and assume risk for a longer period of time than if the holding period were shorter.

CASH AND EQUIVALENTS ASSETS

Cash and equivalents assets are a very broad category defining assets that are highly liquid, very safe, and can be converted easily into cash, such as money market funds, or are already in that form, such as coins and bills. Cash and equivalents usu- ally have a maturity date within one year. The returns of this asset class generally correlate with the rate of inflation. Thus, as inflation rates fall, so too do the rates on money market funds and certificates of deposit (CDs). Cash and equivalents are differentiated by their issuer, maturity date, interest rate (referred to as the *coupon rate*), credit quality, and tax status (taxable or nontaxable).

ALTERNATIVE ASSETS

Alternative assets consist of a very broad category of assets, mostly encompassing what are referred to as *hard assets.* In contrast to the other primary asset classes, alternative assets are more dissimilar in their inherent characteristics than they are similar. Furthermore, most alternative assets are tangible, rather than intangible, as they are with the other primary asset classes.

The principal reason underlying the purchase of alternative assets is to hedge inflation. In practice, this is referred to as *protecting your purchasing power.* Another strong reason to invest in alternative assets is because they tend to have very low, and sometimes negative, correlations with equities. Alternative assets do well in times of high inflation and often capture more investment inflows during times of market weakness, regardless of their valuation.

Some of the primary alternative assets are

- *Real estate*
- *Commodities*
- *Private equity*
- *Hedge funds*
- *Collectibles*

Understanding each asset class, its expected risk-return trade-off profile, and the correlations among the classes is essential to asset-allocation theory and its application to your investment portfolio. Asset classes represent building blocks for the selection of appropriate investments and their weightings within your portfolio.

Given the different asset classes available, you can customize your portfolio in a way most appropriate to achieve your objectives and constraints. Using each asset class is central to enhancing your portfolio's return while reducing its risk. Consider a football team, for example. A team consisting only of linemen most likely will not reach the playoffs. Odds are that the team won't even win a game! It takes a well-balanced team with players in all positions to reach a championship game. Building an optimal portfolio requires this same approach.

Understanding Correlation

An optimal portfolio is not just the sum of its parts. Rather, an optimal portfolio is the sum of its synergies. *Synergies* are created by the interaction of the investments held in a portfolio. This interaction is commonly referred to as *correlation* and is a critical input to the asset-allocation process. *Correlation* is the technical term used to measure and describe how closely the prices of two investments move together over time.

Positively correlated assets move in the same direction, both up and down. Conversely, negatively correlated assets move in opposite directions. Correlations between two assets are expressed on a scale between −1.0 and +1.0. The greater two assets are correlated, or move together, the closer the correlation is to +1.0.

Similarly, the greater two assets move in opposite directions, the closer the correlation is to –1.0. Two assets that move exactly together have a +1.0 correlation, whereas two assets that move exactly opposite each other have a –1.0 correlation.

Example

The correlation between stock A and stock B is 0.8. As a result, for every $1 price movement in either stock, the other will move 80 percent, or $0.80 per share, in the same direction over the same time period.

Correlations between –0.3 and +0.3 are generally considered noncorrelated. This means that the two asset classes move independently of each other. With noncorrelated assets, when one is rising in price, the other may be rising, falling, or maintaining its current price.

A properly allocated portfolio has a mix of investments that do not behave the same way. Correlation therefore is a measure you need to be concerned about. To maximize the portfolio benefits derived from correlations, you will need to incorporate investments with negative correlations, low positive correlations, or even assets that have noncorrelations. Noncorrelated investments move independently of each other. By investing in assets with low correlations, you are able to reduce total portfolio risk without affecting the return of your portfolio. Doing so will help to greatly minimize the overall investment-specific risk attributed to each investment.

The greatest portfolio risk-reduction benefits occur during time periods when correlations across the board are low, noncorrelated, or negative. When correlations increase, risk-reduction benefits are partially lost. Over time, some correlations will increase, and some will decline.

Since you cannot predict which correlations will change or to what degree they will change over time, successful investors will allocate to a number of fundamentally different investments to reap the benefits of asset allocation (see Figure 7–2).

Time Horizon Explained

Your time horizon is another very important input variable. Most investors pay too little attention to time horizon and the important role it plays. Your time horizon affects expected rates of return, expected volatility, and expected investment correlations.

As a result of the important role it plays, time horizon is the first constraint that should be identified. Overestimating or underestimating your time horizon can have

Figure 7-2. Spectrum of hedge fund correlation

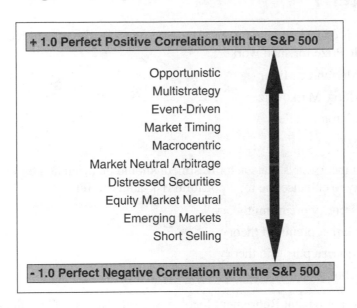

a significant impact on how you allocate your assets and thereby affect your risk-return profile.

The primary role time horizon plays is to help you select and evaluate the appropriateness of each asset class and asset subclass as an investment alternative. Specifically, time horizon helps to determine your balance between equity investments and fixed-income investments. The shorter your time horizon, the more emphasis you should place on fixed-income investments. Conversely, the longer your time horizon, the more emphasis you should place on equity investments. In the short term, equities are simply too volatile and posses too high levels of uncertainty. Said another way, equities exhibit unacceptable levels of risk in relation to their expected returns. On the other hand, fixed-income investments are significantly less volatile in the short term and possess much lower levels of uncertainty. As a consequence, fixed-income risks in relation to their expected returns are more favorable in the short term.

As your investment time horizon increases, so too does the probability of your equity assets experiencing positive returns. Over longer periods of time, equity returns become more stable because there is more time for positive equity returns to offset negative equity returns. The returns of equities become significantly more clear and predictable as your investment time horizon lengthens.

Quiz for Chapter 7

1. Who is considered the father of modern portfolio theory and received a Noble Prize for such work?

    a.   Merton C. Miller

    b.   Harry Markowitz

    c.   Myron Scholes

    d.   Warren Buffett

2. What theory says that each investment should be evaluated based on its ability to enhance the total portfolio risk-adjusted return?

    a.   Security premium theory

    b.   Market premium theory

    c.   Modern portfolio theory

    d.   Allocation efficiency theory

3. The Employment Retirement Income Security Act of 1974 officially recognizes and requires the use of modern portfolio theory.

    a.   True

    b.   False

4. Name the two types of equity stock.

    a.   Limited stock and preferred stock

    b.   Preferred stock and yield stock

    c.   Yield stock and common stock

    d.   Common stock and preferred stock

5. All the following are underlying characteristics of asset classes *except*

    a.   price volatility.

    b.   type of underlying entity.

    c.   factors that influence market prices.

    d.   management structure.

6. Preferred stock does/does not provide voting rights to the shareholder.

    a.   does

    b.   does not

7. Fixed-income assets represent a loan to a corporation, institution, or governmental entity.

   a. True

   b. False

8. For the most part, alternative assets are financial in nature rather than physical in nature.

   a. True

   b. False

9. All the following are considered alternative assets *except*

   a. preferred stock.

   b. collectibles.

   c. private equity.

   d. hedge funds.

10. The longer an investor's time horizon, the more he or she should allocate to equities/fixed-income/alternative assets.

    a. Equities

    b. Fixed-income

    c. Alternative assets

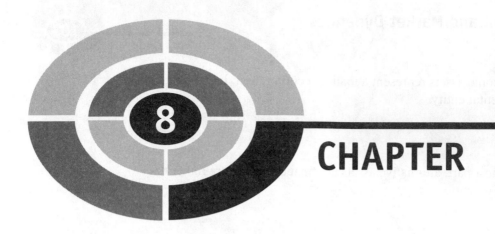

8

CHAPTER

Tools of the Trade

Techniques and Tactics of Hedge Fund Managers

Hedge fund managers operate under a two-tier system framework. This two-tier system consists of the tools and methods hedge fund managers employ and the strategies they commonly use within the context of the tools and methods available. For example, one of the most popular tools employed by hedge fund managers is the use of leverage. However, managers can employ leverage in a number of different ways with the goal of achieving a certain result. This is where the selected strategies of the managers come into play. This chapter is specifically dedicated to those tools of the trade that hedge fund managers typically employ to carry out their desired strategies. The chapters in part two dissect the individual strategies that are commonly used.

An unfitting, yet easily understood analogy to describe the difference between hedge fund tools and strategies is to consider gambling. Your *strategy* is to make money at the local casino while your goal is to go home with more money than you arrived with. But how do you accomplish this? Do you play the slots, take your

chances with blackjack, spin the roulette wheel, or take part in craps? These choices represent the *tools* you have at your disposal. Tools represent the means you have to carry out your strategy, to make money. Depending on your skill and available resources, one such tool may be more ideal for you.

The goal of hedge fund managers is to generate attractive absolute returns. In addition, hedge funds aim to generate a rate of return that has a low correlation with the equity markets and with traditional investment portfolios of stocks and bonds. To accomplish this, hedge fund managers emphasize alternative investment strategies along with the tools discussed in this chapter. Note, however, that many hedge fund managers do not use all the tools of the trade and that some traditional managers even use some of the alternative strategies and tools from time to time. The following are the common tools used by hedge fund managers to carry out their hedge fund strategies:

- Selling short
- Leverage
- Hedging
- Arbitrage
- Futures and options
- Specific markets
- Position limits
- Buy/sell targets
- Stop-loss restrictions

Common Tools of Hedge Fund Managers

USE OF SELLING SHORT

Selling short is selling a security that is not owned by the hedge fund. Here, a hedge fund manager borrows shares of a security from a prime broker and turns around and sells those shares on the open market. The hedge fund receives the proceeds from the sale but then owes the shares back to the prime broker, the custodian of the assets held by the hedge fund.

As long as the price of the security sold short declines, the hedge fund will profit. This follows the tried-and-true investing wisdom of buy low, sell high. But in this

case you sell high and buy low. However, if the price rises, the hedge fund will lose because it essentially will have to replace the borrowed shares by purchasing them at a higher price. This translates into buying high and selling low. This is not exactly what hedge fund managers should be doing.

In order to borrow shares from a prime broker, the hedge fund will need to post some form of collateral, such as other securities. Margin accounts therefore are required. Margin accounts will contain both the assets used as collateral and the borrowed funds. Hedge fund managers use selling short in one of two primary ways. First, hedge fund managers use selling short as a way of reducing exposure to a single investment. For example, a certain hedge fund holds $25 million in equity securities, comprising 90 percent of the entire fund. Given recent strong price increases, the manager believes that the risk and price of equities are too high. To offset some of the risk, the hedge fund manager sells short $5 million, thus reducing open equity exposure to $20 million. Regardless of price change, either up or down, $5 million–out of the $25 million–in long equities is offset by $5 million in short equities. This is considered a "hedging" reason to employ selling short.

The second way hedge fund managers use selling short is to profit from perceived overvalued securities. Thus, if a hedge fund manager believes that a certain investment is priced too high, he or she can sell short shares in the hope that the price will fall, thus allowing for the hedge fund manager to buy back the borrowed shares and return them to the prime broker while making a profit. Unlike the first example, here the hedge fund does not hold an existing long position in the security sold short. As a result, this is considered a "trading" reason to employ selling short.

EMPLOY LEVERAGE

Leverage is best described as borrowing to buy more of an investment. Furthermore, leverage is assuming more investment exposure than what an investor would be exposed to given the assets that particular investor holds. For example, suppose that a hedge fund manager expects that the return on a certain investment will experience strong performance over the next year and will deliver a return that exceeds the cost of borrowing funds. As a result, the hedge fund manager invests $2 million in the investment and borrows funds to buy another $1 million in the same investment. Thus the hedge fund will own an investment worth $3 million dollars, and the fund only used $2 million of its own assets.

For another example, suppose that someone purchases a home for $500,000, where $200,000 is from the homeowner's money and $300,000 is borrowed from the bank. If the home appreciates by 20 percent, or $100,000 ($500,000 x 0.20), over a certain period, then the homeowner will experience a return of 50 percent

($100,000/$200,000) *less* borrowing costs. Now suppose that the home depreciates by 20 percent, or $100,000. This means that the homeowner has experienced a return of –50 percent (–$100,000/$200,000) *plus* borrowing costs. As you can see, the impact of borrowing magnifies return whether positive or negative. Leverage also can create situations where you can lose more than your original investment. In the preceding example, if your home price were to fall 50 percent, or $250,000, then you would have $50,000 in negative equity ($200,000 initial investment – $250,000 loss). Hedge funds work the same way. As long as the return is positive, the return is magnified to the upside. However, when things turn bad, leverage magnifies the bad and can even put the investor in a position where he or she ends up owing money, more than the original investment.

With leveraging, investors and hedge fund managers anticipate a higher return on the borrowed funds in excess of the cost to borrow the funds themselves. Hedge funds borrow these funds from prime brokers, who charge them a rate of interest tied to some standard rate, such as the London Interbank Offered Rate (LIBOR). The use of leverage increases risk, and therefore, leverage should be used cautiously. Leverage magnifies investment performance on the upside *and* the downside. When the market is performing well, leverage will generate greater returns. However, in falling markets or declining price of an investment, leverage can be your worst enemy.

Given the heightened risk with using leverage, many hedge fund managers have found more lower-risk ways of using it to their advantage. There are two common reasons for using leverage. First, hedge fund managers use leverage to increase the exposure of an investment above and beyond what the manager is able or willing to purchase using capital in the fund. Second, managers use leverage to magnify the results of a low-risk, low-return strategy related to pricing discrepancies such as arbitrage opportunities. When used judiciously, leverage can work very well in your favor (see Figure 8–1).

Figure 8-1. Degree of leverage by strategy

Strategy	Leverage
Fixed-Income Arbitrage	20 to 30 times capital base
Convertible Arbitrage	2 to 10 times
Merger Arbitrage	2 to 5 times
Equity Market Neutral	1 to 5 times
Long/Short Equity	1 to 2 times
Distressed Securities	1 to 2 times

CONDUCT HEDGING

Hedging is used when a manager believes that a certain investment offers profit opportunity but does not want to be exposed to other risks, such as market risk. For instance, suppose that a hedge fund manager believes that a select Standard & Poor's (S&P) 500 stock is significantly overvalued. As a result, the hedge fund manager sells short the stock and simultaneously buys an S&P 500 Index fund. Thus the investment is protected from market influences as any change in the stock sold short due to the market will be offset by changes in the index fund. Doing so eliminates market risk and isolates company-specific risk and return potential, or the overvaluation in this example. The same can be done for undervalued securities as well. In this case, a hedge fund manager could buy the security and sell short an S&P 500 Index fund. Thus, if the stock declines owing to the market, then the hedge fund manager will lose money on the long stock position but offset the loss with gains on the short S&P 500 Index fund held. Hedging allows hedge fund managers to eliminate market risk and isolate investment-specific risk and return potential.

USE FUTURES AND OPTIONS

Hedge fund managers can use options and futures either to hedge their positions or speculate. For instance, if an equity hedge fund manager believes that the equity market will decline, he or she can protect the value of the fund by either buying S&P 500 put options or selling short S&P 500 futures contracts. Thus, if the market declines, the hedge fund manager can exercise the S&P 500 put options to offset the loss with the long equity position or will profit on the short futures contract given the decline of the market.

Futures and options are both considered *derivative* instruments. Unfortunately, many people have biases about derivatives because of all the media hype surrounding some high-profile derivative scandals. Nevertheless, derivatives offer investors and hedge fund managers alike the opportunity to protect their positions in the face of adverse price movements or to speculate on the direction of the market.

A *futures contract* is an agreement whereby two parties agree to exchange an asset at a future date at the then prevailing price. In the case of the S&P 500, the futures contract simply states that one party will purchase the S&P 500 from another party, the counterparty. Again, a futures contract is essentially the same as buying the investment, but with a fixed delay built in. This type of an investment thus offers symmetric risk exposure. Options are slightly different but accomplish approximately the same thing—that being speculating on the direction of the market or protecting a portfolio from adverse price movements. Options offer asymmetric risk exposure.

An *option* gives the buyer the right to buy or sell the underlying asset at a predetermined price over a predetermined time period. An option does not obligate the buyer to exercise. However, when the option value is in your favor, an investor would be incredibly foolish not to exercise the option because it would equate to throwing money out the window. Futures contracts, on the other hand, do not give the buyer the right; they obligate the buyer to either buy or sell the underlying investment at a predetermined point in time, but at the price prevailing at contract expiration.

PURSUE ARBITRAGE

Arbitrage is defined in the academic world as a riskless investment. Unfortunately, this word has been overused and used out of context by those in the investment profession as a way to "push" their funds. Arbitrage is the simultaneous purchase and sale of two securities that are explicitly tied in some fashion. One of the most popular uses of arbitrage is to profit from a pricing discrepancy between the price for a particular stock and the price for a convertible bond tied to that stock. For example, suppose that Dynamite Stores stock is selling for $50 a share and that its convertible bond is selling for $1,030. If the convertible bond allows for converting into 20 shares of stock, then the value an investor would receive from doing so is $1,000 (20 shares $\times$ $50 = $1000). However, with the bond selling for $1,030, the investor would be foolish to convert the bond for stock with less value. To profit on this price discrepancy, a hedge fund manager would sell short the convertible bond and buy the stock with the proceeds. The hedge fund would make $30 on each transaction ($1,030 – $1,000). The hedge fund manager would continue to place transactions until pricing equilibrium—the point where no pricing discrepancies exist due to a rising stock price and a falling convertible bond price—is achieved.

TARGET SPECIFIC MARKETS

Hedge funds often target specific markets, sectors, and asset classes. This is done to give the hedge fund focus and to take advantage of perceived opportunities specific to a particular market. Hedge funds often will differentiate between geographic locations, such as European and Asian markets, and asset type, such as equities and fixed-income assets. By targeting specific markets, hedge funds can gain exposure to opportunities not necessarily available in the domestic market or diluted in the overall domestic market. For instance, although many U.S.-based companies have operations in Europe and profit from gains made there, a hedge fund may desire more exposure to European markets than simply buying U.S. companies with European operations. This also can be ideal for investors because modern portfolio theory says that investing in additional markets or asset classes can enhance return and reduce risk.

INCORPORATE POSITION LIMITS

To safeguard a fund from losses on any one investment, hedge funds can institute *position limits* that restrict the size of an investment in any single company to a certain percentage. In addition, position limits also can trigger hedge funds to liquidate certain holdings once losses become too large. For example, suppose that a hedge fund institutes a 20 percent limit on how much any one holding may comprise the fund's overall holdings. Regardless of how well the asset is performing, no new investments can be made in the asset above the 20 percent limit. Furthermore, appreciation of the asset above the 20 percent limit may require the hedge fund manager to sell, or offset with by selling short, some of the investment to satisfy the position limit. This protects the hedge fund from large swings in value if the price of the asset begins to move in the adverse direction.

SET BUY/SELL TARGETS

In simplistic terms, a *buy/sell target* is the point at which a hedge fund manager will either sell a held asset given that it is fairly valued or buy an asset because it is perceived as being undervalued. Hedge fund managers frequently place target prices on securities, and when the investment hits one of the price targets, it triggers a buy or sell transaction.

FOLLOW STOP-LOSS RESTRICTIONS

Regardless of the estimated value of a certain investment, hedge funds are very conscious of the losses they suffer. Investors do not appreciate losses very well either. Consequently, hedge funds are motivated to sell losing investments once a certain investment reaches a predetermined level of losses. This predetermined point is the hedge fund manager's maximum loss he or she is willing to incur on any one particular investment. Hopefully, a hedge fund will not need to institute a *stop-loss provision,* but it can protect itself from additional losses.

Quiz for Chapter 8

1. All the following are tools used by hedge fund managers *except*

   a. arbitrage.

   b. duration.

    c. specific markets.

    d. leverage.

2. Ownership of shares is required prior to selling short those same shares.

    a. True

    b. False

3. In the academic world, which of the following is considered to be a riskless investment?

    a. Selling short

    b. Arbitrage

    c. Hedging

    d. Stop-loss restrictions

4. What is the benefit of employing leverage?

    a. Reduced risk

    b. Can profit in both rising and falling markets

    c. Market risk hedged

    d. Magnifying positive performance

5. Do futures, options, or both obligate the owner to exercise the contract?

    a. Futures

    b. Options

    c. Both

6. When a hedge fund manager borrows shares of stock and then sells them on the open market, this tool is called what?

    a. Specific markets

    b. Position limits

    c. Selling short

    d. Stop-loss restrictions

7. Options and futures are considered derivative financial instruments.

    a. True

    b. False

8. Why are position limits used by hedge fund managers?
   a. To enable more efficient use of leverage
   b. To promote greater use of hedge fund resources
   c. To safeguard the hedge fund against losses from single investments
   d. To offset lack of compliance

9. Which tool is best defined as the point at which a hedge fund manager will either liquidate a current investment or purchase an investment perceived to be undervalued?
   a. Position limits
   b. Stop-loss restrictions
   c. Arbitrage
   d. Buy/sell target

10. Which of the following tools allows hedge fund managers to profit in both good and bad markets?
    a. Leverage
    b. Selling short
    c. Arbitrage
    d. Specific markets

PART

II

Demystifying the Different Types of Hedge Funds

Event-Driven Hedge Funds

Funds that Pursue Opportunistic Situations

Event-driven hedge funds employ strategies that attempt to capture profits from specific one-time opportunistic situations or events. This style is called *event-driven* because the opportunities hedge funds target are not dependent on the performance of the overall market but rather are driven by special events. This means that hedge fund managers can profit from employing this strategy in any market condition. If the market is rising or falling, hedge fund managers will not be affected. What is important to managers is the level of activity that drives these opportunistic situations. As long as the level of activity is robust, opportunities will be identified and pursued.

There are four primary strategies under the event-driven style. These include distressed securities, reasonable value, merger arbitrage, and opportunistic events. Although each is similar, they do differ in important ways. The last strategy mentioned, opportunistic events, is a more broad and general strategy, unlike the other three strategies, which are more focused and targeted.

Distressed Securities

This is a strategy whereby a hedge fund manager invests in the equity or debt of struggling companies at typically steep discounts to their estimated value. The spread between the estimated value and the present market value can be attributed to any number of factors, including the restriction of some institutions from owning non-investment-grade securities and the resulting oversale of those securities. Most of the companies' hedge funds target in this strategy are usually in or facing bankruptcy or reorganization.

There are other times when a hedge fund manager will sell short the securities of companies in distress because he or she expects the share price to fall with worsening conditions. When negative events affect companies, some debt holders will attempt to sell their holdings for any number of reasons. Given the turmoil surrounding such an event, there are times of imbalance given that there are many more sellers than buyers. This imbalance is a ripe opportunity to some hedge fund managers. Consequently, managers will take positions in the company as long as the real value of the security is below that of the current market price, of course. Real value is derived from either intrinsic value, relative value, or the value of similar companies or similar financial instruments of the distressed company that are less affected and thus provide a bogey for valuation. Current market values below both intrinsic and relative values are signals to hedge fund managers that an opportunity for profit may exist.

Many hedge fund managers operate under the premise that the market does not know how to react properly and value companies in or approaching distress. For hedge fund managers who acquire specialized knowledge of the distressed securities marketplace, identifying and taking advantage of opportunities is an ideal way to generate attractive returns. Note that the holding period may be longer when investing in distressed securities than with traditional investments or employing other hedge fund strategies because the companies take longer to turn around their operations.

Many companies that find themselves in serious financial distress will file for bankruptcy protection. As long as the creditors of a particular company have confidence in the future prospects of the company, they will work to help find a financial

solution to get the company back on its feet. This often will include exchanging debt for a combination of new equity and new debt—at lower interest rates, however. These new securities of equity and debt are looked on favorably by hedge funds and are purchased frequently. The holding period could extend many years before positive returns are experienced, however. Hedge funds using this strategy are always on the lookout for companies with solid operations but heavy debt loads that have an impact on the financial performance of the company.

Since the distressed securities strategy is more event-driven than not, hedge funds can find opportunities for this type of investing regardless of how well or poorly the market is performing. One can argue, however, that most such companies fall into distress during times of economic hardship, which often can be during periods of market weakness associated with declining economic conditions.

Typical risk: Low to moderate

Risk-return profile: Return enhancer

Value proposition: Opportunistic returns

Directional bias: Both net long and net short

Reasonable Value

Reasonable value is a strategy whereby a hedge fund manager invests in securities that are selling at discounts to their perceived value as a result of being out of favor or being relatively unknown in the investment community. This strategy is similar to the distressed securities strategy but places more emphasis on securities with lower levels of default risk. As a result, hedge fund managers are presented with greater numbers of opportunities under this strategy. It is therefore important for hedge fund managers to conduct proper due diligence to identify securities that offer the most promising returns with the least amount of risk. Minimizing default risk through the use of this strategy is done because default risk is perhaps the most significant risk inherent in securities facing troubling times. By minimizing default risk, hedge funds will reduce the greatest threat to fund performance, but they also forgo the incremental return potential as well. This is the trade-off hedge fund managers employing the reasonable value strategy are willing to take.

Hedge fund managers using this strategy commonly will purchase a particular security and sell short a comparable security. This will allow the hedge fund manager to isolate the desired company-specific risk and return potential and to minimize market risk from the two offsetting long and short positions. This strategy is not an especially popular strategy among hedge fund managers, but I present it to give you a cursory understanding.

Typical risk: Low to moderate

Risk-return profile: Return enhancer

Value proposition: Opportunistic returns

Directional bias: Both net long and net short

Merger Arbitrage

Merger arbitrage, or what is also called *risk arbitrage,* is a strategy whereby a hedge fund manager invests in event-driven scenarios where there are unique opportunities for profit. As the name of the strategy implies, these opportunities include the following unique situations:

- Acquisitions and corporate takeovers
- Legal reorganizations
- Mergers
- Exchange offers
- Cash tender offers
- Recapitalizations
- Leveraged buyouts (LBOs)
- Proxy contests
- Restructurings

Hedge funds will attempt to generate profits based on changes in price spreads between two securities that historically have consistent spreads but now have changed owing to a merger-related event. The most common aim of hedge fund managers using this strategy is to go long the stock of the company being acquired and to go short the stock of the company that is making the acquisition. Regardless of the merger-related transaction, there is always the risk that the deal will fall through. Consequently, there is commonly a spread between the current valuation based on the announced deal and the value once the deal is finalized. For instance, suppose that company A announces that it will acquire all the stock of company B for $50 when the current market price for company B stock is $44 a share. Almost immediately—after trading for the stock reopens on the exchange—the share price for company B will rise sharply. But the price will not rise to $50 immediately owing to the risk that the deal will fall through. Rather, the price of company B's stock most likely will rise to around $49 per share, with a $1 spread built in to protect against the deal not moving forward. This is where hedge funds will do their research and due diligence on the deal. If a hedge fund manager is comfortable with the deal moving ahead, then he or she will step in and make an investment to capture the $1 spread. More specifically, a hedge fund manager will go long the stock of company B by purchasing shares at $49 and selling short the shares of company A to finance the purchase of company B stock. Once the deal is finalized, holders of company B's stock will receive $50 per share, thus generating $1 profit to the hedge fund. Lastly, the stock of company A will then be purchased to return the borrowed shares given the selling short transaction.

The success of any merger arbitrage deal is based on the deal going to completion. Deals that are terminated typically will lose money for hedge funds. This is the important consideration and drawback of this strategy. For instance, in the preceding example, if a hedge fund had purchased shares of company B and sold short shares of company A, and the deal were to fall through, then the share price of company B would decline—perhaps close to pre-merger announcement levels of $44—whereas the share price for company A would rise to pre-merger announcement levels. Given the short position with company A's stock and long position with company B's stock, the hedge fund would take losses on both sides of the investment. This is not exactly what hedge fund managers want to see happen. This outcome is always possible with merger-related deals and thus must be taken into consideration very seriously before any investment is made.

The primary advantage of this strategy is that it does not depend on the market. Since merger-related transactions occur in both bull and bear markets, prospects to profit are good for hedge funds that target these event-driven opportunities. The disadvantage is that hedge funds in this space are entirely dependent on merger-related activity. As long as activity is robust, opportunities will exist. Once activity declines, then opportunities will be scarce to find. This means that there will be more hedge fund managers chasing each remaining opportunity.

Hedge fund managers who pursue merger-related opportunities tend to be highly specialized in mergers and the process companies go through to make them happen. Furthermore, these hedge fund managers are very good at identifying profitable opportunities and employing strategies for taking advantage of them. Their attempt is to capture the spread between two interrelated securities where the spreads have become temporarily abnormal. As a general rule, the more narrow a spread between the company making the acquisition and the company being acquired, the lower risk the market perceives the deal to have. Conversely, deals with wide spreads mean that the market perceives there to be much risk of the deal falling through. Instead of hunting for companies that exhibit opportunities to be acquired, hedge fund managers emphasize conducting thorough research and making prudent investments after acquisition announcements are made public.

Typical risk: Low to moderate

Risk-return profile: Return enhancer

Value proposition: Opportunistic returns

Directional bias: Both net long and net short

Opportunistic Events

Opportunistic events describe a broad strategy employed by hedge fund managers to invest in securities that are experiencing short-term event-driven opportunities. These opportunities are considered one-time events that offer strong returns. These events have specific beginnings, endings, and time intervals in between. As such, they are very definable. These opportunities include, but are not limited to, the following:

- Initial public offerings (IPOs)
- Seasoned stock offerings
- Earnings release surprises
- New business awarded
- Addition or departure of key executives

The list of possible opportunities is extensive. This strategy covers all possible stand-alone events that can present opportunities. To capitalize on these opportunities, hedge fund managers often will employ multiple and rotating hedge fund strategies. Hedge fund managers will paint themselves into a corner if they commit themselves to using just one particular strategy. They must be flexible, yet proactive.

The opportunistic events strategy is quite similar to the merger arbitrage strategy, but the two strategies are different in two particular ways. First, merger arbitrage strategies focus on merger-related deals, not on extemporaneous opportunities, as opportunistic events strategies call for. Second, merger arbitrage managers will become involved in opportunities once a deal is announced and typically not beforehand. The same is not especially true of opportunistic events managers. Under this strategy, hedge fund managers are proactive in hunting down companies they believe are in strong positions to develop profitable opportunities. Many hedge fund managers will make initial investments in companies they believe will present opportunities even before those opportunities surface. Many traditional investment managers do the exact same thing, so this strategy is not entirely foreign to many people.

As with the other event-driven strategies, the opportunistic events strategy does not rely on the performance of the overall equity or fixed-income markets. As long

as special events present themselves, hedge fund managers employing this strategy will find opportunities to profit. The financial instruments most commonly used by managers in this space include the following:

- Debt securities
- Warrants
- Preferred stock
- Common stock
- Index put options
- Put options spreads

Not only do hedge fund managers emphasize certain financial instruments to make investments, but they also use their specialized knowledge of corporate life cycles and historical price spreads to generate attractive returns. The foundation for this knowledge is derived from appraisal analysis, occurrence analysis, and duration analysis. As long as the prices move as anticipated, given definable short-term events, then the hedge fund will have accomplished its aim and delivered profits to its investors.

Typical risk: Low to moderate

Risk-return profile: Return enhancer

Value proposition: Opportunistic returns

Directional bias: Both net long and net short

Quiz for Chapter 9

1. All the following are event-driven hedge fund strategies *except*
   a. merger arbitrage.
   b. opportunistic events.
   c. distressed securities.
   d. macrocentric.

2. Seasoned stock offerings present opportunities that are best defined as short-term opportunistic events.
   a. True
   b. False

3. Opportunities in merger arbitrage include all the following *except*

    a. stock splits.

    b. exchange offers.

    c. leveraged buyouts.

    d. proxy contests.

4. Purchasing the equity or debt of struggling companies at typically steep discounts to estimated value is which type of strategy?

    a. Merger arbitrage

    b. Distressed securities

    c. Opportunistic events

    d. Emerging markets

5. What is the primary advantage of event-driven hedge funds?

    a. Less expertise is required to implement.

    b. Returns are significantly more certain with the other styles.

    c. Opportunities are independent of how well the total market is doing.

    d. Performance-incentive fees are typically half those of the other styles.

6. What is the aim of event-driven hedge funds?

    a. To capture profits from specific one-time opportunistic situations or events

    b. To profit from directional price movements

    c. To invest according to specific principles

    d. To target significant, yet uncertain profits

7. LBO stands for *legal buyout*.

    a. True

    b. False

8. Based on what do merger arbitrage hedge funds attempt to generate profits?

    a. Sudden increases in prices

    b. Changes in the price spread between two securities

    c. A sudden fall in price captured by selling short

9. What does a wider price spread between the market price and the acquisition price indicate?

   a. The market's low confidence that the acquisition will be consummated.

   b. The market's high confidence that the acquisition will be consummated.

   c. Does not indicate anything of significance.

10. Hedge fund managers believe that the market overvalues distressed companies.

   a. True

   b. False

CHAPTER 10

Tactical Hedge Funds

Funds that Seek Trends and Make Directional Bets

Tactical strategies are very popular with hedge fund managers. In fact, more than half of all hedge fund assets are invested using tactical strategies. Of this style, the macrocentric strategy is by far the most used because it offers significant breadth and depth of available investment opportunities. Many people in the hedge fund trade refer to this style as either *tactical* or *directional*. Both terms are used interchangeably and mean the same thing.

Many people think of hedge funds and envision managers selling short or leveraging their funds. Although this is commonly performed, it is by far not the only way that fund managers operate their funds. Many hedge fund managers employ little to no leverage, and the same goes for selling short. Tactical hedge funds, for the most part, employ minimal leverage and instead operate as long-term and low-turnover investments. At the same time, this low turnover minimizes tax consequences and thus makes tactical hedge funds more tax efficient. Since many hedge fund investors are required to lock up their investment in hedge funds for an extended

period of time, emphasizing long-term investing is therefore a smart move by the hedge fund manager. Note that some strategies within the tactical style do provide for more liberal use of leverage and selling short, such as macrocentric hedge funds. As mentioned in Chapter 2, Warren Buffet was a big player in hedge funds early in his career. His style of choice was the tactical style.

Macrocentric

This is a strategy whereby a hedge fund manager invests in securities that capitalize on the broad markets, both domestically and internationally. This is considered a top-down approach to hedge fund investing. The objective of a macrocentric strategy is to profit from broad changes in markets that are the result of any number of macroeconomic and governmental factors such as influence and intervention. Macrocentric hedge funds are almost always broad-based in nature, such as playing foreign exchange (FX) movements or investing in market indices. Rarely do they invest in a small segment of the overall market, such as buying an oil company to profit from strong earnings. Hedge funds do invest in less broad assets but generally do so using a slightly different strategy. With macrocentric investing, leverage is commonly employed to magnify the results of the investments.

Many macrocentric hedge funds will select a particular market and usually will invest by going long rather than going short. Managers of most other strategies target individual securities, whereas macrocentric hedge fund managers do not. Only the broad markets and broad themes are considered for investment purposes. As a result, macrocentric hedge fund managers will research and make investment decisions based on specific equity markets, foreign exchange markets, and commodity markets, such as gold, oil, copper, and agricultural products.

The objective of macrocentric managers is to identify current valuation and forecasted price movements. Once this is accomplished, investments or bets are made to take advantage of the anticipated price movements. Again, leverage is commonly used to enhance results. These actions taken by hedge fund managers can be either systematic or discretionary.

The advantage of macrocentric hedge funds is in their ability to take advantage of discrepancies in current and forecasted prices. In addition, they can achieve this by allocating a good deal of the hedge fund's assets to the investment and to do so quickly. Given the scale of some macro markets, making even sizable investments will not affect the market as it will with some smaller and less liquid markets. Of importance to macrocentric managers are very specific conditions, such as current asset valuation and flow of investment funds into and out of certain asset classes, which are used in making investment decisions. Knowing these conditions and how best to take advantage of them can provide attractive added returns to this type of hedge fund.

The source of returns for macrocentric hedge funds is the spread between the intrinsic valuation and the current valuation. The greater the spread, the greater is the opportunity. Hedge fund managers employing this strategy seek out these opportunities and quickly take advantage of them. The hope is that when the macroeconomic or political conditions presently driving the asset price abate, the spread will narrow, and the hedge fund will see nice returns. These trends are very important with macrocentric investing.

The great challenge with macrocentric investing is in identifying when is the best time to invest in a certain asset. Hedge fund managers ask themselves if the current trends affecting prices are slowing down, getting better, or are relatively level. If the trend in the macroeconomic or political factor is still declining and getting worse, then the hedge fund manager will delay the investment. However, if the manager determines that things are getting better, then he or she typically will make the initial investment.

Macrocentric hedge funds have performed well over the last two decades; their performance has surpassed that of the Standard & Poor's (S&P) 500 Index by a material margin. In addition, the volatility of macrocentric hedge funds was lower than that of the S&P 500, most likely the result of investing in multiple markets all over the globe. This combination of markets—as with combinations of securities—reduces total portfolio volatility and enhances potential return expectations.

Typical risk: High to very high

Risk-return profile: Risk enhancer

Value proposition: Opportunistic returns

Directional bias: Long bias

Sector-Specific

This is a strategy whereby the hedge fund manager invests in a long holding of equities and sells short equities or equity market indices. Hedge fund managers typically will invest in sectors with which they are familiar and knowledgeable about—thus the name of the strategy. Hedge fund managers are attracted to certain sectors owing to the growth prospects. Therefore, betting on the direction of the sector with a long investment will take advantage of growth opportunities. To minimize total

market risk, hedge fund managers sometimes will sell short the market index, thus increasing the hedge fund's exposure to sector-specific risk. Of course, with increased sector-specific risk comes increased sector-specific return potential. This is what hedge fund managers target by using this strategy.

The typical hedge fund using a sector-specific strategy will hold a core position in the sector and an opportunity position, which is essentially a trading position. The core position emphasizes long-term appreciation and is seldom sold to make a quick profit. Buy and hold is the name of the game with the core position. However, short-term trading and quick turnover to generate profits are the focus of the opportunity position. Here, a hedge fund manager will buy and sell overvalued securities in the sector by either going long for undervalued securities or going short for overvalued securities. The defining objective of this strategy is to use fundamental research and combine that research with sector expertise to generate attractive profits. This research typically emphasizes and filters companies for cash flow and earnings.

The obvious disadvantage to this strategy is the lack of options. If opportunities in this sector decline, then hedge funds will suffer because managers commonly invest in few sectors. There is little asset allocation with this strategy. However, this sometimes can be used to take advantage of the hedge fund manager's expertise. Given the opportunity to sell short, hedge fund managers can profit in both weak markets and strong markets. Hedge fund managers who get to know the sector well will gain an advantage over other investors. Knowing what affects the sector and how to take advantage of that movement is one way knowledgeable hedge fund managers make profits in the sector-specific strategy.

Prior to taking a position in any market sector, hedge fund managers will assess the growth prospects of that sector. This involves forecasting sector growth rates and then comparing the growth rates with those of other sectors and the overall market. Hedge fund managers also will seek out sectors where information is readily available to help the hedge fund management team make sound investment decisions. Lastly, hedge fund managers will gravitate toward sectors that provide numerous opportunities to profit and drive hedge fund returns. These opportunities can be created by governmental influences, the effects of the weather, consumer buying habits, and both the level and direction of interest rates. The greater the number of factors that can affect a sector, the more ways a hedge fund can profit from making directional price bets.

Typical risk: High

Risk-return profile: Risk enhancer

Value proposition: Opportunistic returns

Directional Bias: Both net long and net short

Managed Futures

This is a strategy whereby the hedge fund manager invests in commodities with a momentum focus, hoping to ride the trend to attractive profits. Managed futures are required to register as commodity trading advisors (CTAs) and sometimes as commodity pool operators (CPOs). These types of financial instruments trade on regulated exchanges, although some can trade over the counter (OTC) with banks and brokers.

Many hedge fund managers will employ leverage to magnify the performance of managed futures funds. There are two types of managed futures managers. The first type is the fundamental managers who rely on their experience, research, and judgment to make investing decisions. The second type is the systematic managers who rely on computer models to forecast and make investment decisions. Neither type is really any better than the other. Whatever works best is the key.

Select hedge fund managers will target high turnover and quick but limited profits. This is frequently done as a safeguard against placing larger trades for longer time periods, where the risk of experiencing a large loss increases. Many hedge fund managers using this strategy will do so in a very disciplined fashion. Often they will liquidate their positions if the trend reverses or fails to materialize as expected. This is called *getting stopped out* or *experiencing profits or losses prematurely* (see Figure 10–1).

Typical risk: High

Risk-return profile: Risk diversifier

Value proposition: Countercyclic

Directional bias: Both net long and net short

Figure 10-1. Most actively-traded futures contracts

Chicago Board of Trade (CBOT)	
U.S. Treasury Bonds	U.S. 10-Year Treasury Notes
U.S. 5-Year Treasury Notes	30-Day Federal Funds
CBOT Mini-Sized Down	Corn
New York Mercantile Exchange (NYMEX)	
Crude Oil	Natural Gas
Heating Oil	Unleaded Gasoline
Gold 100 oz.	
Chicago Mercantile Exchange (CME)	
3-Month Eurodollar	S&P 500 Index
E-Mini S&P 500	E-Mini NASDAQ
E-Mini Russell 2000	Euro FX

Long/Short Equity

The long/short equity strategy is essentially named for the practice of going long or going short equity securities. This type of hedge fund is the most fundamental of all hedge funds and was established by Alfred Jones himself.

Hedge fund managers will go long securities they believe will increase in value and will go short securities they believe will decline in value. These hedge funds focus on reducing total portfolio risk by minimizing overall market exposure. Many managers even will use a two-dimensional bet, which means that they go long one particular equity security while going short an entirely different equity security. Thus, when the price of the long position rises and the price of the short position declines, the hedge fund will profit on both positions. This, of course, could go the other way as well, with the hedge fund losing on both fronts if the long position declines in price and the short position increases in price.

The two-dimensional investment is primarily employed to minimize market risk. Additionally, a hedge fund manager can go long an equity security and then sell short an equity index. The net result of any such movement in the market, as expressed by the equity index, will be principally offset by the equity security. The only exposure therefore is the security-specific risk and return potential of the equity security. For managers looking to maximize their stock selections, the two-dimensional investment is ideal since market risk is minimized and security-specific risk is maximized. Pairings, or offsetting investments, with securities in the same sector are done frequently as well. This will minimize any sector-specific risk originating from the initial investment. Exchange-traded funds and stock index put options are frequently used to minimize market risk.

Although the net exposure with long/short equity is often long, holding a net short position is not out of the norm. The degree of long or short positions depends on the manager's forecast of market prospects. Managers typically will emphasize net long positions when they forecast bull markets and emphasize a minimal net long position or even a net short position when they forecast a bear market. As a result, hedge funds can generate profits with this strategy in any market, regardless of whether prices are moving up or down. Many hedge fund managers will employ leverage to further enhance performance from a long/short equity strategy.

Lastly, long/short equity hedge funds typically will underperform long-only portfolios in rising markets, but outperform long-only portfolios in falling markets. Hedge funds employing this strategy can go long or short and take advantage of either market movement to generate attractive absolute returns. In aggregate, long/short equity hedge funds outperform long-only portfolios over time when both bull and bear cycles are included. In addition, given that these hedge funds do not change as much in value as long-only portfolios do in response to market movements, they also have lower volatility. Lower volatility translates into lower investment risk.

The end result is a more attractive risk-adjusted return—higher performance over time combined with lower volatility over time—the ideal scenario.

Typical risk: Moderate to high

Risk-return profile: Risk enhancer

Value proposition: Opportunistic returns

Directional bias: Both net long and net short

Emerging Markets

Emerging markets is a strategy whereby a hedge fund manager invests in securities of companies from less developed, yet emerging countries that typically have emerging financial markets—thus the name of the strategy. These markets commonly offer solid growth prospects that are generally considered volatile with inflation concerns. Given that many foreign markets do not permit selling short, hedge fund managers are limited in the hedging actions they can employ. Certain other countries do allow selling short and using leverage. However, given the high transaction costs found in many emerging-market countries, selling short and leveraging are for the most part not used. Perhaps as the countries improve their financial markets this will change, and so too will the use of leverage and selling short.

Investing in emerging markets takes a good deal of sophistication and expertise. However, once this sophistication and experience are obtained, hedge fund managers become well positioned to take advantage of opportunistic situations. This is often the result of price inefficiencies between related markets. These inefficiencies create undervalued assets, and they instantly become the target of hedge fund managers. Unfortunately, there are many drawbacks and challenges to investing internationally, particularly in emerging markets. These markets are unpredictable, highly volatile, can restrict the flow of capital into and out of the country, and have precarious governmental situations. Managers often specialize in certain types of markets and certain types of hedge fund instruments to best address these issues. In addition, many emerging-market opportunities lack solid business environments, offer poor accounting practices, and can be riddled with dishonest and fraudulent local companies and investors. Expertise thus is very important.

Most successful emerging-market hedge funds employ superior information and possess superior expertise regarding the selected market. Furthermore, they also will use an on-the-ground presence in these markets to foster better cooperation with local contacts. This is all done in the hope of uncovering undervalued or mispriced securities commonly found in emerging-market areas. Without the volatile business climate and lack of suitable information prevalent in these countries,

opportunities simply would not exist to the same degree. Therefore, it is somewhat of a necessary problem in order to achieve strong results using this strategy.

The best way that hedge fund managers can generate superior returns in emerging markets is to assemble their own information and conduct their own research to identify undervalued assets. Once the financial conditions in the country are addressed and corrected over time, hedge funds will profit by being one of the first investors in the country before restructuring is done. Over the last two decades, emerging-market hedge fund managers have done well; they have outpaced the S&P 500 Index with relatively equal volatility. As a result, this strategy has become quite popular with hedge fund managers. Lastly, this strategy is beneficial in that it offers one of the lowest correlations with the other hedge fund strategies. Thus risk can be reduced and return enhanced with an emerging-markets strategy.

Typical risk: High to very high

Risk-return profile: Risk enhancer

Value proposition: Opportunistic returns

Directional bias: Net long

Market Timing

Market timing is a strategy whereby a hedge fund manager invests in asset classes that are forecasted to perform well in the short term. No consideration typically is given to positions held for more than the short term. Rebalancing of the holdings, or asset classes, is commonly done to take advantage of price rotation and price leadership among asset classes. This strategy relies heavily on the skill of the hedge fund manager with regard to the timing of entry and exit points for each investment.

Hedge fund managers will either go long or go short to take advantage of market timing opportunities. Given the breadth of the marketplace, many long and short positions can be held at one point in time. Hedge fund managers will move across the different asset classes opportunistically, looking for that diamond in the rough. Here, the hedge fund manager may invest in commodities, equities, equity indices, bonds, or even foreign currencies. There are few barriers to hedge fund investments.

This strategy requires the utmost attention of the hedge fund manager because opportunities and price discrepancies can disappear very quickly. Many hedge fund managers seek out investments exhibiting a good deal of price momentum, either on the upside or the downside. Regardless of the value of a security, the price simply may advance or decline based on irrational investor cash inflows or cash outflows. Hedge fund managers recognize this and often will capitalize on it to make a profit.

In the past, hedge fund managers used this strategy with mutual funds by placing purchase and sell orders at or just after the close of the market to take advantage of pricing spreads. This practice, viewed by many as borderline fraudulent, caused quite a stir among Wall Street regulators, with many prominent investment companies named as culprits. As a result, few, if any, hedge fund managers presently employ this strategy.

Typical risk: Very high

Risk-return profile: Return enhancer

Value proposition: Opportunistic returns

Directional bias: Both net long and net short

Selling Short

Selling short is a strategy whereby a hedge fund manager sells short securities with the objective of buying them back in the future at lower prices. This strategy is employed when the hedge fund manager believes that the price of a security is over-valued given present earnings or projected future earnings. Thus the hedge fund manager seeks to profit from a decline in the price of the security.

Investments can be made in individual companies, sectors, asset classes, or the overall market, such as the S&P 500 Index. The hedge fund manager must borrow from a brokerage firm the shares of the company that he or she wants to sell. These shares are then immediately sold in the open market at prevailing market prices. The hope of the hedge fund manager is to buy back the shares at a later time and return them to the brokerage firm, all at lower prices, of course. If the hedge fund manager can accomplish this—selling short at a higher price and replacing the shares with a purchase at a lower price—then the hedge fund will have profited. However, if the price of the security rises, then the hedge fund will lose money. This is so because at some point in time the hedge fund manager will need to purchase shares to replace the borrowed shares. Thus, if the price to purchase the replace-ment shares is higher than the price of the borrowed shares that were sold short, the hedge fund will lose the difference in value. The following are two examples of how a hedge fund manager will gain and lose from a selling short transaction.

Scenario 1: Gain

The Miller Hedge Fund sells short 10,000 shares of Mega Company stock at $50 per share. Two months later the price of Mega Company stock has fallen to a price

of $43 per share, not so mega after all. The manager of the Miller Hedge Fund determines that the stock price of Mega Company is reaching a low point and therefore purchases 10,000 shares at $43 per share. The 10,000 shares thus replace the borrowed 10,000 shares. The Miller Hedge Fund will generate a gross profit of $70,000 {10,000*($50-$43)}.

Scenario 2: Loss

At the same time as the Miller Hedge Fund is purchasing 10,000 shares of Mega Company stock, the Smith Hedge Fund sells short 5,000 shares at $43. Unfortunately, the price of Mega Company stock rises and continues to rise to $53 per share six months later. With solid growth prospects forecasted for Mega Company, the managers of the Smith Hedge Fund decide to get out of their losing investment and do so by purchasing 5,000 shares at $53 per share. As a result, the 5,000 shares are returned to the brokerage firm, but the hedge fund has a gross loss of $50,000 {5,000*($43-$53)}.

Under the selling short strategy, hedge fund managers do not have to hold an entire portfolio of short positions. They can simply be *short biased*. This essentially means that the hedge fund will have some long and some short positions, but the net position will be short—thus the short bias.

What we have just discussed is a "trading" reason for selling short. However, there is another reason why hedge fund managers use selling-short strategies exclusively. This reason is to produce monthly income. When a hedge fund manager sells short a security, that transaction produces proceeds equal to the number of shares multiplied by the price per share sold. These proceeds go back to the hedge fund account at a brokerage firm, where they earn interest. Thus the hedge fund manager has artificially created an income stream—the interest payments received—that simply did not exist before. Interesting, huh? This phenomenon is called *short-interest rebate,* and some hedge fund managers are very passionate about using it. Not only can you earn profits if the share price declines benefiting the short position, but so too can interest be earned regardless of the price movement in the stock. If the price rises, then the hedge fund is out of luck. All else being equal, a portfolio that is net short should outperform a portfolio that is net long for the single reason that the short portfolio will receive a short interest rebate.

Typical risk: High to very high

Risk-return profile: Risk diversifier

Value proposition: Countercyclic

Directional bias: Net short

Quiz for Chapter 10

1. All the following are considered tactical hedge funds *except*
   a. sector-specific funds.
   b. arbitrage funds.
   c. managed futures funds.
   d. macrocentric funds.

2. Managed futures funds are required to be registered as commodity trading advisors (CTAs) and sometimes as commodity pool operators (CPOs).
   a. True
   b. False

3. Long/short equity funds typically will outperform or underperform the total market when the market is advancing.
   a. Outperform
   b. Underperform

4. The short-interest rebate is associated with which tactical strategy?
   a. Macrocentric
   b. Managed futures
   c. Selling short
   d. Emerging markets

5. What is going long one equity security and going short a different equity security called?
   a. A two-dimensional bet
   b. Tactical layering
   c. Style-drift focus
   d. Long/short stacking

6. Which tactical strategy has gone out of favor owing to increased Securities and Exchange Commission scrutiny over mutual fund transactions by hedge funds?
   a. Emerging markets
   b. Macrocentric
   c. Sector-specific
   d. Market timing

7. Emerging-markets strategies are considered low to moderate risk.

   a. True

   b. False

8. What is the short-interest rebate?

   a. Difference between shares actually sold short and shares attempted to be sold short

   b. Interest earned on the proceeds from selling short a security

   c. Commission returned owing to selling short rather than buying long

   d. Performance premium from selling short over long only

9. Tactical hedge funds for the most part employ _____ leverage and emphasize _____ turnover investments.

   a. high/high

   b. low/high

   c. low/low

   d. high/low

10. Do macrocentric hedge funds use a top-down or bottom-up approach to investing?

   a. Top-down

   b. Bottom-up

CHAPTER

11

Relative-Value Hedge Funds

Funds That Exploit Small Yet Certain Profits

Hedge fund managers who follow strategies for taking advantage of arbitrage scenarios are thought to be relative-value-style managers. They typically emphasize only one market and make a point of employing hedging in the most profitable way. Relative-value-style managers do not corner themselves into a long or short bias. They do whatever is needed to capture the arbitrage opportunity. This means that the manager will go long to take advantage of the undervalued side of an opportunity and then go short the other side of the arbitrage opportunity. The aim is for the long side to rise in price and the corresponding short side to decline in price and to finance the long purchase. Under this scenario, a narrowing spread between the long and short positions will generate positive returns for the hedge fund, just as a widening spread will lose money for the fund. Of all the different hedge fund styles,

relative-value is the last bastion of hedge funds using pure hedging practices. Capturing profits independent of market movements is the aim of relative-value-style managers while the degree of success for these hedge funds thus is greatly dependent on the decisions the hedge fund managers make.

In the hedge fund trade, three strategies comprise the relative-value style, sometimes referred to as the *arbitrage style*. The managers in each strategy employ generally the same type of hedging techniques and tactics, all with the aim of profiting from arbitrage opportunities. However, these managers focus on different markets, thereby differentiating themselves from the other relative-value-style managers. The three relative-value-style strategies are

- Convertible arbitrage
- Equity market neutral
- Fixed-income arbitrage

Convertible Arbitrage

Convertible arbitrage is a strategy whereby a hedge fund manager takes advantage of perceived price inequality, a scenario that offers low-risk profitable opportunities. This generally involves a hedge fund manager going long one security and going short a related security. The most common financial instruments used include a convertible bond and the underlying security. There is a very good reason for this strategy. Convertible bonds are your typical bonds that pay interest, but they offer one important difference—the option for the bondholder to exchange, or convert, the bond to a predetermined underlying equity security. Convertible bonds are issued with preset conversion ratios, such as 20:1 or 15:1. This means that the convertible bond essentially has two values. The first is the current market price, and the second is the implied value based on the conversion ratio and the market price for the underlying equity security. For example, if a convertible bond with a 20:1 conversion ratio is selling for $900, and the underlying equity security is selling for $47, then the implied value for the convertible bond is $940. To arrive at this implied value, simply take the conversion ratio, which represents the number of shares you would get if you converted, and multiply by the price per share of the underlying equity security, the security you would receive if you exchanged the convertible bond. Thus, in this example, the $940 implied value is the $47 per share price for the underlying equity security multiplied by 20, the number of shares you would receive if converted.

So what does this all mean to you and to hedge fund managers? It means that there is an opportunity to profit. To do so, a hedge fund manager would buy the convertible bond for $900 and sell short 20 shares of the underlying security for $940 which finances the purchase of the bond. Thereafter, the hedge fund manager would convert the bond to the underlying equity security, thus replacing the 20 shares of stock sold short. The manager would receive the difference between the purchase and sold short transactions, or $40. This may not seem like a ton of money, but when a hedge fund buys multiple bonds, then we are talking about sizable profits. Furthermore, many hedge funds will employ leverage, or the use of borrowed capital, to make an even bigger investment. So long as the opportunity exists and the return is greater than the borrowing costs, then the use of leverage will have a positive impact on performance. Furthermore, the proceeds received from the stock sold short will provide financing for the bond purchase.

Now that we have gone through a detailed example of how convertible arbitrage works, I'll pause enough to say that opportunities on this scale do not exist. Hedge fund managers are always on the lookout for profitable arbitrage opportunities and therefore will capitalize on even the smallest opportunity to generate returns. This means that the spread, or difference, in related price between the convertible bond and the underlying equity stock would have been arbitraged away much sooner. The spread never would have reached the level in the example before gaining the attention of hedge fund managers. Narrow incremental arbitrage spread opportunities are what hedge funds typically have to deal with. Leverage becomes all that more important with narrow spreads. Even a narrow spread can provide material profits when substantial leverage is brought to bear. It is rather common for managers who emphasize convertible arbitrage strategies to employ leverage equating to five times or more than the actual hedge fund capital involved.

One of the advantages of convertible arbitrage lies in the hedge fund manager's ability to uncover and exploit opportunities in any market, bull or bear. Since this strategy only involves the mispricing of two related securities, the hedge fund manager does not have to be cautious about how the market will affect the outcome.

Typical risk: Low

Risk-return profile: Reduced risk

Value proposition: Reduced volatility

Directional bias: Both net long and net short

Equity-Market-Neutral

In an *equity-market-neutral* strategy, a hedge fund manager will purchase an equity security and sell short a related equity index. Selling short the equity index will offset the systematic, or market, risk inherent in the equity security first purchased. The objective is to capitalize on the perceived growth prospects of the equity issue and to minimize the risk of the market from driving down the price. For instance, suppose that a hedge fund manager purchases 1,000 shares of an oil company for $50,000 and then sells short $50,000, or an amount that offsets the difference in price movements, in a Standard & Poor's (S&P) 500 Index fund. If the overall market were to decline, then the long stock of the oil company would decline, resulting in a loss, but so too would the short S&P 500 Index fund decline, resulting in a gain. The net result will be close to a zero profit or loss, although it depends on the correlation between the two securities. In essence, this has hedged the downside risk from market factors. At the same time, if the market were to advance owing to favorable economic results, then the hedge fund would profit from the price increase of the oil company but lose from the unfavorable price increase against the short S&P 500 Index fund. The net result of the market movement would be close to zero. Now take a scenario where company- or industry-specific factors affect prices. Since these factors are not totally market-related, the market will see little impact from them. However, the prices for stocks of companies in the oil sector and of the company specifically involved will experience movements. The net result to the hedge fund will either be a gain from favorable price movement or a loss from unfavorable price movement. In summary, the hedge fund has protected itself from market factors, thus leaving the only open exposure to company- and industry-specific factors.

The preceding example provided a scenario where the hedge fund manager was bullish on a particular security. The tables can be turned around if the manager feels strongly about the bearish forecast for a particular security. In this circumstance, a hedge fund manager will sell short the selected security and purchase a stock index fund, again such as the S&P 500. This will minimize market risk and put the onus on the prospects of the individual security sold short.

This strategy places a good deal of the risk on the security-selection skills of the hedge fund manager because the market is more or less hedged. The source of returns under the equity-market-neutral strategy derives from long positions in securities that outperform the market and from short positions in securities that underperform the market. For managers looking to maximize their bets, leverage is employed to purchase more of the investment and sell short more of the market. The results of the security selection thus are magnified.

As with the convertible-arbitrage strategy, equity-market-neutral strategies do not rely on how well or poorly the overall market is performing. Since the aim of this strategy is to hedge market risk, the net result depends only on how well or poorly the individual investment performs. In times of bullish and bearish markets, hedge fund managers always can identify individual securities that they believe are either overvalued or undervalued. No matter which degree of misvaluation they

find, hedge fund managers have the tools to take advantage of the opportunity to generate profits for the hedge fund. But having the tools does not guarantee profits of course. Equity-market-neutral positions also benefit from the short-interest rebate, much like convertible-arbitrage funds do. Again, this is the interest income in which hedge funds receive on the proceeds from the investment sold short.

Two last points of note about this strategy. First, it is not especially easy to perfectly hedge market risk for any one particular security. Hedge fund managers do have statistical models using a number of factors, such as correlation and beta, to help them determine how much of the equity index to purchase or sell short. The amount could be right on but is typically slightly off, thus leaving the fund open to at least a minor amount of market risk. Moreover, relationships or correlations are not static; they change over time. Thus the hedge created originally may need to be modified at a later date. Second, since both long and short positions each are susceptible to market risk, the hedge fund manager can offset incremental market risk from new positions with market risk from opposite positions existing in the fund. For instance, the combination of a newly purchased long security and an existing short security will provide some natural hedging.

Typical risk: Low

Risk-return profile: Reduced risk

Value proposition: Reduced volatility

Directional bias: Both net long and net short

Fixed-Income Arbitrage

Fixed-income arbitrage is a strategy whereby a hedge fund manager purchases an individual fixed-income security and simultaneously sells short a similar fixed-income security. The aim of this action is to capture what is thought to be a short-term mispricing of the spread between the two securities. Two fixed-income securities that traditionally have moved together in price where there is a consistent spread between the prices of the two are sought out when the spread deviates from past norms. Aside from pure pricing spreads, hedge fund managers will pursue opportunities where historically consistent spreads have changed with yield curves, mortgage-backed spreads, credit spreads, and statistical arbitrage.

Hedge fund managers pour over a significant amount of data in the hope of identifying spreads that have become wider or have narrowed abnormally. This presents opportunities for managers to make investments in hope that the spreads return to historical levels, thus driving profits for the hedge fund. Let's look at an example of this strategy used in practice. Suppose that a hedge fund manager identifies the historical prices of bond A and bond B. The spread between the two prices has been relatively consistent over the last several years, but a recent event with one company has caused the price for bond A to decline. The hedge fund manager discovers this and buys bond A and simultaneously sells short bond B. Later on, as the company that issued bond A recovers from the event, the price increases, and the hedge fund profits.

In the preceding example, the hedge fund manager could have simply purchased bond A, which was experiencing price declines, and profited when the bond increased in price as the company recovered. However, by not simultaneously selling short bond B, the hedge fund manager would leave the investment open to market exposure. This means that the profitability of the investment would depend on more than just the company recovering but now must depend also on how well or poorly the market performs. Under the fixed-income strategy, hedge fund managers want to isolate security-specific risk and eliminate or minimize market risk. To accomplish this goal, they sell short another fixed-income security. In this way, when the market moves the price changes of a long fixed-income security and short fixed-income security will offset each other. Isolating security-specific risk thus is accomplished. This strategy is very simple conceptually, and hedge fund managers will scour the fixed-income marketplace to identify where the relationship between two or more securities is out of sync and then buy the undervalued security and sell short the overvalued security. Identifying these out-of-sync abnormal relationships is no easy task, however.

As with convertible-arbitrage and equity-market-neutral strategies, fixed-income arbitrage is not concerned with what the market is doing because good hedge fund managers will have hedged its inherent risk. Therefore, the source of risk and return for a fixed-income investment is entirely dependent on the security selected by the hedge fund manager. Profits under both bull and bear market conditions can be made.

The most important factors affecting fixed-income prices and their yields include credit rating, duration, coupon rate, and special bond provisions and features. Once the fixed-income security is issued, its price can vary for any number of reasons, although the level of market interest rates is by far the most important of all factors. Another important factor is the health of the issuer and its related credit rating. Credit ratings can change favorably or unfavorably depending on a company's current financial position and future prospects.

Another advantage of fixed-income arbitrage is derived from profiting on pricing irregularities rather than on pure market interest-rate plays. Interest-rate investments speculate on the direction of interest rates, whereas fixed-income arbitrage uses the historical relationship between two fixed-income securities and current

mispricings to make profits. Once the out-of-sync spread between the two fixed-income securities returns to more normal levels, the hedge fund will benefit.

As with the other relative-value strategies, fixed-income arbitrage often will identify small but investable opportunities. Consequently, hedge fund managers typically will employ large amounts of leverage to maximize profits.

Typical risk: Low

Risk-return profile: Reduced risk

Value proposition: Reduced volatility

Directional bias: Both net long and net short

Quiz for Chapter 11

1. All the following are relative-value hedge fund strategies *except*
   a. convertible arbitrage.
   b. equity-market-neutral.
   c. principle-directed.
   d. fixed-income arbitrage.

2. Do hedge fund managers typically employ high/low/same leverage with relative-value strategies as they do with other hedge fund strategies?
   a. High
   b. Low
   c. Same

3. A hedge fund manager purchasing an equity security and selling short the S&P 500 Index is an example of which strategy?
   a. Macrocentric
   b. Convertible arbitrage
   c. Equity-market-neutral
   d. Fixed-income arbitrage

4. Relative-value strategies depend on how well the total market is performing.
   a. True
   b. False

5. In relation to other hedge fund strategies, do relative-value strategies place more/less/same emphasis on manager security-selection skills?

    a. More

    b. Less

    c. Same

6. Name the strategy that aims to capture short-term mispricing of two similar fixed-income securities.

    a. Distressed securities

    b. Convertible arbitrage

    c. Equity-market-neutral

    d. Fixed-income arbitrage

7. The leading aim of fixed-income arbitrage is to profit from pure market interest-rate movements rather than from pricing irregularities.

    a. True

    b. False

8. Equity-market-neutral strategies generally have _____ risk than other hedge fund strategies.

    a. more

    b. less

    c. same

9. Of all the hedge fund styles, relative-value is considered the only style to employ what practice?

    a. Pure hedging

    b. Market indifference

    c. Long and short positions together

    d. Profit maximization with leverage

10. With convertible arbitrage, a hedge fund manager can have either a long or a short directional bias.

    a. True

    b. False

CHAPTER

12

Hybrid Hedge Funds

Funds That Blend, Mix, and Match Strategies

Now that we have discussed the primary styles of hedge funds, we turn our attention to hybrid hedge funds—funds that incorporate the other hedge fund strategies to some degree or another. These *hybrid styles* include multistrategy funds, values-based funds, and funds of funds. This chapter discusses all, with particular emphasis on funds of funds, the fastest growing hedge fund style in the investment marketplace today. In 2002, it was estimated that there was close to 1,200 funds of funds. However, in 2003 alone, more than 500 new funds of funds were established. This trend has continued since that time as more financial institutions, such as large banks, have entered the trade and established their own funds of funds. Banks have become a significant force with funds of funds and are making these moves to enhance the product offerings to their wealth-management clientele. Lastly, many estimates show that close to 40 percent of all new investments into hedge funds is flowing into funds of funds. Suffice to say that knowing about funds of funds is very important.

Multistrategy Funds

A multistrategy fund is a hedge fund in which the fund manager employs two or more strategies at one time or different times. Depending on the aim of the hedge fund manager, two strategies may be employed with equal emphasis, or three strategies may be employed where one strategy is given more emphasis. Overweighting or underweighting strategies are common as managers attempt to take advantage of opportunities. For instance, a certain hedge fund manager may believe that a macrocentric strategy coupled with a managed futures strategy is ideal for taking advantage of current opportunities and generating profits for the hedge fund. At the same time, another hedge fund manager may believe that employing two arbitrage strategies would best suit the hedge fund and generate the level of performance he or she desires.

The primary advantage of using a multistrategy style is that the hedge fund will be managed in a more diversified manner. Thus, if one particular strategy is performing poorly, the other strategy or strategies may perform better and offset the poorly performing strategy. The obvious disadvantage with this style is that a hedge fund has more chances of employing a strategy that will not work. The more strategies a hedge fund manager employs, the greater are the chances that one will not work in the current investing environment. However, with this said, hedge funds that offer more than one strategy offer greater diversification over hedge funds that only offer one strategy. More diversification is generally better (see Figure 12–1).

Figure 12-1. Allocation of assets in multistrategy funds

Strategy	% of Funds
Equity Hedge	25%
Macrocentric	19%
Relative Value Arbitrage	15%
Event-Driven	12%
Fixed-Income Arbitrage	8%
Convertible Arbitrage	6%
Equity Nonhedge	4%
Distressed Securities	4%
Equity Market Neutral	3%
Sector-Specific	2%
Merger Arbitrage	2%
Emerging Markets	2%
Short Selling	0%

Funds of Funds

With a fund of funds (FoFs), the hedge fund manager invests in two or more stand-alone hedge funds rather than investing directly in securities themselves. This style provides enhanced diversification from the combination of multiple asset classes and multiple hedge funds. Funds of funds emphasize long-term performance with minimal volatility. Funds of funds are also referred to as *funds of hedge funds*.

To take advantage of different opportunities, funds of funds will *rebalance* periodically. This involves liquidating some positions in one or more hedge funds and making an investment in one or more other hedge funds. Rebalancing can be done to reduce the exposure to a particular hedge fund style, or strategy within that style. In addition, rebalancing can be done to enhance exposure to a specific geographic area or to take advantage of risk-reducing opportunities with a hedge fund that has a low correlation with the total funds of funds portfolio.

Funds of funds are the latest and greatest hedge fund offering. They are the new breed of hedge funds that has the entire industry buzzing. Funds of funds pool money from investors and then invest that money in any number of other hedge funds that make direct investments, namely in securities. There are many benefits and advantages with funds of funds, including important drawbacks. Given the general lack of investor familiarity with hedge funds and how they operate, funds of funds can be a solid entry point into hedge funds as managers can identify hedge funds that are the right strategic fit for investors (see Figure 12–2).

BENEFITS AND OPPORTUNITIES

Managers and other key people in funds of funds management teams recognize the differences among hedge funds and the opportunities they present. Conse-

Figure 12-2. A fund of hedge funds structure

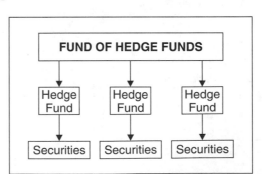

quently, managers blend various strategies and asset classes together to generate attractive long-term investment returns while at the same time delivering lower investment volatility than the stand-alone hedge funds that comprise the funds of funds. The following are the specific benefits and opportunities that funds of funds offer:

Offers a Low Correlation Investment Alternative

Managers of funds of funds recognize that investing in two or more hedge funds is good for diversification purposes. Doing so lowers total risk of standard portfolios with allocations to hedge funds. However, these managers also recognize that investing in two or more hedge funds that are essentially the same provides little to no incremental benefit. As a result, fund of funds managers target hedge funds that are fundamentally different from one another. This means that the correlation of the funds will be low, if not negative. The result is enhanced return and reduced risk. Funds of funds provide a low correlation investment alternative that is rare in the investing marketplace.

Delivers More Predictable and Consistent Returns

One of the aims of funds of funds is to deliver more predictable and consistent returns than stock portfolios, mutual funds, unit investment trusts (UITs), or even stand-alone hedge funds. Funds of funds generate more stable total returns under most market conditions owing to investing in multiple hedge funds where the predictability of fund returns rises with each subsequent new hedge fund investment. Although the return for each stand-alone hedge fund may change from period to period, the average of those returns will change much less. This translates into more predictable and consistent returns. Hedge funds with more predictable and consistent returns are ideal because investors know what to expect and are not blindsided with results.

Provides a Preferred Choice of Institutions

People who manage pension funds and other institutional portfolios are not experts on hedge funds. Although they know a great deal about investing, they also realize that there is much to learn about hedge funds. At the same time, these professionals appreciate the value proposition funds of funds offer and, as a result, most institutions prefer and use funds of funds for their hedge fund investments. These institutions include pension funds, endowments, insurance companies, private banks, and some corporations.

Offers Enhanced Diversification

Funds of funds invest not only in multiple hedge funds but also in asset classes, sectors, and geographic regions that are fundamentally different. In doing so, funds of funds provide enhanced diversification benefits to hedge fund investors, which leads to enhanced return and reduced risk. Multistrategy hedge funds also can provide diversification benefits, but funds of funds are able to accomplish this task quicker and easier through investments in stand-alone hedge funds.

Offers Access to Otherwise Unavailable Hedge Funds

One of the most significant benefits and compelling reasons to invest in funds of funds is the access they provide to hedge funds that are otherwise unavailable to individual investors. Funds of funds provide access to a broad range of styles, strategies, and hedge fund managers. They allow access to a broader spectrum of leading hedge funds that otherwise might be unavailable owing to high minimum investment requirements or closure of the fund to new investors due to demand and strong cash inflows. They also offer an ideal means to gain access to talented investment professionals for a relatively modest investment.

Optimizes Total Portfolio Allocations

Not only do funds of funds provide diversification for hedge fund investments, but they also provide enhanced diversification for an investor's overall portfolio. A hedge fund should not be thought of as a stand-alone investment but rather as a component of a larger portfolio which typically includes hedge funds.

Reduces Single-Fund and Single-Manager Risk

Funds of funds minimize the risk associated with investing in one hedge fund or one hedge fund manager. This provides comfort to the investor and a safeguard to the portfolio in that no single blowup with any hedge fund or hedge fund manager will have a severe impact on the portfolio.

Eliminates Time-Consuming Hedge Fund Due Diligence

Investing in hedge funds is not like investing in stocks or bonds or even investing in mutual funds. Investors need to exercise caution and due diligence with their investing decisions, including monitoring of hedge fund managers. Funds of funds accomplish much of this same work for the investor with a higher degree of effectiveness. Given their contacts and experience, managers are in the ideal position to conduct

due diligence of other hedge fund managers and make informed decisions based on that knowledge.

PERFORMANCE OF FUNDS OF FUNDS

The performance of funds of funds depends on the returns of the stand-alone hedge funds comprising the fund, their weightings in the fund, and their correlations to the other stand-alone funds. Moreover, since funds of funds do not invest in securities directly, risk and return are generated from the component hedge funds. When the component hedge funds are doing well, the fund of funds is doing well. Likewise, when the component hedge funds are doing poorly, so too will the fund of funds. What is the important lesson here? The important lesson is that the performance of funds of funds depends on the skill of the manager in selecting appropriate component hedge funds.

Research has shown that funds of funds and stand-alone hedge funds in general have performed rather equally over the same time periods. However, the real benefit of funds of funds is reduced levels of risk. Given enhanced diversification with funds of funds, this is not necessarily unexpected. Rather, one of the defining characteristics of funds of funds is their reduced risk. It is for this reason and low minimum contribution requirements that funds of funds are becoming so popular.

In addition to reduced levels of risk, funds of funds also provide lower correlations not only with the overall market but also—and more importantly—with other hedge funds. Thus investors in funds of funds experience return-enhancing and risk-reducing benefits.

FEES ASSOCIATED WITH FUNDS OF FUNDS

Funds of funds charge the same two fees as do stand-alone hedge funds. These fees include an investment management fee based on the amount of assets under management and a performance-incentive fee, which is a fee charged against the profits made in a particular year. Since funds of funds do not actively invest in individual securities as do stand-alone hedge funds, they do not charge the same level of fees. The typical stand-alone hedge fund will charge an annual investment-management fee of between 1 and 2 percent and performance-incentive fees of 20 percent. These numbers vary slightly from hedge fund to hedge fund but generally are the same. Funds of funds charge a similar investment-management fee of between 1 and 2 percent with research showing that most charge approximately 1 percent of assets under management. Thus investors with $1 million of assets under management will incur an investment-management fee of $10,000 each year.

Funds of funds also charge a performance-incentive fee, although it is much less than that for a stand-alone hedge fund. Typical funds of funds charge between 10 and 12 percent, which is about half of what stand-alone hedge funds charge. Practically all funds of funds that charge a performance incentive fee—and not all do—have high-water-mark provisions. This protects investors from paying the performance-incentive fee twice on the same gains. Some funds of funds do have hurdle-rate provision safeguards, but for the most part, they do not. For those that do offer hurdle-rate provisions, the index of choice is the London Interbank Offered Rate (LIBOR). Some other fund of funds managers will elect to use the rate of Treasury bills, which are short-term bonds that mature in less than 90 days and are issued by the U.S. government. Treasury investments are considered the safest of all investments in the global marketplace. As we know, however, risk and return are strongly linked. This means that Treasury investments are the lowest returning investments in their particular maturity group.

CHALLENGES AND DRAWBACKS

With funds of funds, there are three primary drawbacks. First, funds of funds charge fees atop the fees already charged by the component stand-alone hedge funds. Thus the component stand-alone hedge funds will charge the customary investment-management fee of 1 to 2 percent and a 20 percent performance-incentive fee. At the same time, the funds of funds also will charge the 1 to 2 percent investment-management fee and tack on an additional 10 to 12 percent performance-incentive fee. The net result is something like a 2 to 4 percent—average around 2.5 percent—investment-management fee and a 30 percent performance-incentive fee. There is no doubt that this two-tiered fee structure is not appealing to investors. Thus investors need to be cautious with investing in funds of funds—but remember, it is the net result that matters, not the gross return and the fees charged. I'd rather pay a 30 percent performance-incentive fee for a gross return of 25 percent than pay a 10 percent performance-incentive fee for a gross return of 11 percent.

The second primary drawback of funds of funds is the lack of transparency, or lack of disclosure information. As with most hedge funds, there is a serious lack of information disclosure on the types of strategies in use and the assets held in the fund. However, this is changing as the hedge fund marketplace becomes more competitive and regulators continue breathing down the necks of hedge fund managers. In this instance, funds of funds are no different from stand-alone hedge funds. They too offer little in the way of information disclosure. As a result, investors sometimes have to take leaps of faith when investing in funds of funds. Even though many funds of funds do not provide the level of transparency that investors would like, this does not necessarily mean that something is foul. All is typically fine.

The third primary drawback of funds of funds is reduced liquidity, even more so than with the component stand-alone hedge funds because funds of funds need extra time to liquidate positions. Stand-alone hedge funds are not especially liquid investments themselves and funds of funds only magnify this characteristic. Most hedge funds have lockup provisions of one year for new money in the fund. Thereafter, hedge funds only allow withdrawals quarterly or annually. Some provide monthly withdrawals, but this is not common. Funds of funds must adhere to the same liquidity provisions as do the other investors in stand-alone hedge funds. Many funds of funds institute more stringent liquidity provisions to give them more time to address the liquidating provisions of stand-alone hedge funds. The most common provisions include lockups of one year for new money and 6- to 12-month redemption periods. The vast majority of funds of funds do not allow for quarterly withdrawals. Some allow for monthly withdrawals but charge a redemption penalty of 2 percent. Now that's motivation to stay in the fund and redeem per the guidelines set in the agreement. Lastly, some funds of funds have what are referred to as *liquidity gate* provisions. These provisions restrict the amount that can be withdrawn from the fund at any one redemption time. The liquidity gate provision is used to safeguard against mass investor defections owing to failing funds. Without doing so, the last investors could be stuck with nothing—a slightly similar case to a run on a bank.

MENU OF FUNDS OF FUNDS

As with stand-alone hedge funds, funds of funds also come in multiple types. In general, there are four different types of funds of funds. These four types of funds of funds, including which stand-alone hedge funds they target, are as follows:

- *Conservative funds of funds.* These funds invest in stand-alone hedge funds that use equity-market-neutral, fixed-income relative-value, and arbitrage strategies.

- *Long-biased funds of funds.* These funds invest in stand-alone hedge funds that use tactical strategies.

- *Defensive funds of funds.* These funds invest in stand-alone hedge funds that use negative-correlation, managed-futures, or selling-short strategies.

- *Diversified funds of funds.* These funds invest in stand-alone hedge funds that use lower-volatility and multistyle strategies.

Most funds of funds target only one style of stand-alone hedge fund. Thus arbitrage funds of funds will target arbitrage stand-alone hedge funds. At the same time, macrocentric funds of funds will target macrocentric hedge funds. This keeps

operations and investment decisions quick, disciplined, and easy. Even within the different styles, funds of funds can offer differing levels of sophistication and varying degrees of knowledge and experience. Often investors will not be aware of a particular fund of funds' style or strategies targeted. Nevertheless, this enhanced focus provides investors with greater expertise and more options (see Figure 12–3).

Figure 12-3.   Assets managed by funds of funds

Year	Assets in Billions
1997	$55
1998	$66
1999	$83
2000	$109
2001	$155
2002	$188
2003	$286
2004	$489

SUMMARY OF INVESTING CONSIDERATIONS

Even with the drawbacks inherent in funds of funds, these funds provide an effective way for investors to invest in hedge funds. As mentioned previously, the benefits of enhanced diversification for investors and the benefit of allowing smaller investors the opportunity to invest in hedge funds often can outweigh the drawbacks. Other benefits, such as access to otherwise unavailable managers and the expertise and management of fund of funds managers, can make all the difference in the world. In contrast, for more experienced investors who have the capital necessary to hold multiple stand-alone hedge funds, bypassing the funds of funds hybrid style can be a good move. This will require more capital to invest in each hedge fund and more time and effort to oversee and monitor how well each is performing.

One good source of information on funds of funds can be found at www.hedge-world.com. This Web site provides basic information on each fund and can be used as a starting point in your preliminary search for a fund of funds.

Values-Based Funds

In many ways, values-based hedge funds are not much different from other hedge funds. These hedge funds employ directional bets, attempt to take advantage of event-driven opportunities, and use the same tools that other hedge fund managers use—leverage and selling short, for example. The primary difference between values-based hedge funds and other hedge funds is the type of assets the hedge fund can or cannot invest in. More specifically, these funds are driven by a unique methodology in which either certain types of investments are off-limits or only certain types of investments are permitted. "Sin" stocks are the most widely screened out type of investment for hedge funds that follow a values-based investment style. Values-based hedge funds thus can be considered funds managed with a higher calling.

For the most part, these hedge funds are established according to specific religious beliefs and follow strict faith-based values in all their investing-related actions. Catholic, Jewish, Islamic, Methodist, and Mormon are some of the most popular types of faith-based hedge funds. Many people may recognize this investing style to be *socially responsible investing* (SRI). This is partly correct and partly incorrect. There is a difference between socially responsible investing and morally responsible investing. Values-based investing does conform to SRI, but there are some hedge funds that take the opposite approach, a sort of "socially irresponsible investing." These hedge funds invest in "sin" stocks—typically shunned by values-based funds—whose companies have ties to armaments, tobacco, alcohol, and gambling. As a result of this and other contrasts, all of these hedge funds are best described as *values-based hedge funds* where some follow good values, such as SRI, and others follow not so good values, such as investing in "sin" stocks.

OBJECTIVES

There are two primary reasons for employing a values-based approach. The first reason is to align one's investments with one's personal or religious values by avoiding companies that do not meet specific guidelines and standards. For example, an investor may screen out companies with ties to gambling and alcohol because its use is forbidden by his or her religion. The second reason is to encourage companies to take action that is more aligned with the investor's personal values relating to social and societal welfare. For example, years ago Nike got a bad reputation for producing many of its shoes in China, where the laws are not as child-friendly as they are in the United States. Investors who were outraged by this could have purchased stock in Nike and then attempted to influence management to make a change. An individual investor's voice generally is not taken seriously or, worse yet, even heard. However, corporations are much more willing to listen to a group and may at times even make changes based on the advocacy of investors.

HISTORY AND ORIGINS

Values-based investing has been around for hundreds of years, with the earliest forms traced back as far as biblical times, when Jewish law directed how a devoted Jew should invest. Many Christian religious groups adhered to ethical investing, where no investing could be made in organizations with ties to enslavement or killings. Specifically, Quakers were known for their avoidance of slavery and war, whereas Methodists have been recognized for their social screening of investments for many years.

It was not until modern times that values-based investing really began to take shape and become a popular investing approach with the general public. With such issues as the Vietnam War, labor-management challenges, and the civil rights movement, the consciousness of many people began to focus on how people were investing their money and thus supporting dubious enterprises. Soon thereafter, individual investors not only began to flock to SRI, but so also did various institutions such as churches, universities, foundations, pension plans, and municipalities. The explosion of new investors reached into the millions. These investors turned their attention and investing strategies against human rights abuses and abusive governments such as that of apartheid South Africa. Positive change was motivated by the decisions of individual investors, who once grouped together, made a significant difference in the lives of so many people.

GROWTH

Most values-based investing is conducted by mutual funds, but a number of hedge funds also have decided to incorporate this type of investing style, such as a Catholic values hedge fund run by Gabelli Funds. Although there are no statistics solely for hedge funds, SRI now totals close to $2.5 trillion in assets under management. This is a substantial increase over the $639 million in assets under management in 1995. This equates to a growth rate of over 250 percent over the aforementioned 10-year period. In addition, findings by Nelson in the *Directory of Investment Managers* indicate that approximately 1 in every 10 newly invested dollars (or 9.4 percent) is invested in an SRI. You can clearly see the considerable explosion in this type of investing.

GROWTH FACTORS

Aside from investors looking to invest according to their principles or to reshape societal enterprises, what are the big draws and reasons for all of the growth in values-based investing? There are a number of factors that help to explain this growth, including solid performance, availability of managers, and more and better information for those looking to get started.

Principles

For most investors following a values-based investing approach, it is the ability to invest based on one's values and principles that is the major draw. Earning solid returns and promoting advocacy are two other areas investors mention, but they still are less important that adhering to one's principles. These principles may be socially-based or perhaps morally-based. Nevertheless, this type of investing offers investors a favorable way to adhere to their principles. Prudent investing and adhering to personal principles can be accomplished with values-based investing. Don't be fooled.

Performance

One of the misconceptions with values-based investing is that investors must be willing to accept lower returns to invest according to their values. Although it is true that some investments are screened out, investors still have a substantial number of investment options, and that means adequate opportunities for gain. The principle of asset allocation supports this very claim in that studies have concluded that *how* you allocate your assets rather than *which* individual investments you select or *when* you buy or sell them is the leading determinant of investment performance over time.

Enhanced Information

Not only has the quantity of information increased, but the quality of information also has increased. To help investors make better-informed decisions, many organizations that manage money using a values-based style are providing more and better information than ever before. The aim is to educate investors and encourage them to make a difference with their investing actions.

Availability

Years ago, very few money managers offered any type of values-based program for investors. This has changed radically over the last couple of decades as more and more money managers have jumped into the field to capitalize on the growing trend. Most of these money managers are passionate about this type of investing and got involved themselves to help others to pursue their own values-based investing. Today there are close to 200 mutual funds that provide some sort of values-based investing style. The total number of money managers increases significantly when you consider all the hedge funds and registered investment advisors that pursue this type of investing. Needless to say, there are many options for the values-based investor.

Women Investors

As more and more women take on the role of managing their money, many of them are conscious of their personal values and want to reflect them in their investing. As a result, the growth of women investors has had a big impact on the number of investors and increase in assets under management. Research has shown that close to 60 percent of all values-based investors are women. As the number of women investors continues to grow, so too will values-based investing.

Investing Adversity

Corporate America and the investing marketplace have fueled the growth of values-based investing through the multitude of scandals and related events that have occurred over the last couple of decades. Events such as the Enron crash and the *Exxon Valdez* oil spill have roused investors to pay more attention to what they are investing in and to play a bigger role in shareholder advocacy.

DIFFERENT APPROACHES

The earliest approaches to values-based investing involved simple screens in which investors excluded certain assets from their investment holdings. As the values-based investing movement gained popularity, other approaches began to appear and were promoted, as follows:

Screening

As mentioned, screening was the initial approach for values-based investing. The most screened investments—including the percentage of money managers that screen them—include companies with ties to tobacco (97 percent), gambling (86 percent), alcohol (83 percent), and armaments (81 percent) and companies with poor environmental records (79 percent). Other factors of lesser importance include human rights abuses, labor concerns, pornography, abortion, animal rights, and contraceptives. Screening adds a more qualitative way to evaluate companies beyond the typical quantitative methods. This approach to values-based investing is considered somewhat passive because generally only screening of investments is done.

Social Venture Capital

Many investors recognize the importance and role certain companies have in our society. To help promote these types of companies, investors provide seed money for their startup and early growth. Without this early funding, many companies would find it significantly more challenging, if not impossible, to get things off the ground. Solar- and wind-power-generating companies are two of the areas these investors target.

Shareholder Advocacy

Shareholder advocacy involves engaging corporate management with the aim of improving financial performance and enhancing the well-being of all stakeholders. These stakeholders include, but are not limited to, corporate shareholders (the owners), employees, customers and clients, suppliers and vendors, the local community, and the surrounding environment. Engaging corporate management can be accomplished in various ways from simple proxy voting and letter writing to more absorbing activities such as filing a formal shareholder resolution.

Community Investing

This approach involves funding community development financial institutions (CDFIs) that, in turn, provide financing to local people, businesses, and community groups in low-income and impoverished areas. The aim here is to improve the local economy by financing small-business development, creating jobs, building affordable housing, and funding projects to build community facilities. Investors are willing to accept below-market rates of return to help rebuild disadvantaged communities that are either underserved or unable to access financing from traditional markets.

Quiz for Chapter 12

1. All the following are considered hybrid hedge funds *except*

   a. multistrategy.

   b. funds of funds.

   c. values-based.

   d. convertible arbitrage.

2. Funds of funds often will invest in securities directly if the opportunity arises.

   a. True

   b. False

3. What is the primary benefit of multistrategy hedge funds?

   a. Lower cost

   b. Enhanced diversification

   c. No net-worth test

   d. Less regulatory oversight

4. Which of the following is a drawback of funds of funds?

   a. Enhanced diversification

   b. Improved asset allocation

   c. Better risk management

   d. Extra layer of fees

5. Funds of funds strive to generate _____ returns.

   a. more consistent

   b. greater variability of

   d. less predictable

   e. relative

6. Most institutional investors prefer which strategy when investing in hedge funds?

   a. Long/short bias

   b. Multistrategy

   c. Funds of funds

   d. Values-based

7. *Funds of funds* and *funds of hedge funds* are different names for the same strategy.

   a. True

   b. False

8. Which of the following is *not* a benefit of funds of funds?

    a. Provides access to unavailable hedge funds

    b. Reduces single-fund and single-manager risk

    c. Minimizes investor due diligence

    d. Minimizes hedge fund fees

9. All the following are drawbacks of funds of funds *except*

    a. Second layer of fees

    b. Lack of transparency

    c. Minimal risk management

    d. Reduced liquidity

10. All the following are approaches to values-based investing *except*

    a. cost reduction.

    b. screening.

    c. shareholder advocacy.

    d. community investing.

PART

III

Demystifying Hedge Fund Investing

CHAPTER 13

Inside Optimal Portfolios

Lessons and Strategies for Peak-Performance Investing

Introduction to Asset Allocation

Please do not get confused by the title of this chapter. This chapter is not necessarily about allocating the assets in your hedge fund portfolio but rather about how to incorporate hedge funds into a properly allocated portfolio. Asset allocation and hedge fund investing can form a very powerful combination. Properly allocated portfolios typically will include equity investments, fixed-income investments, and alternative investments. This is where hedge funds can play a big part. Since this book is about hedge funds and not asset allocation, this chapter will only touch the surface and be more general in nature.

Asset allocation is best described as dividing your investment portfolio and other investable money into different asset classes. The concept underlying allocating your portfolio in such a way is that by splitting your investment portfolio into different asset classes, you will reduce portfolio risk and enhance your long-term risk-adjusted return. In other words, asset allocation provides you with your best opportunity to earn solid returns over time while assuming the level of portfolio risk most suitable for your unique situation. The allocation of your assets is based on a number of very important factors, such as your current financial position, your investment time horizon, your level of wealth, your financial goals and obligations, and your risk profile. There are a few other variables, or *portfolio allocation inputs,* as I like to call them. Specifically, the three most important inputs that determine your asset allocation are your financial objectives and needs, your investment time horizon, and your risk profile. For building an optimal portfolio, your unique risk profile is of utmost importance. Your risk profile includes three variables—your tolerance for risk, your capacity for risk, and your need to assume risk.

Empirical research clearly articulates what drives portfolio performance over the long term—your asset allocation. Let's put this macro viewpoint into a usable set of factors, a micro viewpoint, as follows:

- The asset classes you will employ
- The percentage of your total portfolio that you will allocate to each asset class
- The parameters you set that triggers rebalancing—based on time or deviations
- The investment style you select—active management versus index funds and the like
- The level of portfolio diversification
- The application of low correlations
- The tax status of your portfolio—tax-exempt versus taxable
- The tax bracket you are in (see Figure 13–1)

Al-Location, Al-Location, Al-Location

One of the leading adages of classic wisdom most synonymous with business success is "location, location, location." Nearly everyone has heard of this phrase because it is so very true. Building a successful business is not very different from building a successful portfolio. This exact same classic wisdom applies to investment success as well, but expressed with a twist—"al-location, al-location, al-location."

Figure 13-1. Scale of active-passive management styles

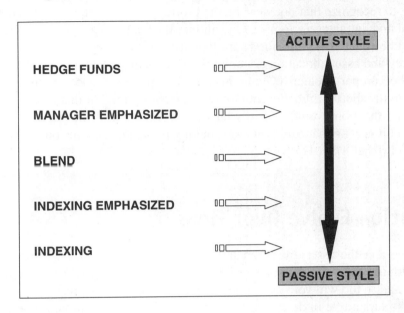

Location, or "al-location" in this case, can mean the difference between feast or famine. Moreover, where you locate can mean life or death for a business, and the same is true with investing. There are no shortcuts, and cutting corners ultimately will be an investor's downfall.

Before selecting a location, business owners do their homework; they do not rely on their own perceived superior instinct. They know that doing so will not get the job done. As an investor, you should approach your investing in the same manner. Prudent investors do not make the mistake of thinking that because their previous investment choice worked out, they are geniuses at picking new successful investments. Through experience, you will know what constitutes a properly allocated portfolio and thus position yourself for long-term success. A factor whose true importance cannot be underestimated or underappreciated is "al-location."

Introduction to Asset Allocation

To better help people understand the significant benefits of asset allocation, I often use a hockey analogy. The analogy goes something like this: Employing asset allocation is similar to a hockey player wearing protective equipment—helmet, shoulder pads, kneepads, etc. If the hockey player were to take off the protective equipment, he or she probably could skate faster, cut easier, and pass the puck better. As a result,

he or she probably would be a scoring machine. However, it doesn't take a rocket scientist to recognize that not wearing the proper protective equipment is not at all practical and, in fact, very foolish. One hit into the boards from your opponent, and you could be out of the game for a very long time, if not forever. So why risk it?

Hockey and asset allocation are quite the same. An investor who does not wear his or her proper protective equipment may experience uncommonly superior returns in the short term but eventually will take the same hit that a hockey player would and therefore would be badly hurt or knocked out of the game completely. Taking a hit may not happen right away, but it will happen at some point. The question is not *if*, but *when*.

Asset Allocation Evolve Over Time

Portfolios and the asset allocation involved in constructing a portfolio will not remain static over time. At some point in the future your personal situation will change, and so too will your asset allocation in response. Many factors can change, and each plays a role in determining your optimal asset allocation. Some of these factors, called *portfolio allocation inputs,* include your risk profile, your current and future financial positions, and your investment time horizon. In addition to a change in your personal situation, market factors affecting your portfolio also will change to some degree over time. These "market-centric" portfolio allocation inputs include expected total returns, the volatility risk, and the trading flexibility of your investments and/or the investments you are targeting. Rest assured, asset allocation promotes quick and easy changes to your portfolio; thus you will not need to spend hour after hour researching what decisions should be made and then implement them.

Key Benefits of Asset Allocation

Asset allocation maximizes the risk-adjusted return of a portfolio. In addition, asset allocation also minimizes portfolio volatility risk and provides for a sound investing discipline. Specifically, asset allocation

- Minimizes retirement-plan losses
- Promotes an optimal portfolio
- Eliminates what does not work
- Supports quick and easy reoptimization

- Maximizes portfolio risk-adjusted return
- Promotes simple portfolio design and construction
- Allows for easy contribution decisions
- Minimizes portfolio volatility
- Minimizes investor time and effort
- Promotes a more diversified portfolio
- Provides maximum avoidance of market weakness
- Delivers the highest impact value
- Reduces trading costs

Common Portfolio Allocation Methods

Once your objectives and constraints are determined, your next task is to work toward allocating your assets in a manner suitable to your objectives. This task involves allocating assets to specific asset classes and subclasses that will enable you to build your optimal portfolio.

Creating your own asset allocation is much like baking your own pie. You will first decide what the purpose of the pie is—perhaps for Christmas, for New Years, or for a birthday. Once you have the purpose established, you will then narrow down what kind of pie you will make. Then you will identify what ingredients you will need and how best to bake your pie. Your choices of ingredients can vary widely from apple, pumpkin, lemon, to blueberry, and more. Toppings also can be added for extra zing. Once you are finished, you have a pie that fits the occasion.

Determining your asset allocation and building your portfolio employ much the same process. The purpose for building your portfolio can vary widely, but most encompass some sort of retirement savings. Thereafter, you will need to select the proper asset classes. There are many methods for accomplishing this task.

The most common methods used by investors and investment professionals include equity overload, simple 110, cash-flow matching, risk avoidance, allocation timing, and custom combination. All these models have their advantages and disadvantages. None is absolutely perfect. A discussion of each method is provided below.

EQUITY OVERLOAD

Not withstanding risk, equity assets have outperformed all other primary asset classes over time. Within equities, small-cap stocks have performed better than

blue-chip stocks. This is the rationale that many investors and financial professionals use as support for a portfolio with nearly all equity, if not all equity. As long as an investor has a long-term time horizon, overloading with equities can be a way to earn solid portfolio performance over time. Beware, however, because this method does not take risk into account; the volatility can be extraordinary, and the risk of substantial loss is uncommonly high. This is not for the faint of heart.

SIMPLE 110

This is one of the most commonly recognized methods for determining asset allocations. However, I have slightly remodeled it for 110 rather than the traditional 100. Under this model, you allocate to equity securities based on the equation 110 minus your age. The remaining portion is allocated to fixed-income securities. For example, a 65-year-old investor would allocate 45 percent to equity securities (110 – 65) and the remaining 55 percent to fixed-income securities.

The underlying assumption of this model is that the investor will live well into retirement years and that his or her risk tolerance, risk capacity, and/or need to assume risk will decline with each passing year. The obvious drawback to this method is that it does not take into account the opposite factors, such as additional wealth, greater risk capacity, or higher risk tolerance.

CASH-FLOW MATCHING

Cash-flow matching attempts to match your anticipated future financial obligations, your cash outflows, with your anticipated cash inflows, both noninvestment income and investment income. The first step in this model is to identify all anticipated future financial obligations. The second step is to identify all anticipated future financial inflows from noninvestment sources. Some sources of noninvestment income include wages, Social Security, and inheritance. Identifying the gaps between future obligations and inflows is step three. The fourth step is to evaluate your current portfolio against what will be needed from your portfolio in the future to fill the gaps in cash flow. This evaluation will determine what performance you will need to achieve, whether this means growth or preservation. For example, an investor determines that she will need to earn 10 percent per year in her portfolio for retirement. Since corporate bonds historically have earned less than 10 percent annually and equities historically have earned greater than 10 percent annually, the investor will need to allocate to both equities and corporate bonds. Other combinations of high-yield bonds, small-cap stocks, international equities, and real estate investment trusts (REITs) can be included as well.

The key is to match anticipated cash outflows with anticipated cash inflows and identify whether your portfolio is large enough to fill the gap. If the gap between what you will need and what your noninvestment sources can provide is small, a conservative portfolio may be appropriate. Although an investor may have the tolerance and capacity to assume risk, he or she may not have the need to assume additional risk, especially useless risk that will provide no benefit.

Forecasting skill, life expectancy, and uncontrollable market factors are the major drawbacks of employing this portfolio allocation method.

RISK AVOIDANCE

Regardless of an investor's risk capacity and need to assume risk to generate desired returns, some investors simply do not want to take risk. They can't stomach it. As a result, allocating to conservatives assets may be the most appropriate thing to do. Although investors in this situation may not be in the best position to accomplish their goals and objectives, they surly will sleep better at night. This gets at the root of behavioral finance and investing.

ALLOCATION TIMING

Under this model, an investor or portfolio manager will change asset allocations in the hope of capturing short-term profits on asset classes that show the most strength. This is obviously a timing strategy that numerous studies have shown to be fraught with error and rarely work. The allocation-timing method involves allocating to asset classes when they are out of favor, such as equities during bearish stock markets, with the hope of selling at the peak of when they are in favor, such as bullish stock markets. Information, care, and skill in making such timing calls are absolutely critical for success.

Building Peak-Performance Portfolios

CUSTOM COMBINATION

Since many of the methods discussed have one or more drawbacks to them, developing a custom combination may prove quite beneficial. Many financial professionals have gone this route and designed their own unique method that uses the best from one or more of the methods. The vast majority employs some sort of cash-flow matching combined with allocation timing. Doing so allows them to establish asset allocations suitable to their investors while allowing them to promote their care and

skill in portfolio management. Using a custom combination may be a smart move for you, depending on your situation. As such, many financial advisory firms offer their own unique methods for portfolio customization.

Over the years, I have had the distinct pleasure of working with many very successful individual and institutional investors. In addition, I have been fortunate to work with a number of very intelligent and influential analysts, portfolio managers, and investment strategists. From my experience, I have discovered some very important strategies that enable investors to gain an edge over other investors. After reviewing and analyzing the strategies exhibited by successful investors, I have compiled a list of the most important ones, or the *immutable strategies*. Note that these strategies target constructing and managing investment portfolios; they do not focus on investment contributions or withdrawals.

1. MANAGE WITH A PRUDENT MIND-SET

The number one golden rule of investing is to manage your portfolio as a rational and informed investor. If you are able to accomplish this task, then everything else will fall into place.

To become a rational and informed investor, you will need to be proactive in learning what rational investors do and do not do. There are many pitfalls along the way. In addition, you will need to learn some of the immutable lessons of investing. By knowing these lessons, you will position yourself to better manage your portfolio going forward.

Who are rational investors? Rational investors do not fall victim to the most common behavioral blunders investors often make. These behavioral blunders include such things as illusion of control, blinders, overconfidence, denial, and herd instinct. Rational investors are objective and do not let emotions cloud their judgment. Rational investors can evaluate investment opportunities and make wise decisions.

By definition, rational investors become informed investors over time. Being informed means that you know and fully understand the key lessons of investing, such as that sector leadership does not continue forever, that market timing is extremely difficult, that no investment is guaranteed, and that you should not invest anything that you can't afford to lose. The list of investment lessons goes on and on. Nevertheless, make it a priority to become a rational and informed investor and manage your portfolio with a prudent mind-set.

2. ESTABLISH SMART FINANCIAL GOALS

Imagine that you are competing in an arrow-shooting contest where you are blindfolded and spun around many times. Now imagine trying to hit the target being

blindfolded with no sense of direction. Do you think that you can hit that target easily? Of course not. The same goes for investing—you cannot hit a target that you are not aiming for. Most people begin investing before truly identifying their financial goals—why they are investing in the first place and what they are looking to accomplish by investing. Establishing financial goals allows you or your professional money manager to tailor the management of your portfolio.

However, establishing your financial goals is only half the battle. Ensuring that they are *s*pecific, *m*easurable, *a*chievable, *r*ealistic, and given a *t*ime constraint (SMART) is the other critical part. Establishing financial goals that do not adhere to this rule will cause some investors to assume more risk than appropriate and others to assume less risk than needed to generate needed returns. This is the direct result of making ad hoc decisions given little to no guidance.

Make it a personal priority to establish SMART financial goals to ensure that you hit your target with prudent investing.

3. UNDERSTAND YOUR RISK PROFILE

Your risk profile is absolutely critical to building your optimal portfolio. What is your risk profile, you may ask? Your risk profile is a measurement of the amount of risk you can, should, and are willing to take in your portfolio to accomplish your SMART financial goals. Let's explore those three variables—can, should, and willing—in greater detail. First, your risk profile is based on your tolerance for risk, or your willingness. Each one of us has a certain point where we are comfortable taking risk but beyond which we simply cannot stomach it. Your tolerance for risk is perhaps the easiest of the three risk-profile components to assess. Second, your risk profile depends on your need to assume risk, the *should* part. The term *need* is used here to communicate how much risk you are more or less required to assume in order to attain your SMART financial goals.

Let's explore an example to help you understand risk need. Consider an investor who owns a portfolio worth $100,000 and needs an additional $20,000 over the next year to keep the portfolio on track to provide a certain amount of wealth at a future point in time. Thus the portfolio will need to generate a return of 20 percent over the one-year period. Given this, the investor has an idea of the amount of risk that he or she needs to assume to accomplish the 20 percent return. Significant risk must be taken in this example, unfortunately.

Finally, the third variable of risk profile is capacity, the *can* part. *Capacity* is best defined as the ability of the investor to assume risk where any losses experienced will not affect attainment of SMART financial goals. Capacity basically indicates how much risk an investor can take, regardless of how much he or she wants to take or needs to take. Your portfolio should be built with your risk profile in mind.

4. IDENTIFY YOUR OPTIMAL ASSET MIX

Numerous landmark studies have concluded that *how* you allocate your assets, rather than *which* individual investments you select or *when* you buy or sell them, is the leading determinant of investment performance over time. Moreover, some studies show that asset allocation is responsible for approximately 10 times more of a portfolio's performance over time than both security selection and market timing combined. As a result, it is essential that you allocate your portfolio properly. *Asset allocation* is defined as the strategy of dividing an investor's wealth among the different asset classes and subclasses to achieve the highest expected total rate of return given that investor's risk profile and SMART financial goals. The advantage of properly allocating your portfolio—even when investing in hedge funds—includes greater certainty of returns going forward, more efficient use of portfolio assets, and a higher portfolio risk-adjusted return over time.

The four primary asset classes that you need to consider when allocating your assets include equities, fixed-income, cash and equivalents, and alternative assets (sometimes referred to as *hard* or *tangible assets*). Although hedge funds are not considered a true asset class, most financial professionals group them under alternative assets, given low correlations with equities and use of alternative strategies and tools.

5. MAXIMIZE ASSET LOCATION

Most investors have heard of asset allocation, but few have heard of its cousin—asset location. *Asset location* can refer to one of two important things. First, asset location can refer to which type of investment account you own—either a taxable or tax-exempt account. Second, asset location can refer to which individual investments you select for your type of account. With a tax-exempt account, you do not need to worry about capital gains taxes or ordinary income taxes on dividends and interest payments received. This means that you are free to select investments that deliver the highest return regardless of the tax consequences. On the other hand, taxable accounts, or your typical investment account, require you to consider the tax consequences of the investment prior to making a purchase or sale. For example, if you are in a high federal income tax bracket, you need to consider municipal bonds because the tax-equivalent yield often will be greater than the yield of fully taxable corporate bonds. It is the net return that matters. Other considerations you will want to explore are those related to investing in asset classes that deliver higher returns for their inherent level of risk. In other words, they offer return premiums. This means that over the long term you can generate higher returns without the corresponding increase in risk. High-yield bonds, small-cap stocks, value stocks, and of course, hedge funds are four such investments.

6. DIVERSIFY, DIVERSIFY, DIVERSIFY

One of the golden rules of investing is *diversify your portfolio*. Diversification is a strategy designed to reduce total portfolio risk by combining a large number of investments within a particular asset class that exhibit similar risk-return trade-off profiles. In doing so, you will reduce the negative impact of any one investment on your portfolio. Diversification within equity securities is most beneficial because equity securities possess the greatest amount of investment-specific risk. Index funds provide a quick and easy method for you to diversify your portfolio because they represent all the securities within that investing space or market.

It is very important to understand that diversification is not the same as asset allocation. This is one of the leading misconceptions of asset allocation. This is a topic discussed in my book, *Understanding Asset Allocation*. Asset allocation involves investing in asset classes that possess certain risk-return trade-off profiles, whereas diversification involves investing in a significant number of securities within each asset class in order to minimize investment-specific risk. The two are vitally important in peak-performance investing.

7. INDEX IT!

It's no secret that most portfolio managers do not beat the return of the market each year. Furthermore, the portfolio managers who do beat the market in any given year have a lower probability of beating the market in the following year. As a result, index funds offer not only a low-cost approach to building out your optimal portfolio but also do so in a quick, easy, and efficient manner.

Index funds are much like mutual funds in that they are pools of investments and are typically highly diversified with low company-specific risk. However, index funds do not employ security selection to guide their investment choices, as do mutual funds. Rather, index funds are considered passive investments that are managed in such a way as to match their return to that of a specific underlying index, such as the Standard & Poor's (S&P) 500 Index. What does this mean to you? This means lower management fees, greater tax efficiency, more complete asset class diversification, maximum liquidity, and higher net investment performance over time than what the average professional money manager can provide. You can build out an entire portfolio using index funds exclusively.

Index funds are most beneficial for large-cap investing. The more specialized a money manager must be to evaluate investment opportunities or asset classes, such as small caps or high-yield bonds, the less benefit index funds provide. Why? The reason is because the asset classes that are more challenging to evaluate typically will have fewer money managers evaluating them. The less an investment is

followed by The Street, the greater is the impact an investment manager can have. This means that more sophisticated investors may want to consider using money managers for these asset classes.

8. EMPLOY TIME, NOT TIMING

Think long term, and emphasize decisions that will affect your portfolio for the long term—do *not* play the market. This is another one of the golden rules of investing. As you can see, this rule is rather simple and straightforward. In addition, do your best to abandon all gambling tendencies and behaviors. Remember to approach investing as a rational and informed investor.

Study after study has shown that market timing determines only a small portion of your total investment performance over time. As a result, trying to time your purchases and sales generally is a waste of time and resources. Rather than attempting to time the market, concentrate your time and resources on employing a sound asset-allocation strategy. A peripheral benefit of emphasizing asset allocation instead of market timing is lower turnover. Many people who use market timing have significant turnover, and this can create problems because capital gains taxes can be triggered.

Lastly, it is difficult, if not impossible, to predict future short-term returns. However, this task becomes significantly less difficult as the holding period increases. Having confidence in future returns allows for the selection of an optimal asset mix. Depending on your goals, investing for the short term can be a form of market timing. As a result, employing time, rather than timing, is by far your best solution.

9. THINK TOTAL PORTFOLIO, NOT COMPONENT INVESTMENTS

One of the most common mistakes investors make is to focus on certain individual investments within their portfolios rather than focusing on their portfolios as a whole. Portfolios behave in a much different way than individual investments comprising portfolios do. Thus a portfolio consisting of only fixed-income investments actually will make your portfolio more risky, with a lower expected return, than a portfolio consisting of both fixed-income and equity investments. Investors who desire a more conservative portfolio therefore should allocate their investments to multiple asset classes.

By focusing on the individual investments in a portfolio, investors tend to lose sight of their overall SMART financial goals. As such, many investors will be tempted to make short-term ad hoc investment decisions that could be detrimental to overall portfolio performance.

The best way to avoid the problem of focusing on individual investments and instead to focus on the overall portfolio is to allocate your portfolio properly, diversify your investments, and employ index funds when and where appropriate.

10. MINIMIZE MANAGEMENT FEES AND COMMISSIONS

Are you looking for a great way to gain performance without even affecting future portfolio gains or adding even an ounce of risk? I am rather confident that you will answer yes. You can accomplish this very goal by minimizing management fees and commissions related to your portfolio. Depending on what financial instruments you employ to build out your optimal asset mix, management fees and commissions can vary quite significantly. If you follow my suggestion and explore the idea of using index funds, then your management fees should be rather low in comparison with what they could be. On the other hand, if you invest in mutual funds or invest with certain money managers, your management fees can be quite expensive—perhaps in the 1.5 to 2 percent range.

Recently, I met with a financial advisor to conduct research for this book, and he told me that he charges his clients over 2 percent for those with portfolio assets under $100,000. Are you kidding me? Remember to always shop around and investigate the management fees of each financial advisor or money manager in whom you are interested. Furthermore, be very cognizant and avoid mutual funds that charge exorbitant fees. It is simply an unfair and unjustified practice. Instead, focus on financial instruments and investment professionals that charge reasonable management fees *and* commissions. Commissions for buys and sells can be excessive as well and eat into your profits. Firms such as TD Ameritrade offer trades for under $10 each. Regardless of the broker or investment professional, minimizing management fees and commissions will lend itself to higher net returns. This, of course, is a very good thing.

11. MINIMIZE TAXES AND EMPHASIZE AFTER-TAX RETURNS

From time to time, I hear financial advisors touting the returns they generated for some of their clients. They always seem to quote gross returns rather than net returns. Although it is not always easy to calculate net returns, in an ideal world, this is what financial advisors and money managers would do. Here's something to think about. If an investor earns an 18 percent return but must pay 5 percent in taxes, did that person really earn 18 percent? If you cannot spend your earnings or reinvest them, did you earn them in the first place? It's the bottom line that ultimately counts.

Unacceptably high capital gains tax consequences can take a significant bite out of your performance. You have to earn those costs back, or else you are losing value.

At the same time, for investors in the highest federal income tax bracket, ordinary tax on interest and dividends also can be severe and rob you of returns. Always think in terms of your *after-tax return,* and minimize your taxes where appropriate.

One final note: Although you need to be aware of taxes and attempt to avoid them, never hold an investment that is not suitable. Tax consequences take a back seat to appropriateness and suitability.

12. DRAFT A WRITTEN INVESTMENT PLAN

Much like a blueprint for building a house, a written investment plan (*investment policy statement*) serves as a blueprint for building your optimal portfolio. First and foremost, a written plan helps you to learn more about what your needs and priorities are, how to best address them, and the risks involved with investing. Second, a written investment plan allows you and your portfolio manager (if you elect to employ one) to gain a better understanding of your objectives and constraints and how to best manage your portfolio to accomplish your SMART financial goals.

Other benefits of a written investment plan are that such a plan (1) defines your optimal asset mix, asset-allocation strategy, and construction method, (2) establishes what management style to follow, (3) provides a benchmark with which to evaluate the performance of your portfolio and manager, (4) safeguards the portfolio against ad hoc decisions that will only impede your long-term strategy, and (5) allows for misunderstandings and miscommunication to be resolved quickly and easily.

13. REINVEST DIVIDENDS, INTEREST, AND CAPITAL GAINS

Unless you need the income earned from your investments to supplement your normal income, reinvesting is a solid way to keep your money working for you. Over time, the accumulation and compounding will become quite significant. This alone will result in strong portfolio growth.

Choosing not to reinvest automatically in a taxable portfolio can be a good decision. Given that you'll need to account for each and every reinvestment when you sell your investments, you may be faced with considerable hassle at tax time. No one wants to match up asset positions that were sold with those that were purchased to identify the gain or loss. One solution is to let your income accumulate in your money market and to reinvest that money every three to six months. Doing so not only will avoid accounting hassles but also will allow you to reinvest in areas that are underallocated in your portfolio. The key point is to always reinvest, regardless of the method.

Also remember that all reinvested dividends, interest, and capital gains must be reported as income on tax returns. Uncle Sam always wants his cut.

14. MONITOR, MEASURE, AND EVALUATE

Once you establish your portfolio, your work, of course, is not complete. Depending on how you look at it, your work is essentially just beginning. What you do after you build your portfolio is arguably just as important, if not more important, than what you do prior to that.

With this strategy, you will take a proactive approach to monitoring not only your performance results but also the continued strategic fit. This means that you need to ensure that the hedge fund has not made any material changes since your initial investment or has underdelivered on any promises it may have made prior to your investing. If you believe that the strategic fit has weakened, you have every right to consider your alternatives and even explore the idea of terminating your relationship. Portfolio performance is only part of the reason you selected the hedge fund in the first place, so any breach of fit justifies your taking action. Monitoring your portfolio also involves keeping watch on how well the portfolio is performing. Poor performance is another strong reason for terminating a relationship.

When you measure your performance, you can measure it against similar hedge fund managers, the market as a whole, or the fund's stated goals if it has them. You also can employ mathematical measurement as well, such as the Sharpe ratio, the Treynor ratio, or beta. These measure the portfolio risk in relation to the portfolio return. Higher returns for the same level of risk are ideal. Once you have a strong grasp of how well your portfolio is performing, you can determine if all is going well, if more scrutiny needs to be conducted by you, or if you want to terminate the engagement.

Regardless of the decision you make, this strategy is very important for keeping you on the right path with your hedge fund investing. Performing this measurement once each year is acceptable, but semiannually or even quarterly is better.

15. REOPTIMIZE YOUR PORTFOLIO

Over time, a portfolio's asset mix, including the resulting risk-return trade-off profile, will change owing to price fluctuations, with some fluctuations being quite large. To address this issue, reoptimization may be appropriate. Reoptimization consists of four different but somewhat similar tasks. These tasks, or what I term the *four R's,* are *r*eevaluating, *r*ebalancing, *r*elocating, and *r*eallocating.

Reevaluating is the task of examining recent changes in your life and evaluating them within the context of your portfolio. Many things may have changed in you life since you last designed and built your portfolio, and these could affect your SMART financial goals and risk profile. As a result, you should take a long and hard look at your original financial plan and portfolio and modify them if needed.

Rebalancing is the task of selling and buying investments in order to return a portfolio's current asset class mix to the previously established optimal asset mix. Rebalancing involves selling a portion of asset classes that have become overweighted and buying a portion of asset classes that have become underweighted.

Relocating is the task of exchanging certain assets for other assets without changing the overall asset mix or risk-return trade-off profile. Relocating might involve exchanging a certain bond to obtain a higher or lower current rate of income depending on how your need for income has changed.

Reallocating is the task of adjusting your contribution mix, specifically what you are buying and in what amount. Reallocating does not change the mix of your existing assets, only how contributions will be made in the future.

16. AMEND YOUR INVESTMENT PLAN OVER TIME

A sound investment plan is only as good as how well it is executed over the entire investment time period. In the short term, investors will find that it is easy to follow through and remain committed to their plans. Unfortunately, committing oneself over the long term is another story and is much easier said than done. However, it is vital that investors do just that.

Be driven, not motivated—good advice I learned early on. Why driven? Because being driven lasts a lifetime, whereas being motivated only lasts in the short term—motivation simply doesn't last. Avoid this very common pitfall, and commit yourself to being driven.

In addition to committing yourself to being driven, you need to revisit your plan from time to time—at least annually—and modify it when and where appropriate. Pay careful attention to your present financial situation, your SMART financial goals, and the plan you have in place to bridge the gap. Changes should be made to your goals or plan if necessary. In addition, evaluate your portfolio within the context of any changes made, and make changes to your portfolio and written investment plan if warranted.

17. OBTAIN PROFESSIONAL HELP WHEN NEEDED

In an endeavor as critical as managing your portfolio, it is not especially wise to handle every situation without the help of a professional. Many individual investors simply do not have the time nor the patience to manage their investments. Managing a portfolio can be quite challenging.

Obtaining professional counsel can be challenging itself and should not be approached lightly. As with investors and their objectives and constraints, professional advisors also differ in their philosophy, processes, services, education,

experience, and ability to add value. Professional advisors work in many fields and hold varied titles, such as investment advisor, financial planner, accountant, estate planner, insurance agent, and stockbroker. Over the last few years, most professional advisors have seen their roles expand, and now the lines between them have become greatly blurred. Today it is commonplace to meet an insurance agent who is also registered as an investment advisor or an accountant who engages in the practice of estate planning (see Figure 13–2).

Figure 13-2. Immutable strategies for peak-performance portfolios

1	Manage with a Prudent Mind-set
2	Establish SMART Financial Goals
3	Understand Your Risk Profile
4	Identify Your Optimal Asset Mix
5	Maximize Asset Location
6	Diversify, Diversify, Diversify
7	Index It!
8	Employ Time, Not Timing
9	Think Total Portfolio, Not Component Investments
10	Minimize Management Fees and Commissions
11	Minimize Taxes and Emphasize After-Tax Returns
12	Draft a Written Investment Plan
13	Reinvest Dividends, Interest, and Capital Gains
14	Monitor, Measure, and Evaluate
15	Reoptimize Your Portfolio
16	Amend Your Investment Plan Over Time
17	Obtain Professional Help When Needed

Quiz for Chapter 13

1. More research than not has concluded that which strategy is the leading determinant of portfolio performance over time?

   a. Security selection

   b. Asset allocation

   c. Market timing

   d. Expense reduction

2. Hedge funds and asset allocation cannot be combined for a more efficient portfolio.

   a. True

   b. False

3. All the following are key benefits of asset allocation *except*

   a. it maximizes risk-adjusted return.

   b. it minimizes portfolio volatility.

   c. it promotes a more diversified portfolio.

   d. it increases trading costs.

4. Allocating based solely on the age of the investor is best described by what allocation method?

   a. Equity overload

   b. Simple 110

   c. Cash-flow matching

   d. Risk avoidance

5. Allocating according to a unique brokerage model is best described as which allocation method?

   a. Equity overload

   b. Cash-flow matching

   c. Custom combination

   d. Allocation timing

6. Overemphasizing equity assets during asset allocation is best described by which method?

   a. Equity overload

   b. Equity 110

    c. Allocation timing

    d. Custom combination

7. Asset allocations evolve over time with changing investor goals and obligations.

    a. True

    b. False

8. Which is the golden rule with peak-performance investing?

    a. Follow what the media say

    b. Manage with a prudent mind-set

    c. Compartmentalize your investments

    d. Minimize tax durations

9. Indexing all portfolio assets is a smart move and highly encouraged.

    a. True

    b. False

10. For which of the following asset classes is indexing most effective?

    a. Large-cap stocks

    b. Small-cap stocks

    c. International stocks

    d. High-yield fixed-income securities

Evaluating Hedge Funds

Sourcing, Screening, and Due-Diligence Considerations

Today there are more than 9,000 hedge funds in operation across the world, with more being established each and every day. This significant number creates logistic challenges for practically all investors, novice and advanced alike. As a result, investing in hedge funds requires a good deal of effort and due diligence to screen out poor hedge fund managers and to identity the ideal hedge fund managers with whom to work.

The task of manager discovery is a significant step unto itself and should not be approached lightly. As with investors and their objectives and constraints, hedge fund managers also differ in their backgrounds, expertise, philosophy, processes, strategies employed, and performance track record. Hedge funds also differ in regard to risk, fees, and taxes incurred. With so many alternatives from which to select, the process can seem daunting. Remember, not all hedge fund managers are equal! Some managers may say the same things as others, but when you investigate further, you will discover significant differences.

As with any other investment, establishing your goals and objectives is the logical first step with investing in hedge funds. Doing so will help you achieve your investment goals. To locate and evaluate hedge fund managers properly, you will need to perform some basic information gathering, ask some specific questions, and then spend time evaluating the hedge funds for proper strategic fit.

Some of the factors you will need to investigate include assets under management, expertise of the hedge fund manager, strategies employed by the hedge fund manager, and the instruments and tools used to initiate the selected strategies. After evaluating these data, you will eliminate certain managers, whereas others will warrant additional investigation. An investigation such as this will uncover many unique management styles and circumstances that either meet your goals or not.

Understand Your Objectives and Constraints

SMART GOALS

Having investment goals and striving to attain those goals will provide not only your hedge fund investing purpose but also your overall investing direction and focus. Do you need money in two years for a new home, or will you be receiving a lump-sum retirement distribution perhaps? For investors who need more income in the form of interest and dividends or need greater liquidity in their portfolios, allocating a small amount to hedge funds is prudent. For investors who have no liquidity need or obligations, allocating a greater amount to hedge funds could be a wise strategy. To best identify your goals, investors should emphasize SMART financial goals. SMART is an acronym that best illustrates the five characteristics of well-designed financial goals:

- *Specific.* Your goals should be unambiguous, clear, and well defined.
- *Measurable.* Your goals should be quantifiable and calculable.
- *Accepted.* Your goals should be acknowledged and motivational.
- *Realistic.* Your goals should be achievable and attainable, not lofty.
- *Time-centric.* Your goals should be for a set period, nothing indefinite.

INVESTMENT KNOWLEDGE

Time and time again we hear, "Invest in what you know." Both Warren Buffett and Peter Lynch propagate this belief. The more knowledgeable you are about a specific investment, the more confident and certain you are regarding whether or not that investment is appropriate and suitable for you. On the flip side, the less you know about an investment, the more apprehensive and uncertain you are about whether or not to hold that particular investment in your portfolio.

All else held constant, the greater your investment knowledge, the higher is your risk tolerance. An investor with strong investment knowledge typically will have a portfolio with higher-risk investments. On the flip side, an investor with weaker investment knowledge will tend to design a portfolio with lower- to moderate-risk investments. Although identifying the assets in a hedge fund is not exactly easy, doing so will help in deciding if that fund is a good match for you.

INVESTMENT OBJECTIVES

The most common objectives investors tend to establish include protecting their portfolios and growing them over time—in other words, earning a sufficient return. Return is the desired financial reward sought by investors for deferring current consumption and making an investment. The reward for making an investment can come in two forms—appreciation of principal and receiving dividends and interest income.

The goal here is to gain a better perspective on what return it is going to take to achieve your SMART goals. Thus you may need a slightly higher return to build a portfolio large enough to fund your retirement some time in the future. Lastly, your desired return should be realistic, neither vague nor unattainable.

CURRENT AND PROJECTED FINANCIAL POSITION

Your level of wealth will play a substantial role in determining your asset allocation and subsequent hedge fund investment. In general, investors with higher levels of wealth tend to have a greater capacity for assuming risk. Simply put, wealthy investors have more room for error in achieving their goals. Of course, this is not always the case, but as a general rule, it usually holds true. For instance, if you were to win the lottery, your capacity to assume risk would increase dramatically. Wouldn't you care less about losing $50,000 if you just won $25 million?

Hedge funds investors, out of sheer screening owing to Securities and Exchange Commission (SEC) regulations, are in much better financial positions than other investors. However, hedge fund investors should take a good look at their current and projected financial positions and identify what their loss capacity may be to better determine how much to invest in hedge funds.

RISK PROFILE

Your risk profile is perhaps your most important investment consideration. Your risk profile will determine not only how you allocate your portfolio from the outset but also how you manage your portfolio over time. Your risk profile consists of three similar yet separate factors. These include your *tolerance* for risk, your *capacity* to assume risk, and your *need* to assume risk. The lowest value in any one of the three factors is considered the maximum level of risk you should assume in your portfolio. For example, although an investor may have a high risk tolerance and high capacity to assume risk, that investor may have a low need to assume risk. Why? This is so because many investors do not have the need to assume risk; their wealth is more than adequate to fund their lifestyle and future goals. Unfortunately, investor risk profile is difficult to measure for three reasons. First, risk is specific to the situation. Second, investment-specific risk is not easily understood, and therefore, people act irrationally and without predictability. Third, an investor's risk profile—tolerance, capacity, and need—may change over time—it is not static. Thus your risk profile could always be moving, not easy to isolate, and thus difficult to work with.

Since you cannot control investment results, risk tolerance therefore is based on your tolerance for volatility. Investments with greater volatility have higher chances of experiencing price declines, which means that you may not achieve your desired return.

TIME HORIZON

Not only is time horizon a key investing consideration, it is also a cornerstone principle of asset allocation—and rightfully so. Time horizon greatly affects expectations for asset class returns, asset class volatility, and correlations among asset classes.

The primary use of time horizon is to help you to determine the portfolio balance between equities and fixed-income securities, namely, bonds and cash. All else being equal, the longer your time horizon, the more equity assets and fewer fixed-income assets you should hold.

The most prevalent type of risk you need to address over the long term is purchasing-power risk, or the loss in an asset's real value owing to inflation. Equity investments provide the best hedge against this type of risk. In the short term, the most prevalent risk is price volatility. Fixed-income investments provide the best hedge against this type of risk.

INCOME AND LIQUIDITY NEEDS AND PREFERENCES

Your needs for current income and liquidity will affect how you allocate your portfolio, including investments in hedge funds. This consideration addresses the degree to which you require cash to accomplish everyday activities and make special purchases. Consider, for example, a retired couple who use their investment portfolio to fund their retirement. In this situation, the retired couple would have a much higher liquidity and income need than would a couple in their prime earning years, where their income exceeds their expenses. As a result, the retired couple would need to build a portfolio that emphasizes income-oriented investments. Hedge funds may not be a smart investment in this scenario.

TAX STATUS AND TAX CONSIDERATIONS

This consideration is central to deciding what asset classes to hold in your portfolio. One of the primary purposes is to aid in deciding what type of fixed-income securities to buy, namely, taxable or tax-exempt. For taxable portfolios, investors with high federal income tax rates will find it more appropriate to invest in tax-exempt securities than in taxable investments. Tax-exempt portfolios should focus on taxable investments because these portfolios do not pay taxes and thus should not invest in lower returning tax-exempt securities.

In addition to aiding in the decision to buy taxable or tax-exempt investments, tax management should focus on realizing, deferring, and avoiding taxes. Consequently, tax management has become one of the hot new buzz words in portfolio management. This is justifiably so because taxes can reduce portfolio performance by a substantial amount. In response, taxes and their impact on your portfolio should be one of your considerations when allocating your assets. As the number and complexity of your tax issues increase, so too does the need to involve either a certified public accountant (CPA) or an estate-planning attorney.

UNIQUE PREFERENCES AND CIRCUMSTANCES

This consideration essentially incorporates anything that cannot be categorized in one of the other inputs but still affects how you should allocate your portfolio. Many of the items incorporated in this input are uniquely specific to the individual investor. These items can range in depth and breadth and may not be common to other investors.

Sourcing Hedge Funds

Years ago, obtaining information on hedge funds was very difficult. Investors had to rely on contacts and referral sources for information. This has changed with the popularity of hedge funds growing exponentially. The hedge fund industry is a well-connected network of professionals, making gathering and disseminating information much easier than in the past. Word of mouth still continues to be the favorite source for investors seeking hedge fund investments. Given the restrictions on hedge fund marketing, this approach seems to work for both investors and managers. With the advent of rating services becoming involved in the ranking of hedge funds, the sources of information will grow. Another solid source of information can be brokerage firms. These firms often host seminars on hedge fund investing and invite hedge fund managers to give quick talks about their funds. Investors may find this venue a good fit. Web sites such as HedgeWorld.com and Morningstar.com provide research on hedge funds. Over time, more sources of information will surface, providing additional help to small and new hedge fund investors.

Gathering information on hedge funds begins with obtaining their offering memorandum, disclosure documents, and legal partnership forms. Some of these documents will prove beneficial in learning more about each hedge fund, but many will not because of a lack of disclosure. Questions that are sometimes answered in these documents include

1. What is the minimum initial investment?

2. What is the investment management fee and incentive-performance fee?

3. What is the hurdle rate, if any?

4. Is there a high-water-mark safeguard?

5. What are the provisions for making withdrawals?

6. When can additional contributions be made?

7. How and when are performance and holdings communicated?

8. What strategies are employed, and what is the stated goal?

Obtaining all other information, whether past or present, is vitally important. This will help you to ascertain the future expectations for the funds under review. Reviewing this information is best using two approaches—a qualitative approach and a quantitative approach. Under the qualitative approach, a review of the hedge fund management team is performed. This will uncover some unique strengths and some previously unknown weaknesses. Much can be learned by looking at the management team. Under the quantitative approach, you will want to review the performance, fees, taxes, and all other relevant numerical data of the hedge fund. This will paint a profound picture of the hedge fund and give you the much-needed ammunition for making a decision on whether or not to invest.

Central Hedge Fund Considerations

During the hedge fund evaluation stage, you will want to concentrate your efforts on four central considerations. These considerations are specific to the hedge fund itself rather than dealing with the manager. The four central considerations include returns, risks, fees, and taxes. I will discuss each one below.

HEDGE FUND PERFORMANCE

The process of screening hedge funds should begin with hedge fund performance. Note that I used the word *performance* rather than the word *return*. Return implies a rate of growth, such as 11 percent capital appreciation or 4 percent dividend yield. Performance, on the other hand, goes a step further. Here, returns are considered in the context of the goal. Thus an 11 percent return is evaluated in the context of a forecasted 14 percent rate of return.

Screening for performance will help to automatically eliminate the bad from the good. Obtaining a complete and accurate performance track record is not easy; thus this process should be considered only a preliminary screening step. Some of the areas where you will want to concentrate the bulk of your time and resources include historical returns, dispersion of returns, and consistency of returns. Each will give you a solid look inside the performance of a hedge fund.

Historical returns demonstrate how well or poorly a hedge fund has done in the past. As we all know, past performance is not a guarantee of future performance however. Given that hedge fund managers possess a high degree of influence over the hedge fund, knowing past performance gives some indication of how the fund is managed. Are the returns all over the board, or are they fairly consistent? Are the returns meeting the hedge funds objective of generating attractive absolute returns? Are the returns exceeding the hurdle rate? Once you know the strategy the hedge fund manager is employing to manage the fund, identifying the historical returns will help you to evaluate how good of a job the manager has done.

Dispersion of returns is best described as how the return of a single hedge fund compares with the average return of its peer group. This provides a big-picture view of the hedge fund. Be cautious of hedge funds with wide dispersions of returns around the peer average return as this could indicate a haphazard approach to managing the fund. Why? Because if the majority of hedge fund managers are experiencing returns of 12 to 15 percent each year but a certain hedge fund is experiencing returns of 10 to 17 percent, then one must question its effectiveness in implementing and managing the same strategy that others are using to generate more consistent returns.

Dispersion of returns leads into the third area of discussion, consistency of returns. Ideal hedge funds demonstrate high levels of consistency regardless of how well the peer group is performing. High levels of consistency provide security in future performance. The more consistent a fund is now, one can argue the more consistent it will be in the future. Of course, consistency itself as a screening tool is not enough. Hedge funds can have high levels of consistency while generating poor performance. Year after year a hedge fund could generate poor returns. This isn't an ideal hedge fund. Attractive consistent returns should be sought by hedge fund investors.

A Brief Caution with Performance Screening

Screening performance in an attempt to identify good hedge fund managers presents two problems. First, with the growth in the number of hedge funds in the marketplace, the sample average returns used for comparison purposes involve more managers at the end of the holding period than it did at the beginning of the holding period. Second, the return data exhibit a survivorship bias. This bias, extremely prevalent with mutual funds, means that as the poorly performing funds close and drop out of the performance data, the average return rises. This rise is purely cosmetic and biased.

HEDGE FUND FEES

Hedge funds typically charge two types of fees. These two include a fixed investment-management fee and a variable performance-incentive fee. The standard performance-incentive fee is 20 percent, although some can be found that differ from this amount. This fee is charged on all gains, whether realized or unrealized, including dividends and interest payments received. This fee is based on the total return of the fund. Investors will from time to time pay this fee only to see the value of their investment decline. To protect the investor from paying a fee for gaining that value back, hedge funds have high-water marks. These safeguards ensure that investors do not pay fees twice for the same gain in value. For instance, suppose that an investor contributes $1 million to a hedge fund and over the subsequent year the fund earns 10 percent. The portfolio at the end of the year then will be $1.1 million. The hedge fund will charge the standard 20 percent performance-incentive fee against the 10 percent earned, or $100,000. This translates into a fee of $20,000. The high-water mark has now been set at $1.1 million. Now suppose that in year two the investment declines by $50,000, thus no performance-incentive fee is charged—although the typical investment management fee based on assets under management is charged. In year three the hedge fund generates strong returns with the investor's portfolio appreciating to $1.5 million. The performance-incentive fee is charged on the gain in excess of the high-water mark. This gain equates to $400,000 ($1.5 – $1.1 million). No performance-incentive fee is charged against the $50,000 loss experienced in year two that was earned back in year three.

The 20 percent performance-incentive fee is commonly applied to the gain in value *after* the standard 1 percent investment-management fee is charged. For example, suppose that an investor earns 14 percent in a particular year, giving that investor $3 million in total value. The 1 percent investment-management fee then is charged against the $3 million. This equates to $30,000. The performance-incentive fee then is charged against the gain less the $30,000 investment-management fee. Note that many hedge funds deduct the 1 percent fee prior to the performance-incentive fee, but some do not. These managers charge the performance-incentive fee first, followed by the investment-management fee. The common investment-management fee is charged to cover the operating expenses of the hedge fund. These expenses include, but are not limited to, accounting and auditing, payroll, marketing, and compliance.

Another safeguard provision some hedge funds use is a hurdle rate. A *hurdle rate* is the point at which a return higher than the hurdle rate is charged the performance-incentive fee. Performance below the hurdle rate is not charged the fee. The hurdle rate is most always based on a short-term rate, such as the London Interbank Offered Rate (LIBOR). Rates based on the Standard & Poor's (S&P) 500 Index are not used because this would cause hedge funds to abandon their pursuit of absolute performance and instead focus on relative performance and equity securities.

The use of fees depends on the individual hedge fund. Some hedge funds charge performance-incentive fees of more than 20 percent and some less. At the same time, some hedge funds charge the standard 1 percent investment-management fee, and some charge more and some less. The use of the high-water mark and hurdle rate safeguard provisions is also variable. Most hedge funds do implement high-water-mark provisions, but most do not have hurdle rates. Furthermore, hedge funds typically are willing to negotiate fees. The greater the assets an investor brings, the greater is the negotiating leverage.

One final note regarding performance-incentive fees: Many people think that hedge fund managers will try to maximize this fee by assuming high levels of risk. This is not the case for two simple reasons. First, the top hedge fund managers have their own money in their hedge funds. Thus, if they take too much risk with the fund, they will put not only the assets of their investors at risk but also their own money. Second, hedge fund managers for the most part want to stay in the business long term. Compensation generated over their lifetime is significantly more appealing than earning more in one year and losing it the next. For these reasons, hedge

fund managers recognize the need to take calculated and smart risks. Doing so will help both investors and the manager to sleep better at night.

HEDGE FUND TAXES

Hedge funds are considered *pass-through entities*. This means that hedge funds themselves do not pay taxes but instead pass all gains and losses to individual investors. Since hedge funds typically engage in active trading, realized gains and losses are common. This translates to more challenging tax planning and reporting. Schedule K–1s, or Form 1065, are supplied to investors of hedge funds, given that the limited partnership form is the structure of choice for hedge funds. Schedule K–1s are not due to investors until close to the tax filing deadline, so investors will find filing their taxes a chore in patience and discipline. Tax-reporting extensions are common with hedge fund investors.

Limited partners, or the investors, receive capital gains or losses in proportion to their interest in a hedge fund. For instance, if an investor held a 10 percent interest in a hedge fund, and that hedge fund generated $400,000 in capital gains for a tax year, then the investor would incur $40,000 in capital gains. Capital gains are taxed against the investor's personal tax rate. As with mutual funds, investors are responsible for reporting earnings, both income and capital gains, even if the investor did not withdraw money from the fund. This is similar to the "phantom tax" that investors in CDs must pay even when their earnings are locked up in the CD.

The frequency and amount of hedge fund investors' tax obligations depend on the specific hedge fund and, more important, on the type of strategy employed by the manager. The actions of the hedge fund manager to carry out each stated strategy will be a factor in any tax consequences generated. As mentioned previously, the degree of active trading is a big factor in tax implications. Selling existing investments will generate either capital gains or losses. Capital gains and losses can be classified as either short- or long-term. The tax rate on long-term gains is lower because it gives investors incentive to hold investments for more than a year rather than "flipping" to make a profit. Capital losses are offset against capital gains to minimize taxable consequences. However, there is a maximum capital loss amount that investors can use to offset against capital gains. A portion of excess capital losses, if they exist, can be carried over to the next tax year and perhaps offset against new capital gains.

The second type of tax that hedge fund investors incur is ordinary income tax. Ordinary income consists of the dividends and interest received from the holdings in the hedge fund. This type of income is received in the form of stock dividends and interest payments from bonds. Depending on the type of hedge fund, an investor may

or may not be exposed to this tax consideration, but most will be. Many stocks do pay dividends, so investors will incur some taxes on current income.

Not only does the type of hedge fund make a difference in the taxes investors incur, but also does the type of investor matter. Individual investors for the most part hold taxable portfolios. However, many not-for-profit institutions are tax-exempt. Thus tax considerations are not a significant issue with this type of investor. However, for the vast majority of investors, taxes are a priority issue because they can take a serious bite out of your earnings. Remember, it is not what you earn when the day is all said and done but rather what you take away and retain. Keep tax considerations at the forefront of your evaluation of hedge funds. Specifically ask the hedge fund management team about this consideration.

Characteristics of Top Hedge Funds

Throughout this book I have discussed the fundamentals of hedge funds—their benefits and risks and the different types of hedge funds. But what characteristics are common among the top hedge funds, you might ask? Since this chapter is all about screening hedge funds to meet your goals and objectives, I thought it appropriate to include this section. Emphasizing these characteristics in your screening can help you to find suitable hedge funds. These characteristics are as follows (see Figure 14–1).

Figure 14-1. Characteristics of top hedge funds

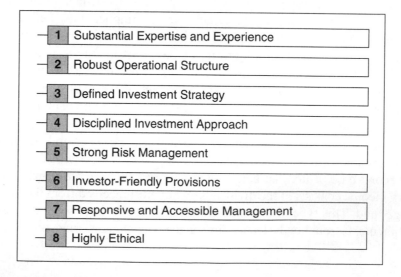

1. Substantial Expertise and Experience
2. Robust Operational Structure
3. Defined Investment Strategy
4. Disciplined Investment Approach
5. Strong Risk Management
6. Investor-Friendly Provisions
7. Responsive and Accessible Management
8. Highly Ethical

SUBSTANTIAL EXPERTISE AND EXPERIENCE

The top hedge funds are operated by very talented investment professionals. These people typically are highly educated and possess a strong grasp not only of the financial marketplace but also of hedge funds in particular. In addition, these people have a true passion and drive to manage money and run hedge funds.

ROBUST OPERATIONAL STRUCTURE

Given that operations are the core of hedge funds, the operational structure of a hedge fund can mean life or death for that particular hedge fund. Operational structure consists of such things as trading operations, broker-dealer effectiveness, pricing and valuation, and executive leadership. A hedge fund could be operated by some of the brightest minds in the field, but without a robust operational structure, nothing will get accomplished. The top hedge funds strive to build, enhance, and protect their operational structure, thus enabling management to run the fund effectively without issue.

DEFINED INVESTMENT STRATEGY

For the most part, investment strategy is how hedge funds differentiate themselves from the competition. This provides a way for hedge funds to offer unique expertise, experience, and investment accessibility to investors. Investors with the greatest amount of clout and sophistication will seek hedge funds that offer very specific types of strategies. Funds of funds will allocate their capital to many different investment strategies in order to diversify and maximize their risk-adjusted return. The top managers rarely deviate from established investment strategy because they know where their competitive advantage lies. This also helps to brand the hedge fund manager at the same time.

DISCIPLINED INVESTMENT APPROACH

The top hedge funds clearly have defined approaches to making investment decisions. Going outside their set guidelines typically is unacceptable to them. Hedge funds that have policies against the use of leverage beyond a certain point are generally highly disciplined to ensure that this threshold is not breached. Demonstrating consistency in a disciplined investment approach is very important to the top hedge funds and a positive indicator for institutions that are evaluating hedge fund managers for potential investments.

STRONG RISK MANAGEMENT

Risk management is perhaps the number one characteristic of top hedge fund managers. They recognize that they need sound systems and processes in place to identify when and where the fund might be assuming greater risk than is acceptable. A strong risk-management group not only will provide comfort and confidence in the hedge fund but also will provide the necessary oversight so as to ensure that the fund does not stray from established guidelines and thresholds for risk. Strong risk-management groups will apply the brakes and handcuff hedge fund managers when they deviate from set policy and goals and potentially place the fund at unacceptable levels of risk.

INVESTOR-FRIENDLY PROVISIONS

One of the biggest drawbacks in investing in hedge funds is the restrictive provisions placed on investors. These provisions include lockup restrictions, limitations on when withdrawals can be made, and transparency. To attract the biggest and most sophisticated investors, hedge funds need to make their provisions more investor-friendly. The top hedge fund managers aim for enhanced transparency, shorter lockup periods, and more opportunities to withdraw invested capital.

RESPONSIVE AND ACCESSIBLE MANAGEMENT

Hedge funds are established as partnerships, not typically as corporations. Why, then, should investors or partners in a hedge fund not have access to hedge fund management? They should, of course. The best hedge funds recognize that they need to develop and cultivate an environment of open communication. Large institutions will demand it. Being responsive to investor issues relating to account management or client service is also a priority of the top hedge funds. They recognize that it is much more difficult to gain new investors than it is to retain existing investors.

HIGHLY ETHICAL

Nothing can bring down a hedge fund like unethical actions. As you read in Chapter 5, fraud, mispricing, and theft caused some of the largest hedge fund failures to date. The top hedge fund managers want to remain in this business over their entire careers and therefore highly value ethical behavior. Building a top hedge fund can take a significant amount of work, time, and money, but only one unethical action can cause it to come crashing down. The top hedge fund managers are at the pinnacle of the industry and therefore do not want to risk this happening.

Quiz for Chapter 14

1. What is the smart first step with hedge fund investing?

    a. Investigating hedge fund managers

    b. Conducting regulatory background checks

    c. Talking with a referral source

    d. Identifying your SMART financial goals

2. Clearly defined financial goals must be measurable but can be somewhat unspecific.

    a. True

    b. False

3. Which of the following is *not* a characteristic of SMART goals?

    a. Measurable

    b. Tactical

    c. Specific

    d. Realistic

4. Which of the following is *not* considered an "objective and constraint"?

    a. Risk profile

    b. Time horizon

    c. Risk management

    d. Current financial position

5. In regard to portfolio construction, what is the primary purpose of time horizon?

    a. To identify appropriate hedge funds

    b. To determine the balance between equity and fixed-income allocations

    c. To determine the allocation of alternative assets

    d. To ascertain which risk metric is most appropriate

6. Risk profile includes all the following variables *except*

    a. capacity to assume risk.

    b. need to assume risk.

    c. tolerance for risk.

    d. credit for risk.

7. Regardless of net worth, investors should have an emergency fund equal to three to six months of expenses.

   a. True

   b. False

8. Name the document investors receive from hedge funds that is necessary for them to file their taxes.

   a. Schedule K–1

   b. Form 1099-H

   c. Form 1040-H

   d. W-H1

9. Risk management often can restrict hedge fund managers from taking extra risk. Is strong risk management a sign of a well-run or poorly run fund?

   a. Well run

   b. Poorly run

10. All the following are characteristics of top hedge funds *except*

    a. investor-friendly provisions.

    b. strong risk management.

    c. shifting investment strategies.

    d. robust operational structure.

CHAPTER 15

Selecting a Hedge Fund

How to Find and Pick the Right Manager

Now that you have learned how to evaluate hedge funds and hedge fund management teams, we shift focus to making the initial investment in a hedge fund or hedge funds. In this chapter I will expound on the preceding chapter and discuss how to select a hedge fund. Specifically, this chapter will cover three important considerations for finding and picking the right manager, including final investigative work, employing sensible selection strategies, and building a hedge fund portfolio.

As with traditional investments, investments in hedge funds should be approached rationally and prudently. This process begins with making important decisions that ultimately will affect how well your investment objectives are accomplished. For investors with some experience in hedge funds, this process is relatively simple

and straightforward; however, other investors will discover this process to be more challenging. Nevertheless, the next section on final investigative work will help investors gain a better perspective on the hedge fund selection process and how best to use it to their advantage.

Final Investigative Work

Manager discovery and the pursuit of an ideal hedge fund manager constitute the key first step in selecting a hedge fund. Regardless of your experience with investing, you need to ensure that some very basic and important processes are followed to ensure a successful hedge fund investment. The following are some of the final critical issues you should investigate to find and pick the right hedge fund manager.

IDENTIFY HEDGE FUND OFFERINGS

The first step you should undertake is to identify the various hedge fund offerings available to you. Are the hedge funds high-risk, high-potential-return funds; low-risk, low-potential-return funds; or a combination of the two? Can the hedge fund manager integrate the fund's offerings with the portfolio you presently have, or will this be a stand-alone investment? Does the hedge fund manager offer multiple hedge funds to provide investors with a choice of strategy? Once the question of hedge fund offerings is answered, you then can make an informed decision on whether or not to go any further in your investigation of the manager. This initial step will help you to avoid serious problems in the future.

INVESTIGATE HEDGE FUND PERFORMANCE

Most hedge fund managers will provide you with some type of performance composite for you to review. When reviewing performance, be sure to learn which benchmarks are employed, how well the manager performed against his or her peer group, how consistent performance has been over long periods of time, what type of volatility is typical in the hedge fund, what the growth of assets under management has been, and how and when the performance composite was created. A statement claiming that the performance composite conforms to CFA Institute standards is your best assurance that the results are accurate. Some hedge funds even go a step further and have an external party review their performance composite and give it

their stamp of approval. If any of these items are not offered, ask the manager to provide them.

OBTAIN DISCLOSURE DOCUMENTS

All on-shore hedge funds are required to provide an offering memorandum, a limited partnership agreement, and a subscription agreement. Make sure that you understand the level of risk, the initial investment minimum, any withdrawal provisions, and other important considerations. Evaluate this information within the context of your goals and objectives to ensure that they are suitable to your investing goals, time horizon, and risk profile (tolerance, capacity, and need). As with any investment, the higher the potential returns for a given hedge fund, the higher is the potential risk that you must assume. Risk and return are linked.

ASK ABOUT ASSET VALUATION METHODOLOGY

To take advantage of unique opportunities, some hedge funds will need to invest in highly illiquid securities that may be difficult to value. In addition, many hedge funds exercise significant discretion in the method and timing of valuing securities. Make every effort to find out when the valuation will be performed (e.g., monthly or quarterly) and how the assets are valued. It is always wise to fully understand the valuation process and to learn if the assets in the hedge fund are valued internally or externally.

INVESTIGATE FEES

Fees have a big impact on your net return. Most hedge funds typically charge an investment-management fee of 1 to 2 percent of assets under management plus a performance-incentive fee, which is typically 20 percent of profits. This performance-incentive fee is used to motivate the hedge fund manager to generate positive returns. If the hedge fund manager does not perform, then the investor will not have to pay. This is a win-win situation for both. At the same time, however, this performance-incentive fee could motivate a hedge fund manager to take greater risks than warranted in pursuit of even greater returns and thus generate more fees. Most hedge funds will charge both the annual investment-management fee and the performance-incentive fee. However, funds of funds typically charge only the annual investment-management fee and not the performance-incentive fee because the stand-alone hedge funds comprising the fund already charge one. Note that some funds of funds do charge a performance-incentive fee. Remember to get all of

this information on the table from the outset. By the way, the expression "1–20" refers to the typical hedge fund pay structure of a 1 percent investment management fee and a 20 percent performance-incentive fee.

UNCOVER RESTRICTIONS ON WITHDRAWING INVESTED CAPITAL

The vast majority of hedge funds have restrictive provisions on the withdrawal of invested capital by investors. These provisions include withholding the right to withdraw from the hedge fund during the first year and establishing the periods of time when withdrawals can be made. Most funds implement provisions where an investor's initial investment cannot be withdrawn for a period of one year or more. Thereafter, funds typically are available only on a quarterly or annual basis. These provisions are instituted to give hedge fund managers the opportunity to employ their strategies and to give these managers the required time to liquidate investments—to cover withdrawals—that are difficult to sell or otherwise illiquid.

INQUIRE ABOUT TAX CONSIDERATIONS

Some managers underemphasize tax management, whereas other managers overemphasize it. Specifically, ask about the general degree of turnover, how the fund incorporates tax management into its management process, and how the fund approaches the issue of loss harvesting and exchange strategies. Many hedge fund managers will strive to maximize the top line, or gross return, but top managers will focus on maximizing the bottom line, or net return. Remember, if you cannot walk away with the gain, did you really earn it in the first place?

CONDUCT BACKGROUND CHECKS

This is perhaps the golden rule of hedge fund investing. Know with whom you are investing your money. Make sure that the hedge fund manager and other key decision makers are qualified to manage your money. Investigate what type of education the manager has—a bachelor's or perhaps a master's degree? Investigate whether or not the manager has earned a professional designation, such as chartered financial analyst (CFA), certified public accountant (CPA), certified financial planner (CFP), or chartered financial consultant (ChFC). Having a designation illustrates commitment and specialized knowledge, both of which separate top managers from the rest of the pack.

Investigate how long the manager has been managing hedge funds and how much experience he or she has with investments and portfolio management. Also

inquire how long the manager has been in his or her present role. You will find many hedge fund managers with very little experience not only with hedge funds but also with portfolio management. Given the lure of hefty compensation from the performance-incentive fees, more and more people with little direct experience are entering this field. This does not mean that a manager with little experience will fail at generating suitable returns; it means that you should exercise extra caution.

INVESTIGATE ETHICAL CONSIDERATIONS

This step is obviously very subjective and not always easy to address when you first meet a hedge fund manager. A good way to approach this is to investigate whether or not either a regulatory organization or a private association to which the manager belongs publicly disciplined him or her. You can obtain this type of information by reviewing the manager's Form ADV-II, if available. Depending on whether or not this form is available, it may be possible for you to review the firm's Form ADV-II using the Security and Exchange Commission's (SEC) Investment Adviser Public Disclosure (IAPD) Web site. For managers with less than $25 million in assets under management, the state securities regulator where the manager's principal place of business is located might be able to provide this type of information. Lastly, you may get additional information from the National Association of Securities Dealers (NASD) or any association of which the manager is a member, such as the Certified Financial Planning Board of Standards (www.CFP.net) or the CFA Institute (www.CFAInstitute.org).

ASK ABOUT THE MANAGER'S PERSONAL INVESTMENTS

Hedge fund managers should have a substantial amount of their investable assets in the hedge funds they are managing. Moreover, the hedge fund manager should not have any investments of similar type outside the hedge fund. Ask the hedge fund manager both these questions. Exercise caution with hedge fund managers who invest actively in similar investments outside the hedge funds they are managing. Owning nonsimilar assets such as Treasuries or real estate is not a concern because it does not cause conflicts of interest or signal that better investments can be found outside the fund. Hedge fund managers who invest a substantial amount of their personal assets in the fund also will have an extra incentive to generate attractive returns. This is a win-win for both parties involved and provides the investor with more confidence, knowing that the interests of the manager and the investor are aligned. If hedge fund managers are investing outside their funds, perhaps investors should do the same.

CONSIDER THE PERSONALITY FIT

Usually after the first meeting, you will know if there is a fit or not. Is the manager more serious or humorous? Is the manager intense or low key? Is the manager more professional or down to earth? Did the manager graduate from the same university as you graduated? Does he or she play golf? Did a friend refer you? Are your interests similar? Personality fit is not a high-priority item, but not having a good relationship with your hedge fund manager will make things more difficult.

DO NOT BE AFRAID TO ASK ADDITIONAL QUESTIONS

Investing in hedge funds is not quite the same as picking stocks and bonds or investing in mutual funds. With hedge funds, you are entrusting your money to someone who wields a significant degree of freedom in making investment decisions that affect your portfolio. As a result, you should know where and how your money is being invested, who the key decision makers are, what strategies will be employed, how and when you can redeem your investment or make additional contributions, what safeguards are in place to protect your investment, and what your rights are as an investor.

Decision-Making Considerations

Evaluating a hedge fund manager based on the information you gathered in the interview and in researching the disclosure documents can be challenging at best. After speaking with the hedge fund management team, you may get a negative feeling and end the investigation right then. At other times, you may get a positive feeling and decide to continue or perhaps invest at that point. Managers who are unable to answer simple questions about their hedge funds, the hedge fund company, or the current and anticipated investing marketplace provide a good reason to stop the process. As with experience in investigating homes for purchase, having experience with investigating hedge fund managers is invaluable and will serve you well.

No single positive response should motivate an investor to select a certain hedge fund. This is justly unwise. However, one such negative response to any of the items investigated could motivate the investor to move on to another hedge fund manager. Identifying the best hedge fund manager can be a Herculean effort. Focus on finding good hedge fund managers, and select the one or more managers who best fit your needs and personality. It is smart to diversify your hedge fund managers rather than concentrating on only one. This will elevate manager-specific risk similar to how hedge fund managers minimize investment-specific risk by investing in numerous securities. Evaluating and selecting a manager is not always easy and therefore should be handled with the utmost care, skill, and patience.

Seven Strategies for Selecting a Hedge Fund Manager

There are no guarantees in hedge fund investing, and there are no shortcuts. Some investors will have bad experiences with investing in hedge funds, whereas many will have positive experiences. To give you an idea of how best to maximize your opportunity to experience a successful hedge fund investment, I have provided the following seven sensible strategies.

STRATEGY 1: DO YOUR PRELIMINARY BACKGROUND RESEARCH AND DO IT WELL

Managing your portfolio always begins with you. Selecting a hedge fund manager or hedge fund based on a recommendation from a friend or advisor is not good enough. Investors need to take a more proactive role in screening hedge funds and managers and then evaluating them thoroughly. Background investigations should be done, as well as asking many questions to identify proper fit. Reading the required disclosure documents is also highly encouraged. Investors should never rely on someone else to do what they should be doing.

STRATEGY 2: SEEK OUT HEDGE FUND MANAGERS WITH DEMONSTRATED SUCCESS

Little is more important in hedge fund investing than investing with managers who have demonstrated success. Of course, past performance is not a guarantee of future performance, but consistent, attractive performance over many years speaks volumes. Performance numbers can be obtained from the hedge funds or from an external source. Hedge funds with solid to strong performance will make every effort to communicate to you how well they have done. Conversely, hedge funds with not so attractive performance will not be as forthcoming. One external source for hedge fund information is Morningstar, the same company that was built on providing information and rankings on mutual funds.

STRATEGY 3: PURSUE HEDGE FUNDS WITH INVESTOR-FRIENDLY PROVISIONS

Although the performance track record of a certain hedge fund is very important, it is not the only factor to take into consideration. Other very important factors that should be evaluated include a high-water-mark provision, hurdle-rate provision, fee structure, and redemption provisions. All else being equal, hedge funds with

hurdle-rates and high-water-mark provisions are ideal. At the same time, hedge funds with flexible (instead of stringent) redemption provisions offer investors more opportunities to withdraw their investments with minimal challenges or, worse yet, headaches. Last but surly not least, pay attention to the hedge fund fee structure, namely investment management fees based on assets under management and performance-incentive fees. Ensure that both are not excessive compared with other hedge funds.

STRATEGY 4: EVALUATE HEDGE FUNDS WITHIN THE CONTEXT OF YOUR OVERALL PORTFOLIO

Hedge funds should not be viewed as stand-alone investments. Rather, they should be considered within the context of your overall portfolio. This means that you understand how your overall portfolio will be affected when determining how much to invest in hedge funds and what hedge fund strategies to pursue. At the same time, managing the remaining allocations of your portfolio, such as equities, fixed-income securities, and money market instruments, should be accomplished with your hedge fund investments in mind. For example, if you build a portfolio heavily emphasizing equity investments and believe that your exposure to equities is excessive given your objectives and constraints, then equity-long hedge funds may not be the most appropriate investment. An equity-short hedge fund may be more suitable because it not only will limit your equity exposure but also will reduce your total equity exposure because the shorts will offset, or neutralize, some of the long positions.

STRATEGY 5: DIVERSIFY YOUR HEDGE FUND PORTFOLIO

Funds of funds provide many benefits that other hedge funds do not. First and foremost, funds of funds provide immediate and enhanced diversification. This is the result of investing in multiple hedge funds and with multiple hedge fund managers. Diversification is ideal because it reduces the risk that any one fund or manager will perform poorly and affect your portfolio negatively. Second, funds of funds provide a means for the investment masses to invest in hedge funds. Most funds of funds have low initial minimums, which is in stark contrast to other types of hedge funds. Other benefits include risk management and professional oversight of where to invest and with whom. The obvious drawback to funds of funds is the second layer of fees charged. Thus investors need to take this into consideration when evaluating this type of fund. Nevertheless, funds of funds provide an excellent way for investors to diversify their hedge fund portfolios.

STRATEGY 6: SWITCH HEDGE FUND MANAGERS WHEN APPROPRIATE

Regardless of the background research you conduct, some hedge fund investments simply do not work out. Perhaps the issue is performance-related, perhaps the key manager retired, or perhaps the issue is the relationship between the manager and investor. Nevertheless, some investors at some point in their investing will find it necessary to walk away and move to another manager. When situations such as this arise, make sure that you understand what is expected of you prior to beginning the process of withdrawing your investment. Some hedge funds have flexible provisions for withdrawing investments, whereas others do not. The most important lesson here is to make the switch when the time arises. Waste little time if things are just not working out.

STRATEGY 7: BE A RATIONAL AND INFORMED HEDGE FUND INVESTOR

The golden rule of investing is to manage your portfolio as a rational and informed investor. This is smart advice for both hedge fund investing and general investing. If you are able to accomplish this goal, then everything else will fall into place.

To become a rational and informed hedge fund investor, you will need to be proactive in learning what rational and informed investors do and do not do. There are many pitfalls along the way. In addition, you will want to learn the key attributes of hedge funds and general investing basics. Chapter 18 of this book provides a quick and simple discussion of key hedge fund attributes. By knowing the key hedge fund attributes, you will position yourself to better manage your portfolio going forward.

What are rational investors? Rational investors do not fall victim to the most common behavioral blunders investors often make. These behavioral blunders include such things as illusion of control, blinders, overconfidence, denial, and herd instinct. By definition, rational investors become informed investors over time. Being informed means that you know and fully understand the key lessons of investing, such as that no investment is guaranteed and not to invest anything that you cannot afford to lose. Make a point of becoming a rational and informed hedge fund investor.

Building the Hedge Fund Portfolio

As with traditional investing, smart decisions backed by thorough research are important with hedge funds. Having realistic goals and objectives is critical. For investors

to have realistic goals and objectives, they must first understand basic investing lessons and prudent ways to manage their portfolio for long-term growth. But what are some of the benchmarks for hedge fund investing? In particular, how much should you invest in hedge funds and how many hedge funds should you hold?

HOW MUCH IN HEDGE FUNDS

Determining how much to allocate to hedge funds is one of the most important questions in hedge fund investing. Unfortunately, this question is also one of the most subjective as well. The best response to give is, "It all depends." It all depends on the type of investor, the risk profile of the investor, the time horizon of the investor, the investor's need for liquidity, the investor's desired returns, and more. These considerations provide a strong look inside what helps to determine how much to invest in hedge funds. Many investing gurus say that investors, depending on their level of wealth and risk profile, should allocate anywhere from 0 to 20 percent in alternative assets, including hedge funds. However, remember that hedge funds are not really an asset class themselves but rather a different strategy for investing. This approach has made people label them as alternative.

Allocating anywhere from 0 to 20 percent is the view commonly held by traditional investment managers. However, many hedge fund managers will say that allocations significantly higher than this figure should be considered. Some research has shown that allocations close to 60 percent should be invested in hedge funds. This is much too high for the typical hedge fund investor. Sticking with conventional wisdom of 20 percent or less is probably a smart move for most investors.

HOW MANY HEDGE FUNDS

Again, *it all depends*. What level of portfolio diversification are you looking to achieve? What level of oversight are you willing and able to accommodate? With diversification, both the hedge fund management team and the strategies employed, should be taken into consideration. Given the numerous hedge fund strategies available, investing in multiple hedge funds that employ different strategies will help to diversify your hedge fund portfolio. For example, an investor may invest in a hedge fund that employs a macrocentric strategy and a hedge fund that employs a distressed-securities strategy. In doing so, the investor will incorporate investments that are more value-oriented and with a somewhat longer-term time horizon. As with asset classes, at different points in time different hedge fund strategies will do better than others. Investors with multiple hedge funds or hedge fund strategies will benefit from this rotation of which strategy is doing best. One good and easy solution to diversifying across multiple strategies is to invest in a hedge fund that employs

multiple strategies rather than just one. Diversifying with two or more hedge fund managers could prove beneficial when a multistrategy hedge fund is held.

Research shows that investing in multiple hedge fund managers provides for more diversified and optimal hedge fund portfolios. As with the research relating to the allocation to hedge funds, research on the number of hedge fund managers to use is across the board. Some researchers indicate that over 15 managers is optimal. Doing so is simply not practical for individual investors but is for institutional investors. The best advice is to consider more than one hedge fund manager, where appropriate.

Funds of funds provide one of the best ways for investors to diversify across a broad number of hedge fund managers. The managers of funds of funds are experts at knowing hedge funds and hedge fund management teams and at determining which is ideal to invest in. As a result, they offer one of the best ways to diversify in terms of both hedge fund strategies and hedge fund managers.

Quiz for Chapter 15

1. During hedge fund discovery, which of the following steps occurs first?
   a. Investigate fees
   b. Identify hedge fund offerings
   c. Ask about manager's committed capital
   d. Consider the personality fit

2. Given privacy concerns and the desire for secrecy, most hedge funds do not provide offering documents.
   a. True
   b. False

3. All the following are typical offering documents *except*
   a. limited partnership agreement.
   b. subscription agreement.
   c. offering memorandum.
   d. fund registration certification.

4. When someone mentions a "1–20," to what are they referring?
   a. A typical hedge fund organizational chart
   b. The days of the month when withdrawals are permitted
   c. 1 percent investment-management fee and 20 percent performance-incentive fee
   d. The timing of capital gains tax consequences

5. What is the duration of a typical lockup provision?

 a. One month

 b. One quarter

 c. One year

 d. Two years

6. What will Form ADV-II tell an investor about a certain hedge fund?

 a. Background of key people

 b. Approval process for becoming an accredited investor

 c. Approved withdrawal limit

 d. Deadline to make a second investment in the hedge fund

7. It is not necessary to investigate the backgrounds of hedge fund managers with strong performance track records.

 a. True

 b. False

8. Diversifying your hedge fund portfolio is a smart idea. Which of the following hedge fund styles provides the most diversification?

 a. Multistrategy

 b. Event-driven

 c. Funds of funds

 d. Tactical

9. What is the optimal portfolio allocation range for alternative assets, including hedge funds?

 a. 0 to 5 percent

 b. 0 to 10 percent

 c. 0 to 15 percent

 d. 0 to 20 percent

10. For investors seeking to invest in a stand-alone hedge fund, it is smart to consider investing in multiple stand-alone hedge funds, if applicable.

 a. True

 b. False

CHAPTER 16

Hedge Fund Benchmarking

Monitoring and Measuring Progress and Performance

Now that we have discussed how best to make the initial hedge fund allocation, we turn our attention to what to do after that step is complete. Here we will be concentrating our time and effort on proper oversight and related due diligence. Monitoring your hedge fund investment thus takes on the utmost importance. Many people may wonder if monitoring hedge funds is beneficial, let alone possible, given the lack of disclosure by many hedge fund managers. It is true that many hedge funds will not communicate everything you will want; however, they will communicate enough to help you keep a good handle on how well your hedge fund investment is working out. Monitoring is definitely not one of the more interesting activities of hedge fund investing, but it is one of the most important. Here are a few reasons why you should place emphasis on monitoring your hedge fund investment:

- Monitoring allows you to keep tabs on the manager, the person most responsible for your hedge fund performance.
- Monitoring allows you to gain a better insight into how your portfolio is being run, what is affecting the performance, and what value the hedge fund manager is adding.
- Monitoring guards the portfolio against managers making ad hoc decisions that will impede your long-term strategy.
- Monitoring allows you to quickly identify performance and ethical issues and to take early action to resolve such issues.
- Monitoring greatly decreases miscommunication and misunderstandings and allows for such occurrences to be resolved quickly and easily.
- Monitoring is a form of risk management and control.
- Monitoring helps to keep the hedge fund manager in tune with your needs.
- Monitoring assists the manager in understanding your objectives and guidelines.
- Monitoring ensures that your asset allocation does not stray from the optimal mix.

Regardless of how you stay in contact with your hedge fund manager—telephone, e-mail, office visits, or social events—staying in contact is very important. Keeping up on the latest happenings in the investment marketplace is another smart move. This is important because you do want to become and remain knowledgeable on the types of investments and markets your hedge fund is invested in. For example, if your hedge fund invests in opportunities presented by global macro events—oil, gold, etc.—then keeping up on these is essential. For investors who want to play a more active role in monitoring their managers and understanding their hedge fund investment, knowing the different strategies available to your manager and how they affect your portfolio is highly recommended. Monitoring your hedge fund manager is definitely a worthwhile and somewhat complex event. Strive to become an informed and prudent investor capable of making sound investment decisions.

Many hedge fund investors think that open communication with their hedge fund manager is difficult to achieve. In addition, many think that hedge fund managers will be cold and unreceptive. This is more fiction than fact. Most hedge fund managers are very approachable and are willing to sit down and talk with you. Before talking with your hedge fund manager, be mindful of the time commitment you require and the number of contacts you make.

Gaining access to your hedge fund manager is much easier when you have a large portfolio or you are a general partner rather than a limited partner. Given that general partners share in the risk, they are provided with the greatest amount of

transparency and disclosure of material information. This, of course, comes with a price in that general partners have relatively unlimited risk for losses. Limited partners are only liable to the amount of their investment. Furthermore, when you have your own hedge fund account rather than pooling your investment with those of others, you will gain greater access to hedge fund managers. It all boils down simply to money and influence. The larger your portfolio, then the greater access to managers you command.

Potential Areas of Concern

Hedge funds, like traditional investments, have certain areas that historically exhibit greater concern than others over time. Consequently, your due-diligence monitoring warrants a review of the following areas that could affect the performance and success of your hedge fund investment.

CHANGE IN KEY PEOPLE

Most hedge funds rely on one or two key people to make all the decisions. These are the very people who have generated solid returns and attracted the attention and interest of investors. If these key people leave, their talent and skill will leave with them. Filling the vacuum will be an unproven person, or at least a person unproven with that particular hedge fund. A change in key people commonly triggers investors to follow the key people or simply to seek out another hedge fund altogether.

DECLINE OF IMPORTANCE

Over time, good hedge funds will gather more assets. The higher the performance, the more assets the fund will gather. When this occurs, hedge funds typically increase their minimum initial contribution requirements as the number of available slots for investors decreases. This means that smaller investors will become overshadowed and thus lose their importance in the eyes of the hedge fund. Some hedge fund managers probably would love to see the small investors leave to open slots for larger investors. Nevertheless, more investors and more assets dilute the influence and importance any one specific investor holds.

FRAUD AND UNETHICAL PRACTICES

Nothing can cause an investor to terminate his or her relationship with a hedge fund and transfer his or her investment like an incident of fraud or other unethical practice.

Trust is so important in hedge fund investing because of the substantial capital involved and the limited disclosure of information. Hedge fund managers command significant control over their investors' portfolios. Contrary to what the media say about hedge funds, fraud is not widespread. Furthermore, questionable managers can be screened during the hedge fund discovery stage. Exercise caution and keep an eye out for information that appears to be misrepresented or omitted altogether. More severe problems could be lingering as a result.

PRUDENCE ISSUES

A good hedge fund manager will be placed on a pedestal at some time in his or her career. Managing hedge funds is a wonderful profession, but it is also laden with opportunities for managers to become overconfident and egotistical. This may cause the manager to believe that he or she can deviate from the existing strategy and try something else. Rational and prudent hedge fund managers recognize this risk and safeguard the portfolio from any such scenarios.

CHANGE IN STRATEGY

A very popular adage with investing is "the trend is your friend." With hedge funds, this simply means that the investment strategy presently being used is working as needed. Why, then, would a hedge fund manager change his or her strategy? The primary reason is that the current strategy is not working. Thus a change in strategy could signal bigger performance issues. In addition, one of the central reasons for investing in a particular hedge fund is the strategy employed. Changing strategies could mean that there is no longer a reason to continue investing in that hedge fund.

IGNORING STATED SAFEGUARDS AND PROVISIONS

Safeguards are put in place to protect the hedge fund and the investor. They also give the hedge fund manager guidelines on how to manage the fund. When these safeguards are ignored, it could mean trouble in keeping with the stated plan. Pay particular attention to how the manager is adhering to stated provisions, such as types of instruments used, exposure to asset classes, number of positions permitted, frequency of trading, and the sizes of positions allowed.

EXCESSIVE ASSETS UNDER MANAGEMENT

Successful hedge funds will attract investors who are more than happy to make generous investments. Unfortunately, the bigger a fund gets, the more difficult it

becomes to manage. The result could be missed opportunities or limited benefit from taking advantage of opportunities. This is so because many hedge funds profit from small inefficiencies that must be seized quickly. Consequently, the activity that made the hedge fund successful in the first place cannot be used when the fund becomes successful. Additionally, hedge fund managers may find it necessary to invest in securities with greater risk to make up the difference. Now you have a portfolio with questionable performance opportunities and more risk. This is not the best direction for the fund to take.

DECLINE IN TARGETED INVESTMENT OPPORTUNITIES

Over time, the opportunities a hedge fund targets for investments begins to become less and less profitable. The lure of higher returns is too great, and that attracts additional interest and competition from other hedge fund managers. Before you know it, returns are lower, and the opportunity altogether is gone or at least severely limited. For example, suppose that a hedge fund manager invests in a relatively unknown investment in the marketplace, a small growth company. As the company generates strong earnings, the stock price increases, and the hedge fund profits. Other hedge funds, always on the lookout for additional opportunities, discover this and buy the stock. The original hedge fund will benefit from the new interest in the short term, but given the increased stock valuation, risk has increased, and the probability of earning strong returns over time declines.

INVESTMENT TRENDS CONCLUDE

Some hedge funds rely heavily on certain investment trends. These trends could include movement of interest rates, direction of foreign currency rates, or strength of market sectors. Once these trends decline and finally conclude, the hedge fund is left without an opportunity, and the performance of the fund could suffer as a result.

IMPACT OF LEVERAGE

Leveraging the holdings in a hedge fund can be both good and bad. When things are going well, leverage will enhance and magnify performance. When things are going poorly, leverage will magnify the losses. At the same time, having leverage leaves the hedge fund susceptible to the decisions of the investment firm granting the loan. When rates tick up, hedge funds typically are faced with greater interest payments. An increase in the leverage requirements is another potential risk to hedge funds employing leverage.

Progress Benchmarking

The primary challenge in monitoring hedge funds is transparency, or the ability to investigate the hedge fund and identify its holdings. This is much easier said than done, of course. Nevertheless, transparency is key to learning how well the hedge fund is complying with its stated objectives and provisions, such as investment objectives and risk safeguards. Investors deserve to know if the hedge fund is delivering on the representations made prior to the initial investment. Not only is this important to individual investors, but it is also important to institutions that ultimately have a fiduciary responsibility to the individual investors whose money they manage. Lack of disclosure makes the job of monitoring difficult but not impossible. External sources can fill the void and provide insights into how well the fund is operating.

PARAMETER MONITORING

Prior to investing in a hedge fund, an investor will learn a great deal about how the fund is run and what parameters are established and adhered to. A wise investor from time to time will investigate whether or not the hedge fund is following the parameters it communicated before the start of the engagement and the initial contribution. Although a lack of transparency will make this challenging, investigating the use of leverage, degree and type of exposure to asset classes, types of financial instruments used, number of asset positions held, and size of the asset positions held should be done.

PERFORMANCE MONITORING

Monitoring hedge fund performance is much more complex than comparing the performance with a set benchmark. The primary difficulty arises because hedge funds commonly invest in many markets and asset classes, use leverage to magnify performance, and hold both long and short positions. This means that performance results are not entirely comparable with other general benchmarks, such as the Standard & Poor's (S&P) 500 Index, the benchmark of choice for traditional investment managers. Benchmarks incorporating returns from peer groups thus are the best solution. Comparing against the S&P 500 is essential, however, because it provides the bogie for justifying hedge fund investing in the first place.

Before beginning your monitoring and evaluation of hedge fund performance, it is a good idea to keep in mind that hedge fund managers are limited by specific capital market–related constraints. It is true that hedge fund managers do bring a wealth of skill in profiting from select market opportunities; however, those opportunities do not exist for extended periods of time. By understanding these challenges, investors gain a better grasp of how best to evaluate the performance of a hedge fund manager.

Hedge fund monitoring requires performance comparisons with appropriate benchmarks and related peers. Performance attribution is a key element in succeeding in hedge fund investing. Many hedge fund managers evaluate the performance of a fund or portfolio on a quarterly basis in order to appease investors. However, evaluating performance is not as easy as it might appear initially. Why? First, there is the issue of evaluating a portfolio's short-term results when you have designed and implemented a long-term strategy. Second, there is difficulty in comparing a multi-asset-class portfolio to a benchmark. Which benchmark or benchmarks do you select? Simply selecting the S&P 500 for a multi-asset-class hedge fund or fund of funds will not suffice. The S&P 500 consists of equity securities only. Thus a portfolio consisting of fixed-income securities or real estate investment trust (REIT) assets simply would not be appropriate. The solution is to segment each asset class and compare it against an appropriate benchmark, such as the S&P 500 for U.S. equity securities and the EAFE for international equity securities.

Lastly, hedge funds should be compared against their primary performance aim—to generate attractive absolute returns. Here, you will want to assess how consistent the fund is with generating positive returns. The degree of positive returns is not as important as the consistency of generating those returns. People invest in hedge funds primarily to receive consistent absolute returns. Hedge funds should be judged on attaining this objective.

RISK MANAGEMENT AND CONTROL

Monitoring portfolio risk is a wise move, especially for those who do not want to assume a high degree of risk volatility. Some of the things to look for when monitoring your hedge fund portfolio for risk include degree of leverage, use of derivatives, degree of going long or short, and finally, the risk of the underlying investments targeted given the strategy employed. For example, emerging-markets investments will be more risky than strategies pursuing convertible arbitrage. Other factors to consider include investment in public or private securities, degree of investment concentration, and adherence to stated objectives and goals. Identifying some of these factors will be challenging because some hedge fund managers will not disclose this information. The best strategy is to work with the information you have.

Regardless of how well the hedge fund investment may be going, risk management and control are essential given ever-changing circumstances. Hedge fund managers change, as do their strategies for generating returns. At the same time, investor objectives and constraints also change over time. Take risk profile, for example. As an investor ages, his or her need for risk will decline while risk capacity and perhaps even risk tolerance will rise. As we know, however, the appropriate

risk is the lowest of the three risk profile variables. Thus the portfolio will need to incorporate less risk over time. The monitoring process is definitely not static and will evolve over time with changing factors.

REVIEW AND COMPARISON

Investing in hedge funds can be expensive. With the annual investment-management fee and the performance-incentive fee, investors need to exercise caution by evaluating performance against other investments, specifically index investments and hedge fund peers. Intuitively, evaluating against peers is just plain common sense. But why, then, do we judge against index investments? Because index investments are your bogie, your true long-term hurdle rate. Since index investments offer the lowest-cost method of diversified investing, measuring a hedge fund against an index can uncover just how much an investor is paying in fees for the difference in performance. There is simply no need to pay extra unless you receive extra performance. If the performance of your hedge fund is not keeping up with the market index, you will want to think long and hard about making a change. The same goes for evaluating your hedge fund against peers. One or two periods of lackluster performance are not necessarily something to worry about, but more than that, and a change should be made. Many people invest in hedge funds for performance reasons, so why should anyone stay with funds that cannot deliver? Hedge fund managers know this as well. Live by the sword, die by the sword.

There is some obvious leeway with performance measurement that investors need to consider when evaluating returns against an index fund. Correlation and consistency of returns—as demonstrated by absolute returns—play an important role in building an optimal portfolio and enhancing risk-adjusted returns. Modern portfolio theory says that investors should not evaluate each investment on a stand-alone basis. Rather, each investment should be evaluated based on its ability to enhance the overall risk-return profile of a portfolio. Hedge funds are masters at accomplishing this very aim. This is why investing in hedge funds is so important and performance measurement should therefore keep this in consideration.

One final thought about performance measurement and monitoring: It is very important to ensure that the performance data are created using geometric returns rather than arithmetic returns. Why? The reason is because the results can be misleading. For instance, suppose that your $1 million hedge fund investment suffers a huge loss and is worth $500,000 after one year. This is a negative 50 percent return. Suppose that the following year your investment gains the $500,000 lost in the preceding year, giving you a total market value of $1 million at the end of the second year. Thus you earned a return of 100 percent for year two. Using arithmetic returns, your manager may claim to have earned you a positive 25 percent (–50 percent +100

percent ÷ 2) during the two-year period. As you can see, your portfolio has not appreciated whatsoever, thus the +25 percent is not accurate. Using geometric returns, your portfolio manager would report a 0 percent return rather than a +25 percent return. This is something to keep in mind.

Firing Your Manager

As you progress with the monitoring of your hedge fund manager, you may come to a point where a change in managers is warranted. This may be the result of lack of performance, comparably high fees, restrictive provisions for withdrawing invested capital, or simply a breakdown in the relationship. Nevertheless, making the change is not an especially easy task. Monitoring is a nonstop evaluation of whether or not to hire or fire a hedge fund manager—as it is with traditional investing. In general, there is no set rule or provision as to how, where, or when to fire your manager. This process is rather subjective but must be approached with an objective mind-set to collecting, understanding, and balancing the pros and cons.

When the point in time arrives when you need to make a change of managers, there are some important factors you should take into consideration. First, the termination process is not the same as with other investment relationships given the partnership format. This means that the entire termination process from start to finish could take as long as 90 days. Most take a minimum of 30 days. For audit and paper trails, most hedge fund managers require a written letter from an investor that communicates his or her request to exit from the partnership. This traditionally occurs and finalizes on fixed periods of time, specifically calendar quarters. The offering memorandum and other disclosure documents will outline in writing everything that an investor must do to exit from the partnership. Some even charge you a redemption fee on leaving to cover costs and as a deterrent to leaving, although they will not say that it is for this purpose.

On leaving, some managers will give you cash, whereas others will give you securities in lieu of cash. Receiving securities has its drawbacks. First, securities that otherwise should have been sold in the fund may have embedded capital gains that also should have been spread out among the entire group of investors, not just one. Second, securities may be relatively illiquid and thus be difficult to sell at the stated market value.

Although the process is difficult at best, most hedge fund managers are sensible people who will sit down with you and try to work out the issue. If no resolution can be found, the hedge fund manager will help to facilitate the termination and transfer of assets. Many investors terminating their relationship will discover that the process resembles that of traditional investment portfolio terminations. In this case, however, the investor may want to take the lead role in identifying how best to transfer the securities. Some may want to transfer the entire lot, whereas others may want to transfer only some of the securities, with the rest transferred in cash. Investors who find themselves in this situation will want to take the lead role because hedge fund managers may not have the best interests of the terminating investor at heart.

FUNDS OF FUNDS CONSIDERATION

Funds of funds are growing steadily in popularity. One of the primary reasons for this growth is the professional management and oversight of stand-alone hedge funds. This means that an experienced investment professional is reviewing and evaluating other hedge funds for hiring and firing purposes. Thus the monitoring process that many investors will do is managed by a professional. However, this does not excuse the investor from his or her responsibility of reviewing the hedge fund for performance, fees, taxes, risks, fit, and other factors related to due diligence. The best person to look after your interests is you. Managers of funds of funds do a superb job in evaluating performance, talking with hedge fund managers, and making good decisions for the hedge fund, but this does not mean that investors can outsource this role.

Performance Benchmarking

With traditional investing, measuring performance against a specific index or benchmark is necessary to ascertain how well the portfolio has performed. This, of course, is relative-performance benchmarking. Absolute-performance benchmarking does not require an index per say because you only need to generate a positive return to accomplish the aim of absolute performance. The same is not true of relative performance. With relative performance, a benchmark is selected that accurately reflects the investments in the portfolio or fund you will use to compare. For example, the most widely used performance benchmark with traditional investing is the S&P 500 Index. This is so because many of the stocks in the S&P 500 are held in traditional investment portfolios. This means that comparing against this index is the most appropriate approach.

Until recently, the challenge of hedge fund investing was the lack of appropriate indices to benchmark performance. This has changed recently because more and more sources are establishing indices to track either one particular hedge fund strategy or the entire field in aggregate. The very first basic indices appeared in the 1980s, but they were not widely followed.

In 2004, the *Wall Street Journal* began publishing several hedge fund indices to enable readers to make quick and easy relative comparisons. Investors thus are better informed as to how well or poorly their funds have done compared with others. Other indices also have been established for the same reasons. You also will find that some of the indices are established by hedge fund managers simply to get their names out in the hedge fund investing marketplace. Nevertheless, Figure 16–1 lists some of the more well-known hedge fund indices.

Figure 16-1.   Selected hedge fund indices

INDEX	INCEPTION	NUMBER OF STRATEGY INDICES	WEIGHTING METHODOLOGY
Standard & Poor's Indices	2002	10	Simple Mean
HFR	1994	37	Simple Mean
Dow Jones	2003	5	NAV Calculation
Altvest	2000	14	Simple Mean
CSFB/Tremont	1999	14	Asset Weighted Mean
MSCI Indices	2002	4	Asset Weighted Mean & Simple Mean
Van Edge	1994	25	Simple Mean
Hennessee	1987	24	Simple Mean

Some of the indices, owing to construction flaws, have built-in biases and inconsistencies. However, they do provide a nice way for investors to gauge the direction of hedge fund performance. Over time, the hedge fund industry will move to one or more primary indices for evaluating performance, much like what traditional investing has done. This may involve the S&P 500 Hedge Fund Index owing to name and investor confidence or not. Only time will tell.

INVESTABLE INDICES

There are essentially two primary strategies for managing investments—active management and passive management. Hedge fund investing is predominately active management, whereas index funds and exchange-traded funds represent an approach to passive management. Holding an S&P 500 Index fund is passive investing at its fundamental level. There are many index funds available for investors to hold in their portfolios. With hedge fund investing, investing in indices is not as easy. There are only a couple of indices available for investors to buy to gain returns comparable with the hedge fund strategy the index tracks. Three of the more popular indices are the S&P Hedge Fund Index, the Financial Times Stock Exchange, and Morgan Stanley Capital International (MSCI). Each of these strategies attempts to track and deliver a return that mirrors the return of the aggregate hedge fund market. In the future we will most definitely see more investable indices hit the marketplace. In addition, I would not be surprised to see passive traditional exchange-traded funds established to track any number of hedge fund strategies.

DRAWBACKS OF HEDGE FUND INDICES

Most hedge fund indices are created using information collected on a monthly basis involving performance numbers from thousands of hedge funds. These performance numbers are collected and entered using either analyst entry or manager entry. Altvest and HedgeFund.net employ the manager-entry method, whereas the rest of the commercial databases employ analyst entry, according to a study entitled, "A Comparison of Major Hedge Fund Data Sources," conducted by software company Strategic Financial Solutions. This study also found errors in the data assembled by the data sources, such as fee requirements, performance, required minimum investment, and hedge fund strategy employed. Nevertheless, the information provided by these data sources is more beneficial than not.

One of the big reasons for the discrepancy in information stems from the inconsistency of hedge fund managers in reporting to hedge fund databases. Some managers do not provide data, whereas others pick and choose to whom they will report data. This creates issues among indices. In addition to the inconsistent reporting, hedge fund managers sometimes will not report numbers if performance is poor. This means that performance could be biased to the high-return side because offsetting poor returns are omitted. Lastly, if a hedge fund were to close, some funds do not account for this and simply continue to emphasize existing funds. When benchmarks only reflect existing funds and not closed funds, then these indices are said to have *survivorship bias*. This means that performance numbers are distorted and higher than they should be under actual conditions. The performance of closed funds should be included in historical performance.

Another issue with hedge fund indices relates to the classification of hedge fund strategies. One company may classify all hedge fund strategies in 10 distinct groups, whereas another company may classify all hedge fund strategies in 15 distinct groups. Thus there is confusion among investors as to which index is best for benchmarking purposes. Over time, I suspect that we will see more accepted categories and thus standardized hedge fund indices.

BENCHMARKING SUMMARY

Even given the aforementioned issues involving hedge fund indices, they provide a more than adequate means for investors to benchmark the performance of their hedge fund investments as compared with the hedge fund industry. This benchmarking will give investors better knowledge of how well their managers are doing and whether or not to move their investments to other hedge fund managers. In the not so distant future hedge fund indices will become significantly more standardized and thus even more valuable to hedge fund investors.

Quiz for Chapter 16

1. Monitoring your hedge fund provides many benefits. Which one of the following is *not* a benefit of monitoring?
   a. Greatly decreases miscommunication and misunderstandings
   b. Enhances risk management and risk control
   c. Guarantees strong performance
   d. Helps to keep up to date with the performance of the fund

2. Monitoring a portfolio is the sole job of the hedge fund manager and not the investor.
   a. True
   b. False

3. Which one of the following is a potential area of concern in hedge fund investing?
   a. Stable managers
   b. Ethical management
   c. Modest level of assets under management
   d. Shifting investment strategies

4. What is the drawback of growing assets under management too quickly and becoming a supersized hedge fund?
   a. Exponentially increasing costs
   b. Fewer investable opportunities
   c. Greater compliance issues
   d. Forces conversion to a mutual fund

5. Why is a change of managers a cause for concern?

    a. Outgoing managers naturally will take investors with them.

    b. Incoming managers demand sign-on bonuses.

    c. Outgoing managers will redeem their invested capital.

    d. Incoming managers are not proven and come with uncertainty.

6. What are the two types of progress benchmarking?

    a. Level and advancing

    b. Parameter and performance

    c. Performance and backfill

    d. Backfill and trend analysis

7. One of the concerns in hedge fund investing is a decline in targeted investable opportunities caused by other managers jumping on the bandwagon and making investments that dilute opportunities.

    a. True

    b. False

8. Which index is the preferred choice for measuring and evaluating hedge fund relative performance?

    a. S&P 500

    b. Nasdaq

    c. Dow Jones

    d. NYSE

9. What is relative-performance benchmarking?

    a. Evaluating performance against dissimilar portfolios

    b. Evaluating performance against an appropriate index

    c. Evaluating performance against concentrated indices

    d. Evaluating performance against historical returns over the last five years

10. Name the two forms of performance benchmarking.

    a. Relative and peer group

    b. Peer group and targeted

    c. Relative and absolute

    d. Tactical and strategic

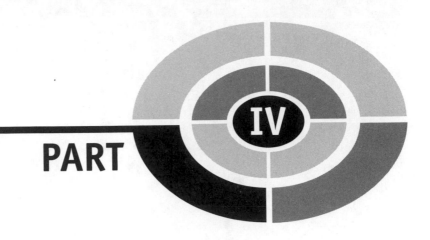

PART IV

Demystifying Special Considerations

CHAPTER 17

Leading Misconceptions and Fallacies

Separating Hedge Fund Fact from Fiction

Many people view hedge funds as mysterious and secretive in terms of not only the strategies they employ but also the financial instruments they buy and sell and the objectives they aim to achieve. There are simply many misconceptions and fallacies in the financial marketplace about hedge funds. This is to be expected and easy to understand because many hedge funds do seem to operate in a shroud of secrecy. However, much of what people think of hedge funds is actually more fiction than fact. To better help you to understand what hedge funds are all about, a chapter on what they surely are *not* may put things into a clearer and better perspective. The following are some of the more prominent misconceptions about hedge funds with a brief discussion of each (see Figure 17–1).

Figure 17-1. Leading misconceptions about hedge funds

1	Hedge Funds Hedge Risk
2	Hedge Funds Are Always Taking Significant Directional Bets
3	Hedge Funds Employ Extreme Leverage
4	Hedge Funds with Zero Leverage Are Most Ideal
5	The Use of Derivatives Is Rampant with Hedge Funds
6	Hedge Funds and Mutual Funds Are Nearly Identical
7	Profitable Hedge Fund Strategies Will Continue into the Future
8	Hedge Funds Are Considered Speculative Investments
9	Hedge Funds Trade Rather than Invest
10	Hedge Funds Are a Distinct Asset Class
11	Hedge Funds Are Structured and Managed Relatively the Same
12	Hedge Fund Strategies Cannot Be Implemented by Common Investors
13	Hedge Funds Emphasize Rare and Unusual Financial Assets and Instruments
14	Hedge Funds Have No Place in Most Investors' Portfolios
15	Greater Transparency Will Lead to Safer Hedge Funds
16	Hedge Funds Always Make Positive Returns
17	Only the Most Sophisticated Investors Can Invest in Hedge Funds
18	All Hedge Fund Managers Are Highly Qualified

Hedge Funds Hedge Risk

The first misconception that many investors have is that hedge funds actually hedge risk. Although this aim may have at one time been the single focus, today it surely is not. Many hedge funds in the marketplace today do hedge risk, be it hedge-fund-specific risk or portfolio risk, but most hedge funds simply do not hedge risk at all.

Many actually create additional risk. This is not a big surprise to most people, I suspect. Use of the name *hedge fund* has remained with us since the early days of hedge funds, when selling short and building a low-correlated portfolio helped to reduce total portfolio risk. Perhaps this misconception was triggered by the hedge fund trade itself when it began employing riskier strategies in the hopes of generating higher returns. From a portfolio vantage point, hedge funds typically do hedge risk because they have low correlations with the equity component of a portfolio; however, on an investment-specific basis, hedge funds can be considered risky. Remember, however, to always think in terms of your overall portfolio rather than just the individual assets comprising your portfolio—that's basic modern portfolio theory stuff. Doing so provides support for investing in hedge funds.

Hedge Funds Are Always Taking Significant Directional Bets

The second misconception is that hedge funds make substantial investments or take sizable bets on the price direction or movement on particular investments, notably global assets. Given the number of hedge funds in the marketplace, this absolutely is the case with a select few but is not for most hedge funds. In reality, fewer than 5 percent of hedge funds are macrocentric—the hedge funds most active in directional or tactical investments. Thus more than 95 percent of hedge funds take little to no directional bets whatsoever. From a best practices viewpoint, hedge fund managers recognize the inherent risk to the hedge fund and to their own jobs if they were to take substantial positions and bet on macroprice movement. Hedge fund managers want to keep their jobs as much as you want them to judiciously grow and protect your wealth. Finally, remember that you have the means to avoid this type of risk because you can screen out these types of hedge funds from the very beginning.

Hedge Funds Employ Extreme Leverage

Many people have the notion that hedge fund managers love leverage and use it to the extreme. On the contrary, many hedge funds do not employ any leverage at all, and those that do employ leverage on a full-time basis only do so under certain conditions, typically to take advantage of arbitrage opportunities. Leverage can be both good and bad, depending on how well or poorly the investments in the fund are performing. Leverage will magnify both a gain and a loss. For example, if a hedge fund

were to be 100 percent leveraged, then a gain of 5 percent all on assets would turn into a 10 percent gain for the overall hedge fund. However, if the same assets were to experience a –7 percent return the following year, then the fund would experience a total loss of –14 percent. As you can see, leverage can have a significant impact on the total return of a hedge fund. Consequently, hedge fund managers need to employ leverage judiciously, and hedge fund investors need to be aware of the risk associated with substantial leverage and make their decisions accordingly.

Hedge Funds with Zero Leverage Are Most Ideal

Leverage itself does not mean that a hedge fund will not report losses or become a top-performing fund. Some of the top-performing hedge funds employ significant leverage and generate strong returns simply from magnifying modest gains. The important point to remember is that leveraging only magnifies the gains or losses with the underlying asset. Thus, if you were to magnify a conservative asset, then you might not greatly increase your total risk. However, if you were to leverage a risky investment, then your total portfolio risk almost assuredly would rise. Consider banks, for example. Banks are typically very highly leveraged, somewhere around 12:1. Most people consider banks to be rather conservative to moderately risky investments. This is so because banks generally leverage less risky investments. For another example, think about your own home and the mortgage you have on it. Some homeowners are 70 percent financed, whereas others may have 50 percent or perhaps even 80 percent. The amount financed does not greatly increase the risk of the home from an investment standpoint because homes generally are considered less risky than other types of assets.

The Use of Derivatives Is Rampant with Hedge Funds

Derivatives have received a terrible reputation over the years. There is perhaps no other financial instrument that has such a negative connotation than do derivatives. Much of this hysteria is due to media hype, with no real examination of the benefits of derivatives. Derivatives are absolutely needed to foster an efficient market, regardless of whether or not that market is stocks, bonds, or even energy. They are vitally important and essential. Unfortunately, many people do not know what derivatives really are. If you have heard of put options, call options, and even futures contracts, then you know something about derivatives. Nevertheless, some people assume that hedge fund managers employ derivatives extensively and think that their use is rampant. For the most part, this is not true. The bulk of managers do not use derivatives at all or only for true hedging or safeguarding purposes. In addition to employing derivatives to hedge risk in the fund, some managers will use derivates to generate a modest amount of cash by writing or selling options and gaining the respective premiums. There are many ways to use derivatives and many ways that hedge fund managers employ them; most do so to reduce total portfolio risk rather than to increase it.

Hedge Funds and Mutual Funds Are Nearly Identical

As we saw in Part I of this book, there are significant differences between mutual funds and hedge funds. These differences include the type of investment strategies and tools managers are permitted to employ and the types of investors each can manage money for. Hedge funds can only invest for institutions and wealthy individuals that satisfy certain SEC guidelines, whereas the same is not true for mutual funds–they can accept and manage money for nearly anyone. And finally, mutual funds provide daily liquidity to their investors, whereas hedge funds hold investments for a long period of time, with withdrawals restricted during the first year. It is true that mutual funds and hedge funds do pool money together from investors and then invest in somewhat similar financial instruments, but this is where most of the similarity ends. Mutual fund companies tend to be quite large and cumbersome and make decisions by committee. This is in contrast to hedge funds, which typically are very small in both the number of employees and the amount of assets under management and make decisions much more quickly.

Profitable Hedge Fund Strategies Will Continue into the Future

This leading misconception is not exclusive to the hedge fund trade. Many investors have the same misconception about mutual funds and even traditional stock and bond strategies. Investors have this misconception because they believe that higher-ranked mutual funds must have top managers who employ a strategy that can deliver solid performance consistently. This, of course, is not the case at all. Most investors are quite familiar with the investment lesson of "past performance is not a guarantee of future performance."—a lesson exemplified by all investment

managers and often communicated in print and television advertising. Hedge funds managers do have an advantage over traditional investment managers given their freedom to employ alternative investment strategies such as selling short and employing leverage. However, this advantage does not mean that any particular hedge fund will outperform mutual funds over the long term on a consistent basis. Research has demonstrated that there is a rotation among hedge fund strategies as to the best-performing strategies in any single year. One strategy may do well one year and not do so well the following year. Smart investors, regardless of whether or not they are investing in hedge funds, recognize this and make decisions appropriately.

Hedge Funds Are Considered Speculative Investments

Many investors mistakenly believe that hedge funds are always risky investments and only for investors with high risk profiles. I tell many people that it is not the hedge fund itself that makes the investment risky but how the hedge fund is managed. Some managers will operate funds conservatively, some aggressively, and some with a balanced approach. Hedge fund strategies that employ leverage are more risky than hedge funds that do not employ leverage. Also, investors need to emphasize the risk-return trade-off profile of their total portfolios rather than the component individual investments. By doing so, an investor will build a more optimally allocated portfolio that delivers a higher risk-adjusted return over time. With over 9,000 hedge funds in the marketplace, there will be opportunities across the board for people to invest in a hedge fund with which they are comfortable.

Hedge Funds Trade Rather than Invest

Some people have the misconception that hedge funds emphasize trading, or short-term transactions, over investing, or long-term transactions. Moreover, some people probably have it in their mind that hedge fund managers are on the telephone or glued to their computer screens every minute of the day, placing quick buy and sell orders, much like day traders. On the contrary, many hedge funds will invest in traditionally less liquid assets and require investors to lock up their invested capital for certain time periods to enable the hedge fund to capture the anticipated profits.

There are some hedge funds that operate more like traders and less than investors, but they are much less prevalent.

Hedge Funds Are a Distinct Asset Class

This is certainly not a cut and dry misconception. Many investors believe that hedge funds are a distinct asset class because they learned this from a trusted financial advisor. As with mutual funds, hedge funds are not exactly an asset class. Rather, they are the portfolio or pool that contains the assets that can be classified in one of the asset classes. For example, a hedge fund may invest in equity assets or perhaps in fixed-income assets. Thus it may be appropriate to classify hedge funds that invest in equity assets as being part of the equity asset class and to classify hedge funds that invest in fixed-income assets to be part of the fixed-income asset class. Doing just this is not the wrong thing to do. However, most financial professionals will present hedge funds as being part of the alternative asset class. This is done because hedge funds provide a hedge to typical stock and bond portfolios, with emphasis on the equity side. Since they provide a hedge to traditional portfolios, they are frequently seen as alternative assets and thus classified that way. Remember to always think of hedge funds as the portfolio, pool, or shell that holds assets that individually are classified in one of the asset classes. Given the ability to hedge traditional portfolios, classifying hedge funds as alternative assets is appropriate.

Hedge Funds Are Structured and Managed Relatively the Same

Many people who lack knowledge and exposure to hedge funds incorrectly assume that all hedge funds are rather the same. However, with the significant numbers of strategies, tools, and financial instruments available to hedge fund managers, there exist many different types of hedge funds. Once you consider hedge fund size, decision making, and provisions, investors will quickly see that hedge funds can be very unique. One hedge fund may target commodities, whereas another may target collateralized mortgage obligations, or CMOs. The greater the different types of hedge funds, the greater is the probability that an investor will find a hedge fund that is most appropriate and suitable for his or her financial goals and obligations.

Hedge Fund Strategies and Tools Cannot Be Implemented by Common Investors

Although some hedge funds do employ very complex investment strategies and tools, for the most part the strategies and tools they employ can be implemented quickly and easily by the common investor. Tools such as selling short, employing leverage, and position limits all can be implemented. There are some arbitrage strategies that are not exactly feasible for common investors given the sophistication and responsiveness of their computers. Nevertheless, investors still can use many of the simple strategies and tools that hedge fund managers use to grow and protect their funds.

Hedge Funds Emphasize Rare and Unusual Financial Assets and Instruments

There is no doubt that hedge funds have a mysterious aura and a perception of secrecy. However, this does not mean that hedge fund managers trade in rare, unusual, or exotic securities. The truth is that the vast majority of hedge fund managers actually trade traditional securities, but in much different ways than the common investor. Hedge funds differ from traditional investing in the strategies they employ and the tools they use, not necessarily in the financial assets and instruments they buy or sell. It is the trading techniques that truly set hedge funds apart from the rest of the investing marketplace. With this being said, however, there are some hedge funds that do participate in buying and selling exotic securities, but they are not the norm. Think of hedge funds in terms of the strategies and tools they employ, not in terms of the financial assets and instruments they buy or sell.

Hedge Funds Have No Place in Most Investors' Portfolios

As mentioned previously, many people have the notion that hedge funds are relatively speculative investments. These people therefore conclude that hedge funds have no place in the portfolios of most investors. Hedge funds can be speculative, and they can be highly conservative. Most hedge funds fall somewhere in between these two extremes, however. Research has shown that it is not which specific investments you buy or sell, or when you buy or sell them, but how you allocate your portfolio among the fundamentally different asset classes. As a result, allocating to alternative assets, which includes hedge funds, is considered a smart move by most investment professionals. Yes, there may be added risk of doing just this, but the benefits of building a more optimally allocated and more diversified portfolio outweigh the potential added risk from hedge funds. Furthermore, prudent investors recognize that they should not focus on the individual component investments but on the total portfolio. When you do this, you build a portfolio that stands the best chances of helping you achieve the returns you need to accomplish your SMART goals.

Greater Transparency Will Lead to Safer Hedge Funds

This misconception is not entirely black and white. There are many shades of gray in this case. There is some truth to the premise that greater transparency will lead to safer hedge funds, but for the most part this will not occur. Greater transparency will help investors to make better and more informed investment decisions. Greater transparency will not force nor significantly motivate hedge funds to alter their investment strategies, thus reducing overall risk. Simply providing more information on the holdings of a hedge fund will not trigger that hedge fund into changing its investment strategy or allocating to safer assets. Allowing investors to enhance their decision making is what greater transparency is all about.

Hedge Funds Always Make Positive Returns

Many investors have the preconceived notion that hedge funds make money in nearly all market environments under all market conditions. Aside from the unusual hedge fund collapse, the reining position with the majority of investors is that hedge funds make money and make significant positive returns. This is probably driven by investors' lack of exposure to and knowledge of the hedge fund trade rather than anything else. Further complicating the issue is the steadily increasing number of hedge funds that managers are starting. They mistakenly believe that a growing field is a sure sign of strong performance and moneymaking. As we have learned, however, the number of hedge funds is growing rapidly because of their allure to investment professionals. Earning 20 percent of a solid return can make anyone's pocketbook large. This is why many hedge funds are started in the first place. Investors need to recognize that hedge fund managers are not infallible and can easily make costly errors, with some devastating. History has illustrated that even the most gifted hedge fund managers can make errors from time to time, and this can cause any hedge fund to underperform.

Only the Most Sophisticated Investors Can Invest in Hedge Funds

This misconception is relatively easy to understand given that most investors were restricted not too long ago. Recently, however, funds of funds have opened the gates to hedge funds for the mass of investors. Investors looking to invest in a stand-alone hedge fund still will need to adhere to the accredited investor rule as set by the SEC, but investors in funds of funds will not. Today, there are many opportunities for less sophisticated and less wealthy investors to gain access to hedge funds and better allocate their portfolios for growth and preservation.

All Hedge Fund Managers Are Highly Qualified

In the investment marketplace, there are few jobs that garner as much attention and profile as hedge fund managers. Being a hedge fund manager is considered the domain of the highly talented few. Although this is by far an accurate statement, there are hedge fund managers who probably should not be managing money for clients. There are a number of reasons why hedge fund managers may not be fully qualified to manage your money. First, they may not have the knowledge of the trade and how best to manage money. When you don't know this trade inside and out, this is a sure-fire warning sign. Second, some hedge fund managers may lack the support and technology systems to operate their hedge funds properly. Although they have the intellect, they may suffer from a lack of support that can hinder implementation of specific investment strategies. By asking questions and carefully reviewing the offering documents, you can avoid many of these issues.

Quiz for Chapter 17

1. *Fact or fiction*? All hedge funds employ significant leverage.
   a. Fact
   b. Fiction

2. Many people have the misconception that hedge funds are fully engaged in hedging risk.
   a. True
   b. False

3. *Fact or fiction?* Hedge funds are always taking substantial directional bets.

   a. Fact

   b. Fiction

4. *Fact or fiction?* Profitable hedge fund strategies will lose value over time.

   a. Fact

   b. Fiction

5. Although hedge funds are clearly not a distinct asset class, they are typically grouped with which class?

   a. Equities

   b. Fixed-income

   c. Alternatives

   d. Cash and equivalents

6. *Fact or fiction?* Most hedge fund strategies can be employed by common investors.

   a. Fact

   b. Fiction

7. Hedge funds emphasize short-term trading over long-term investing.

   a. True

   b. False

8. *Fact or fiction?* Hedge funds emphasize rare and unusual financial assets and instruments.

   a. Fact

   b. Fiction

9. *Fact or fiction?* Less transparency will lead to riskier hedge funds.

   a. Fact

   b. Fiction

10. *Fact or fiction?* Some hedge fund managers are not properly qualified to manage.

    a. Fact

    b. Fiction

CHAPTER

18

Key Attributes of Hedge Funds

Highlighting the Top 10 Defining Characteristics

As there is with nearly anything, there are very specific and definable characteristics that comprise a certain concept. Hedge funds are not much different. Hedge funds can be defined easily by a number of different characteristics that present them in a truly unique light. Throughout this book I have discussed each one of these characteristics to some degree, but I want to zero in on what I consider the most important of these characteristics. I call these the top 10 defining characteristics of hedge funds and bring each of them together in one chapter to reinforce their importance.

If there is anything or any lesson that you should take away from this book, it is an understanding of these top 10 defining characteristics that is most important.

These top 10 defining characteristics are presented in no particular order, with no one defining characteristic any more important than another. After reading each defining characteristic, you may want to review the material in this book relevant to the topic to gain a solid grasp.

1. Unique Structure and Organization

Hedge funds are quite different from other investment organizations, including mutual funds. Hedge funds typically are established as limited-liability companies or limited partnerships. Sometimes hedge funds are established in such a way that the general partner, or the person with unlimited liability, is actually a limited-liability company. Hedge funds also differ slightly in where the fund is domiciled—either domestically as an onshore hedge fund or in a hedge fund haven as an offshore hedge fund. Other forms include commodity pools and separately managed accounts. Each has its own benefits and merits.

Hedge funds ascribe to a small is better philosophy. As such, hedge funds typically are much smaller in size, scope, and key people. Most hedge funds are run by one or two key people rather than an investment committee, much like mutual funds are run. Smaller can be both good and bad. The bad is that the margin for error is exceptionally small given fewer people to make important decisions. The good is that fewer decision makers means faster decisions and faster accommodation of investment opportunities. Many hedge fund companies are dominated by one or two key people.

Another drawback of having a smaller investment company is that it typically has fewer assets given the lack of framework to handle more investors. Restrictions on the type and number of clients also serve to impede asset growth.

Lastly, hedge fund managers commonly do something that most other investment managers do not do—invest a substantial amount of their own personal assets into the fund. This is frequently done to give the client confidence in knowing that the hedge fund manager believes in the story and invests in it.

2. Unconstrained with Minimal Regulatory Oversight

The investment industry is regulated on many fronts. However, in aggregate, hedge funds are far less regulated than mutual funds and other traditional investments. Unlike mutual funds, hedge funds are not required to provide daily liquidity to their

investors, nor must they disclose the same level of information that mutual funds are required to provide. This minimal oversight and regulation allow hedge fund managers to stretch their arms and employ investment strategies that more traditional managers are not permitted to employ.

Some of the major players involved in regulating some aspects of hedge funds include the Securities and Exchange Commission (SEC), the Commodity Futures Trading Commission (CFTC), the Federal Reserve, and the U.S. Treasury, as well as indirectly by banks, brokerage firms, and the National Association of Securities Dealers (NASD) via their business relationships with hedge funds.

The most important regulations affecting hedge funds include, but are not limited to, the Investment Company Act of 1940, the Investment Advisers Act of 1940, antifraud laws, inside-trading laws, and the Commodity Exchange Act.

3. Restricted to a Low Number of Accredited Investors

Hedge funds are severely restricted by the number and the types of investors they are allowed to accept. This restriction is placed on hedge funds by the SEC as a trade-off for the freedom to employ nearly any investment tool desired. The SEC permits hedge funds to accept only investors that fit the definition of "accredited investor." To qualify, investors must pass some basic net worth hurdles, such as having earned at least $200,000 annually in income for the past two years—and have a reasonable expectation of doing so into the future—and having a net worth of at least $2.5 million after excluding personal residences and automobiles. In addition, hedge funds are limited to a low number of investors, essentially 99 or fewer. Compounding the situation for hedge funds are the restrictions on marketing and promotion. Thus hedge funds have to exercise more effort to find suitable investors for their funds.

4. Restrictive Liquidity and Redemption Provisions

Unlike mutual funds and other traditional investments, hedge funds for the most part have restrictive liquidity and redemption provisions. With mutual funds, if an investor wants to withdraw his or her investments, he or she only needs to call the fund company and request a redemption. Days later a check will show up in the mail. In addition, shareholders in mutual funds can determine the price and value of their investment on any given day because mutual funds provide such information daily. The SEC requires mutual funds to provide not only daily liquidity but also daily pricing. The same is not true for hedge funds.

Hedge funds do not provide daily valuations nor monthly valuations. Furthermore, hedge funds have tough restrictions on withdrawing or redeeming invested capital. Most hedge funds have what is called a *lockup period* for new investors. This means that new investors are not permitted to withdraw their invested capital for a certain predetermined period, typically one year after the initial investment contribution is made. This is implemented to protect the hedge fund manager from making otherwise long-term investments with the new money and then being forced to sell after only a brief time to accommodate a request for capital.

In addition to lockup provisions, hedge funds commonly only permit the withdrawal of funds at certain times during the year. This is typically done on a quarterly basis. Some permit monthly withdrawals, whereas others opt for longer periods of one year. Once a new investor passes the lockup period, then he or she must follow the standard redemption provisions of all hedge fund investors. These provisions are spelled out in the offering documents hedge funds provide to interested and accredited parties prior to making the initial investment contribution.

5. Limitations on Marketing and Promotions

The SEC places strict regulations and limitations on how and to whom hedge funds can market their offerings. Since the SEC is out to protect the general investing public, it wants to minimize any contact and investment possibilities with investors who are not qualified to invest in any given hedge fund.

Hedge funds are restricted from airing radio or television commercials so that the general investing public will not be exposed to the message and investigate making an investment. The SEC also has provided restrictions on the type of person that hedge funds can market to. Also removed from the publicity arsenal for hedge fund managers is print advertising and advertising with any other medium where the general investing public will hear or see it. As a result, most hedge fund manager Web sites are password protected to ensure only accredited investors can gain access to online information.

6. Extensive Tools of the Trade

Perhaps there is no more significant difference between traditional investing and alternative investing, including hedge funds, than in the tools of the trade—more

specifically in the tactics and techniques hedge fund managers employ to manage their funds. These tools include using leverage, selling short, trading derivatives, investing in deeply discounted securities or overly valued securities, and pursuing arbitrage opportunities.

Traditional investment managers are for the most part restricted from using these tools. This is attributed to safeguards implemented by the SEC and forced on managers if they wish to deal with the general investing public. The SEC believes that these tools increase risk, and they can. Therefore, the SEC places handcuffs on managers if they want to invest money for investors who lack knowledge and experience in dealing with these tools.

In contrast, hedge funds use these tools extensively to take advantage of opportunities and make the best of certain special situations. These tools provide hedge fund managers with substantially greater flexibility than mutual fund managers or other traditional managers. The simple ability to sell short provides the hedge fund manager with an opportunity to offset risk associated with the market or a certain sector. In addition, funds can be developed that can generate profits in any market regardless of overall market declines or advances. Another important tool hedge fund manager's use is that of leverage. Leverage allows the hedge fund manager to magnify performance. Leverage is essentially borrowing capital from a prime broker or bank and then using that capital to buy more of a specific asset. As long as the return of the invested asset is greater than the borrowing cost, then the hedge fund will have made a smart move and enhanced performance. The remaining tools are all used by different hedge fund managers at different times. Most hedge fund managers stick with one or two tools and emphasize only those. They do not use all the tools available to them at any one point. This would create a jack of all trades and master of none.

7. Absolute Returns

In the world of investing, most pooled funds seek good relative performance. Relative performance is essentially performing well against the peer group. Regardless of how well or poorly a mutual fund manager has performed, the real comparison is in how well or poorly the rest of the peer group performed. Hedge funds, on the other side of the pendulum, seek good absolute performance. Absolute performance and relative performance are not the same. With absolute performance, a hedge fund manager strives to generate positive returns, not returns that knock the cover off the ball. Hedge funds are all about reducing risk and enhancing returns smartly. Absolute performance is aligned with this aim.

Many people think hedge funds are a means to reduce risk. This is an excusable consideration given the name and history of hedge funds. Unfortunately, most hedge funds do not reduce total risk. Many actually create additional risk. Specifically speaking, hedge funds seek strong performance and this means attractive historical returns, low dispersion of historical returns, and high consistencies of historical returns.

The benefits of absolute returns include positive returns and holding an asset class that exhibits low volatility. Low volatility is the result of the pursuit of absolute returns, not the objective per say. When returns are fluctuating all over the place, volatility will be high. And as we know, higher volatility means higher risk. Hedge funds do not have these same big swings in value given the strategies they employ to generate absolute returns, or positive returns in any investment market.

Lastly, hedge funds and mutual funds have different sources of return and risk. The sources of risk and return for mutual funds include market timing, the strategy employed by the manager, and the care and skill of the manager to implement, monitor, and manager the strategy to take advantage of profitable opportunities. Given the ability and willingness of hedge funds to sell short securities, market risk can be minimized. As a result, hedge funds face only investment-strategy risk and the risk associated with how the strategy is implemented.

8. Ideally Low Correlations

Hedge fund managers can employ many different tactics and techniques to manage their funds. As a result of their use of these tools, hedge funds exhibit low correlations with the equity markets and other asset classes. Correlation is a measure of how closely the market prices of two assets move together over time. Thus high correlation means that the prices of two assets are changing and moving in very similar ways and patterns. On the flip side, low correlation means that the prices of the two assets are moving differently from one another. The lower the correlation, the less the prices move together. Low correlation could mean that they still move in roughly the same direction–positive correlation—or even in opposite directions—negative correlation.

Holding a portfolio of assets with low correlations to other assets is ideal because when one asset is moving down in price, another will not fall as much or even will rise in value. Hedge funds have low correlations and thus move differently from the market, especially the equity markets. Although the assets held in hedge funds do play a role in determining fund correlation, it is the tactics and techniques that really drive low correlations. Since hedge fund managers have the ability to sell short, the inverse correlation thus is incorporated. For example, if two stocks have

high correlation close to +1, which means that they move in perfect lock-step form, then selling short one of those stocks will create a correlation that is close to –1, which means that they move in perfectly opposite lock-step form. Note that the two stocks will continue to have a high positive correlation, but the effect of the sell-short will deliver negative correlation to the fund.

To enable hedge fund managers to deliver on their aim of absolute returns, holding low-correlation assets is essential to counter the movement in the equity markets. Thus, when the market is declining, a low-correlation fund still may deliver gains.

9. Incentivized Fee Arrangement

Hedge funds charge two primary types of fees. The first is an investment-management fee, and the second is a performance-incentive fee. Nearly all traditional investment managers charge the standard investment-management fee, typically around 1 percent—or higher for mutual funds. This figure could be slightly more or slightly less. Hedge funds generally charge the same fee which covers the expenses of the fund. The second fee is what differentiates hedge funds altogether, the performance-incentive fee. This fee is charged against the profits generated by the hedge fund. The typical performance-incentive fee is 20 percent, with some higher and some lower, and is assessed annually based on the performance of the previous year. If the fund does not generate a positive return and make money for the investor, then the fee is not charged. Furthermore, certain safeguards are often used to protect the investor from paying twice or even more on gains the fund had earned in the past but lost in subsequent years. Please see the following defining characteristic for more on these safeguards.

Some people may become uncomfortable when they hear that hedge funds can charge 20 percent fees on profits generated. The point to remember is that hedge funds earn this fee, or at least it had better, by delivering on the aim of absolute returns or positive returns even when the equity market is declining. It's better to pay a 20 percent fee on a 10 percent annual return than a 0 percent fee on a –5 percent annual return. Many hedge funds earn their keep.

10. High-Water-Mark and Hurdle-Rate Safeguards

Given the high fees that hedge funds charge investors in the form of a performance-incentive fee, safeguards typically are implemented to protect the investor. The two safeguards most prevalent with hedge funds include the high-water mark and the hurdle rate. Most hedge funds have the high-water mark, but few have the hurdle rate.

The high-water mark is a safeguard established to protect investors from paying the performance-incentive fee on the same gains. The high-water mark is the point where all gains above this level are charged the fee. Thus, if a $1 million portfolio loses $100,000 in one year and the next year gains $200,000, then the performance-incentive fee is only charged on $100,000 because the other $100,000 only returned the portfolio to its original starting point, which incidentally was the high-water mark. Given the gain, the new high-water mark moves to $1.1 million, and only gains above this amount are assessed the performance-incentive fee.

The hurdle rate basically says that only gains above a certain rate will be charged the performance-incentive fee. Most hurdle rates are tied to the London Interbank Offered Rate (LIBOR) or the rate on Treasury bills. Funds that implement hurdle-rate safeguards typically still will implement the high-water mark. In a certain year if the LIBOR rate is 4.5 percent, then only gains associated with returns above 4.5 percent are charged the fee. Thus, if a certain fund generated a return of 5 percent, then the performance-incentive fee will be charged against the excess 0.5 percent (5.0 – 4.5) return only, as long as this gain is above the high-water mark, of course.

Quiz for Chapter 18

1. All the following are key attributes of hedge funds *except*
   a. minimal oversight and regulation.
   b. restricted to a low number of "accredited investors."
   c. favorable liquidity and redemption provisions.
   d. limitations on marketing and promotions.

2. Most hedge funds are run by one or two key people.
   a. True
   b. False

3. All the following are involved in regulating some aspect of hedge funds *except*
   a. the American Association of Individual Investors.
   b. the Securities and Exchange Commission.
   c. the U.S. Treasury Department.
   d. the Federal Reserve.

4. Hedge funds are limited to how many accredited investors?

   a. 49

   b. 99

   c. 149

   d. 199

5. How much net worth must an individual have to satisfy the accredited investor status?

   a. $1.5 million

   b. $2.2 million

   c. $2.5 million

   d. $3.5 million

6. What is a *lockup period*?

   a. Period of time during which invested capital from all investors is not available for withdrawal

   b. Period of time during which invested capital from new investors is not available for withdrawal

   c. Period of time during which the hedge fund is closed to all investors

   d. Period of time during which the hedge fund is closed to new investors

7. Most hedge funds do not have lockup period provisions.

   a. True

   b. False

8. Are hedge funds permitted to use television and radio to advertise their business?

   a. Yes

   b. No

   c. Only within 30 days of opening the fund

9. Do hedge funds tend to have high/low/no correlation with equity investments?

   a. High

   b. Low

   c. No

10. Which safeguard protects investors from paying a performance-incentive fee on the same profit earned in a previous year?

   a. High-water mark

   b. Hurdle rate

   c. Protection trigger

   d. Shielding mechanism

CHAPTER 19

Hedge Fund Alternatives

Mutual Funds and Exchange-Traded Funds That Hedge

For investors looking to invest like a hedge fund without actually investing in one, finding alternatives can be a challenge. Why would an investor want to forgo investing in a hedge fund and instead investigate hedge fund alternatives? Perhaps an investor does not find the liquidity provisions ideal or does not want to make the financial commitment necessary to invest in a particular hedge fund. The reasons for bypassing hedge funds can be numerous, including the simple desire and passion to manage your own portfolio and overcome the related challenges.

Investors who find themselves in this position essentially can pursue one of three strategies. First, they can employ hedge fund strategies and manage their own portfolios without the assistance of professional money managers. For example, an investor can employ leverage, sell short, or use derivatives in his or her portfolio. Second, the investor can invest in a new breed of mutual fund that has many similarities to hedge funds. Finally, the investor can invest in certain exchange-traded funds (ETFs) that are actively managed based on selected hedge fund strategies.

This last strategy is a combination of the two aforementioned strategies of self-management and professional management with mutual funds. This chapter provides an introduction to both mutual funds and ETFs that have much in common with hedge funds. This book does not cover individual hedge fund–related strategies that investors can employ for themselves. However, if you are interested, my book, *Understanding Hedge Funds,* (McGraw-Hill 2006) presents a chapter on this very topic.

Mutual Funds

Mutual hedge funds, is that correct? Yes. Over the last couple of years, mutual funds that behave much like hedge funds have been established to compete for investors looking to optimize their portfolios. These funds are registered with the Securities and Exchange Commission (SEC) under the Investment Company Act of 1940 and focus on delivering returns that have low correlations with the equity market. This means that portfolios will experience smoothed performance volatility—and therefore lower risk volatility. The end result is a higher risk-adjusted return. This type of mutual fund is often referred to as a *market-neutral mutual fund*. This term is representative of mutual funds that sell short but not of those that employ leverage.

Mutual hedge funds—for lack of a better name—can go long or short, employ leverage, and use other more "alternative" investment strategies—just as hedge funds do. This new investment phenomenon has not gone unnoticed by investors and investment advisors alike. According to Morningstar, there were 48 long/short mutual hedge funds at the end of 2006, and the number is growing. This figure is double the number that the firm tracked at the end of 2003. Furthermore, according to Strategic Insight, a mutual fund research and consulting company, there was approximately $4.8 billion in new capital flowing into these types of funds, up from the $1 billion range the year prior.

MANAGEMENT FEE STRUCTURE

One of the most compelling reasons for investing in mutual hedge funds is the management fee arrangement. Hedge funds typically charge a 1 percent annual investment-management fee regardless of performance and a 20 percent performance-incentive fee that is charged against all profits earned above the high-water mark. Mutual hedge funds, on the other hand, charge only one fee, the annual investment-management fee.

There is no performance-incentive fee with the majority of these funds. The trade-off, however, is the higher-than-normal annual investment-management fee of 2.5 percent. This can be more or less depending on the manager. Thus, if your investment loses money in a particular year, you would be better off in hedge funds, all else being equal, because you would only incur the 1 percent annual investment-management fee and not the performance-investment fee because the fund lost money. If the same person were invested in a mutual hedge fund, then he or she would incur the typical 2.5 percent fee, which is 150 percent more than the typical hedge fund fee. However, if the investor made a profit in his or her portfolio, then he or she would be better off in the mutual hedge fund than in the hedge fund from a fee standpoint only, of course. This is due to the fact that the investor would not incur the 20 percent performance-incentive fee and would only have to pay the 2.5 percent annual investment-management fee. We can calculate the typical performance breakpoint mathematically where an investor would be better off in a hedge fund or better off in a mutual hedge fund, again from a fee standpoint only. This breakpoint is around 8.1 percent. Investors experiencing returns above this number will pay lower fees in a mutual hedge fund. Likewise, investors experiencing returns below this number will pay lower fees in a hedge fund. This is something important to keep in mind.

Keep an eye on this new type of investment, I suspect that we will see a great number of new funds along these lines over the next decade.

BENEFITS OF MUTUAL HEDGE FUNDS

- *Potentially lower fees.* Mutual hedge funds do not charge performance-incentive fees but do charge higher investment-management fees. Since performance-incentive fees can be quite substantial, not paying them can potentially lower total fees incurred.

- *Better tax reporting.* Mutual fund investors receive 1099s and by law must receive them by January 31. In contrast, hedge fund investors receive K–1s and often times very close to the tax filing deadline.

- *Greater liquidity.* Mutual hedge funds do not have lockup provisions for new investors and allow for frequent withdraws of invested capital.

- *Enhanced transparency.* Investors know exactly what asset positions are held in the fund and receive this information on a more frequent basis.

- *Daily valuation.* Since these funds are technically mutual funds, daily valuation and pricing are available to shareholders.

- *Reduced manager departure risk.* Hedge funds typically are managed by one or two key people. This creates added risk for investors because any manager departure could greatly affect how the fund is operated. Although

there is manager-departure risk with mutual hedge funds, these funds generally are part of a larger mutual fund family, and any departure can be resolved more quickly with other managers or analysts working for the same organization.

- *Financial advisor friendly.* For investors looking to have someone in their corner helping to manage their money, mutual hedge funds provide the means to do just that. Since mutual hedge funds are technically mutual funds and not hedge funds, there are simply more financial advisors who have access to mutual hedge funds than to hedge funds. Hedge funds are more specialized, and therefore, not all financial advisors can provide help with investing in them.

- *Enhanced flexibility.* Given shareholders' ability to redeem their shares in a mutual hedge fund and to turn around and invest in a different fund, there is far greater flexibility for investors. Furthermore, given the high income and net-worth hurdles for investors to invest in hedge funds, many investors in stand-alone hedge funds may have to limit the number of hedge funds they can invest in. With mutual hedge funds, investors can invest money in a number of different funds, thus creating a more diversified hedged portfolio. Funds of funds also provide this same benefit because they invest in a number of stand-alone hedge funds and require far smaller initial investments from investors.

- *Pursue absolute returns.* Mutual hedge funds pursue many of the same goals as do hedge funds. This means that mutual hedge funds pursue absolute returns, or positive returns, for their investors. The benefits of achieving this objective are smoother returns, lower risk volatility, and higher risk-adjusted returns for the total investor portfolio (see Figure 19–1).

Figure 19-1. Selected mutual funds that employ alternative strategies

FUND	TICKER
Analytic Global Long/Short	ANGLX
Calamos Market Neutral A	CVSIX
Diamond Hill Long-Short A	DIAMX
Hussman Strategic Growth	HSGFX
James Market Neutral	JAMNX
Laudus Rosenberg Global Long/Short	MSMNX
Laudus Rosenberg U.S. Large/Mid Long/Short	SSMNX
Merger	MERFX
Templeton Global Long Short A	TLSAX

Exchange-Traded Funds

Given the incredible explosion in the quantity and complexity of ETFs over the last decade, it was only a matter of time before money managers saw the potential and established ETFs that resemble hedge funds. These ETFs are a cross between actively and passively managed funds. ETFs historically have been passively managed funds and have only recently begun taking on a more active management focus. *Passive management* is an investing strategy that tracks a market index and does not attempt to beat the market through security selection or market timing. This precludes managers from making ad hoc decisions in the hopes of making excess profits, which can often lead to losses. *Active management* is an investing strategy that relies on the judgment and skill of the manager to select investments and time purchases and sales. Active managers use analytical research and forecasts to supplement their own decision making. Money managers using this strategy emphasize security selection and market timing approaches.

ABOUT ETFs

ETFs are stocks that trade on organized stock exchanges, such as the American Stock Exchange (AMEX), with the aim of generating a return that mirrors a predetermined index, such as the Standard & Poor's (S&P) 500 Index. ETFs can be purchased and sold just like any stock during any time of the day as long as the stock market is open. ETFs can be purchased using leverage and can be sold short. Many hedge funds sell short and sometimes go long ETFs as a way to gain quick and easy exposure to specific indices or hedge market risk. ETFs track nearly all indices existing in the marketplace today, even many you may not have heard about before. Many investors believe so strongly in the power and benefits of ETFs that they build their entire portfolios using them and avoid individual company stocks altogether.

BENEFITS OF ETFs

ETFs provide significant benefits to investors, and I personally and professionally invest in them and encourage others to strongly consider them as well. First, ETFs provide instant diversification because each share typically will represent every company operating in that market. Second, ETFs provide tax benefits in that minimal capital gains distributions are made to shareholders. Mutual funds cannot make this same claim because they frequently distribute much larger capital gains. By basic definition, ETFs have minimal turnover, which translates to minimal capital gains tax consequences. Therefore, the only taxable consequences incurred by investors include minimal capital gains from the ETF, dividends received from the ETF, and capital gains once the investment is sold outright by the investor. Third,

ETFs provide access to multiple asset classes with only one investment, and this means a better-allocated portfolio and an enhanced risk-adjusted return. Fourth, ETFs provide a low-cost investing method. Many actively managed investments, such as mutual funds, charge management fees in excess of 1 percent. In contrast, nearly all ETFs charge management fees of less than 0.75 percent, with many below 0.40 percent. Given that most traditional money managers do not beat the return of the market each year, why, then, would any investor want to pay the higher fee and still have a greater chance of underperforming than to invest with a low-cost ETF or index fund and perhaps beat the return of most money managers? The more efficient the market—such as large-cap stocks—the more effective indexing will be for the investor. Indexing of less efficient markets—such as small-cap stocks and some international markets—will not be as effective for an investor. Less efficient markets are sometimes, but not always, best served through active management given a manager's knowledge, skill, and experience in that market.

ETF EXPENSES

ETFs that follow a strict passive management strategy typically have very low management fees, sometimes less than 10 basis points, or 0.1 percent. For ETFs that employ a more active management style, management fees will be higher, often around 60 basis points, or 0.6 percent. In addition to management fees, investors will need to transact these shares on an exchange—typically the AMEX—and this means that commissions will be charged for both purchases and sales. ETFs that specifically employ specialized strategies, such as those that hedge funds employ, will charge more. As a result, be mindful and consider the expenses of these funds prior to building a portfolio of them. ProShares, a money manager that specializes in actively managed ETFs, charges 0.60 percent on the funds it manages using alternative strategies, namely, leverage and selling short.

ETFS AND HEDGE FUND STRATEGIES

Of all the alternative strategies hedge fund managers use to manage their funds, three of them standout as the preferred strategies for ETF managers. First, most of the ETFs in this group sell short the index they are mirroring. Thus the price of the ETF moves inversely with the price of the underlying index. Second, many ETFs in this group employ leverage to magnify their returns. Thus, if the underlying index returns 10 percent for a year, an ETF that is 50 percent leveraged will generate a 15 percent return for shareholders. Third, some ETFs in this group target specific sector indices rather than broad market indices. Thus the ETF manager is betting that the underlying index in the sector selected will advance in price at a faster rate than will broad market indices.

One such money manager that offers an impressive line of ETFs that employ alternative investment strategies similar to those of hedge funds is ProShares. This money manager offers ETFs that sell short the underlying index with the aim of producing a 1:1 inverse price relationship. The company also offers what it calls "ultrashort ETFs," which leverage the selling short of the underlying index with the aim of producing a 2:1 inverse price relationship. Thus, if the underlying index declines by 10 percent in a given year, the ultrashort ETF is expected to rise by 20 percent in that same year—a 2:1 price relationship. This company also offers sector ETFs as well.

If you are interested in learning more about specific ETFs that employ hedge fund strategies, visit ProShares.com. I strongly encourage you to consult with your financial advisor and do your due diligence to ensure that investing in these or any other ETFs that employ hedge fund strategies is right for you.

Quiz for Chapter 19

1. Which of the following are two financial instruments that offer management similar to that of hedge funds?

   a. Mutual funds and annuities

   b. ETFs and CDs

   c. CDs and annuities

   d. ETFs and mutual funds

2. Perhaps the most compelling reason for bypassing hedge funds in favor of mutual funds that hedge is the elimination of the performance incentive fee.

   a. True

   b. False

3. All the following are benefits of mutual funds employing alternative strategies *except*

   a. more liquidity.

   b. greater variety of managers.

   c. enhanced transparency.

   d. daily valuation.

4. For tax reporting, hedge fund investors receive _____, whereas mutual fund investors receive _____.

   a. Form 1040-H/Form 1099

   b. Form 1099/Form K–1

   c. Form K–1/Form 1099

   d. Form W–7/Form W–9

5. Which of the following is *not* a benefit of ETFs?

   a. Low cost

   b. Instant diversification

   c. Zero tax consequences

   d. Access to multiple asset classes

6. The two most popular hedge fund strategies employed by ETFs are

   a. selling short and arbitrage.

   b. arbitrage and leverage.

   c. leverage and market timing.

   d. leverage and selling short.

7. Mutual hedge funds typically charge a lower annual investment-management fee than do hedge funds.

   a. True

   b. False

8. By what date must mutual fund shareholders receive their 1099s?

   a. January 31

   b. February 28

   c. March 15

   d. March 31

9. ETFs historically have been _____ managed and sold _____.

   a. passively/over the counter

   b. actively/over the counter

   c. actively/on an exchange

   d. passively/on an exchange

10. Mutual funds that employ alternative strategies pursue strong relative returns and deemphasize absolute returns.

   a. True

   b. False

Future of Hedge Funds

Outlook, Perspectives, and Developing Trends

Hedge funds have become a significant force in investing and wealth management. The growth of the trade is truly astounding. Today, there are over 9,000 hedge funds with approximately $1.4 trillion in assets under management. The market over the most recent couple of decades provided the foundation and support for hedge funds to grow and flourish, with the conditions ripe for an industry with strong potential and interest. However, let's put the past behind us for a moment and think about the future and what it may hold for hedge fund investing. Many questions quickly surface when we think about this topic. Will present-day conditions continue into the future, or will they disappear? Will government regulations squeeze the industry, essentially turning hedge funds into glorified mutual funds, or will government continue to provide minimal regulation? One thing is for certain: The hedge fund trade will experience changes over the foreseeable future. But what will these changes specifically affect? Figure 20–1 illustrates the 10 changes I predict will occur in the future to hedge funds.

Figure 20-1. Ten probable changes to the hedge fund trade

1	Hedge Fund Companies Will Increase in Size and Offerings
2	Hedge Fund Regulation Will Rise
3	Reduced Hedge Fund Fees
4	More Robust and Additional Hedge Fund Indices
5	Enhanced Investor Liquidity
6	Improved Transparency
7	Greater Use of Niche Strategies
8	Increase in the Number of Hedge Funds
9	Greater Geographic Diversification of Hedge Fund Managers
10	Merging of Alternative and Traditional Managers

1. Hedge Fund Companies Will Increase in Size and Offerings

This trend has been developing for some time now as existing hedge fund companies expand in size and scope and establish new hedge funds in their product offerings. Over the next few years, hedge fund companies will strive to add more funds and grow their companies, thus capturing economies of scale. With the money many of these hedge funds earn, financing more expansion will not be especially difficult. This expansion most likely will create mega-hedge fund companies that offer hedge funds in each strategy, with multistrategies and funds of funds offerings included to enhance and complete what they offer to institutional and high-net-worth investors. A push to become more consultive also will occur over the next several years.

2. Hedge Fund Regulation Will Increase

This is another trend that has been ongoing for some time and is fully expected to continue into the foreseeable future. Without a doubt, the Securities and Exchange Commission (SEC) will hunt for ways to regulate hedge funds. We have seen this in practically everything the SEC does and says regarding hedge funds. The end result of this heightened regulation most likely will include the following:

- Full registration of hedge fund managers
- Greater disclosure of hedge fund holdings and tools employed
- Modest limitations on tactics and techniques used
- Increased liquidity
- More stringent regulations on who is an accredited investor (occurred in 2007)

Entities that will bring their influence—both positive and negative—to bear on the hedge fund trade include governmental regulatory entities, related third parties such as broker-dealers and institutional investors, and political entities. It is only a matter of time before regulatory entities sink their teeth into hedge funds.

3. Reduced Hedge Fund Fees

The question is not if but when hedge fund fees will decline overall. Asset-based fees are most likely to remain largely intact and untouched, but performance-incentive fees will see pressure owing to two primary factors. First, with so many new hedge funds being established, managers will reduce their rates from the typical 20 percent of profits to give them an advantage over other managers. This will set them apart and attract additional investors. Second, with many institutional investors increasing their allocations to hedge funds, pressure to reduce rates will increase. These institutions will swap capital invested for a reduced rate—a quantity discount of sorts. Many managers will continue to keep their 20:1 (performance-incentive and investment-management) fees steady given strong historical performance and resulting demand for their services. However, for the most part, hedge fund managers will experience declines in the fees they charge, much like what mutual funds experienced many years ago.

4. More Robust and Additional Hedge Fund Indices

Index-based investing is not a new approach to traditional investing but is new to hedge fund investing. Over time, more standardized investable indices will emerge that will enable investors to generate returns that mirror the performance of any one of the different hedge fund strategies. Soon hedge fund investors will be able to hold index-based derivatives, now in their infancy. In addition, hedge fund indices themselves will improve because there is a concerted effort by data providers and hedge fund managers to provide the best data possible to construct acceptable indices. Given the pressure from institutions to provide greater transparency, hedge fund managers will improve the data provided not only to their institutional investors but also to those who construct indices. This means that both institutional and retail investors will have better and more reliable benchmarks to facilitate performance measurement and ongoing investment decisions.

5. Enhanced Investor Liquidity

Most hedge funds impose one-year lockup periods for new money and 90-day notice periods for withdrawing money from existing investments. For hedge funds that invest in long-term investments such as venture-capital projects or highly illiquid assets, requiring long periods of time before withdrawing money is more than fair and appropriate. However, many of the remaining investments held in a hedge fund can be liquidated in a relatively short period of time, such as weeks or even days. This means that hedge fund managers have the flexibility to change their requirements and thus enhance investor liquidity. In doing so, hedge fund managers will set themselves apart from other managers, and this will help them to attract additional investments from both institutional and high-net-worth investors. Many hedge fund managers will move toward enhancing investor liquidity on their own, whereas others will be either highly motivated or required to do so by institutional investors and governmental entities. The end result will benefit investors and help hedge funds to compete with more traditional investments that, in today's investing marketplace, are more advantageous in this regard.

6. Improved Transparency

Today, institutional investors want and demand more transparency from hedge funds. Individual investors are no different. As competition for investors heats up, hedge funds will increase the disclosure of information to help win over clients. Regulators most assuredly will push for greater disclosure as well. Information that will see improved transparency includes assets under management, strategies employed, tools used, and investment positions held. Full disclosure will not happen overnight, nor will disclosing the same level of information as mutual funds

anytime soon. Rest assured, however, that improved transparency is on the horizon.

7. Greater Use of Niche Strategies

As the number of hedge funds increases, the desire for hedge fund managers to set themselves apart will grow. One way to accomplish this will be to focus on one particular area or niche. Many managers are already doing this, but more will continue into the future. Today, many managers are already focusing on specific strategies such as macrocentric investing, funds of funds, and merger-arbitrage investing. The future will see these managers continue to become more specialized while including customized and unique tactics and techniques for profiting from opportunities. The result will be more niche managers who know their respective markets well and thus how to position their hedge funds for above-normal profits and/or less risk.

8. Increase in the Number of Hedge Funds

With the future of hedge funds, nothing is a forgone conclusion. However, one trend that is most predictable is the continued growth in the number of hedge funds both in the United States and abroad. Given the lure of significant compensation, less government oversight and regulation, and a reputation as a prized profession, hedge funds will continue to attract the best and the brightest from not only the traditional side of investing but also other professional areas that are not exactly related to investing. These people will come from legal, accounting, and marketing professions. Not only will new hedge fund management companies start from the ground up, but so too will the numbers of hedge funds grow at existing hedge fund companies. Low barriers to entry will help to pave the way for ever-increasing numbers of hedge funds. More hedge funds will equate to more options and opportunities for hedge fund investors.

9. Greater Geographic Diversification of Hedge Fund Managers

Today, the majority of hedge fund managers are located on the East Coast of the United States, specifically New York and Connecticut. This will change. Over time, the geographic diversification of hedge fund managers will increase as hedge funds open around the country and throughout the world. Money-center cities such as

Chicago, Charlotte, and San Francisco will experience much of the new growth. Smaller cities and other major cities also will see new hedge funds established in their areas. This means greater accessibility to hedge fund managers for investors, which is usually a good thing.

10. Merging of Alternative and Traditional Managers

As hedge fund companies grow in size and complexity, so too will the services they offer. In doing so, hedge fund companies will start to look more and more like other traditional investment companies. Hedge fund companies will begin to offer more separate accounts, corresponding traditional investment accounts, and perhaps even financial planning related services. Many of these services are years away but definitely on the horizon. The most sophisticated companies that want to attract more high-net-worth investors will be very motivated and at the forefront of offering traditional services seen as most ideal to this group. At the same time, many traditional investment managers also will enter the hedge fund arena by establishing either their own hedge funds or perhaps jumping on the bandwagon of opening their own mutual hedge fund. Given the potential benefits of mutual hedge funds, I suspect that there will be explosive growth in their number and complexity over the next decade. One of the big areas where more traditional money managers have begun encroaching on hedge fund turf is with exchange-traded funds (ETFs) and mutual funds that employ alternative strategies used by hedge fund managers. The marketplace will experience a substantial increase in the number of these types of investments over the next decade. You can take that to the bank.

The hedge fund industry continues to change and mature. Over the next dozen years, factors such as increased competition, heightened governmental regulation, additional institutional involvement and pressure, and challenging market environments will help to transform the hedge fund trade into a more investor-friendly marketplace. This will attract more investments and open opportunities to the masses of investors.

Quiz for Chapter 20

1. All the following are probable future changes in hedge funds *except*
   a. greater transparency.
   b. higher fees.
   c. more regulation.
   d. improved liquidity.

2. It is anticipated that hedge fund managers will focus on more niche strategies in the future.

    a. True

    b. False

3. The number of hedge funds in the world is anticipated to rise/fall.

    a. Rise

    b. Fall

4. In the future, there will be a greater geographic diversification of hedge fund managers.

    a. True

    b. False

5. In the future, traditional managers and hedge fund managers will continue to diverge.

    a. True

    b. False

6. Over time, the number of hedge fund indices will rise, as will their robustness.

    a. True

    b. False

7. Although the number of hedge funds is expected to rise, the size of hedge fund companies is expected to decline.

    a. True

    b. False

8. All the following are reasons why the number of hedge funds is expected to rise *except*

    a. low barriers to entry.

    b. acceptable startup costs.

    c. attractive manager compensation.

    d. loosening of regulatory restrictions.

9. Which of the following is least likely to play a role in tightening hedge fund regulation?

   a. Governmental agencies

   b. Industry associations

   c. Prime brokers and those who lend margin

   d. Political entities

10. Who will have the most influence on hedge fund managers to reduce their fees?

   a. Prime brokers

   b. Governmental agencies

   c. Individual investors

   d. Institutional investors

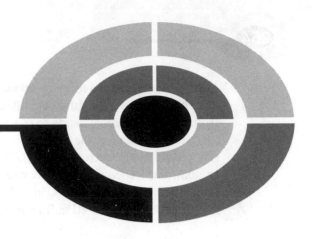

Conclusion

Hedge Funds Demystified was written for investors who want to learn more about one of the most misunderstood investments in the financial marketplace today. It is my aim that the information provided here will help investors to allocate their portfolios properly for solid portfolio performance over the long term. Hedge funds may be that missing component for many investors who are looking for an edge.

Please feel free to visit www.HedgeFundsDemystified.com the official author Web Site for this book. If you are interested in learning more about how my firm can help to protect and grow your wealth, please contact me for a brochure and more information.

Scott Paul Frush, CFA, CFP, MBA
Frush Financial Group
37000 Woodward Avenue, Suite 101
Bloomfield Hills, Michigan 48304
Voice: (248) 642–6800
E-mail: Contact@Frush.com
Web site: Frush.com

For more information on the basics of asset allocation and why allocating your portfolio is so important, I highly encourage you to read my book, *Understanding Asset Allocation* (McGraw-Hill, 2006). *Understanding Asset Allocation* explains

exactly what you need to know about how to allocate your assets. This comprehensive, highly accessible guide clearly explains the key principles of asset allocation from selection to rebalancing to risk versus return. You'll discover how the different asset classes behave, the leading misconceptions about asset allocation, and how risk profile, time horizon, and SMART financial goals can affect your investments. In addition, I encourage you to visit my official author Web site, which provides information on all my books, including the latest news and information on upcoming books, at www.ScottPaulFrush.com.

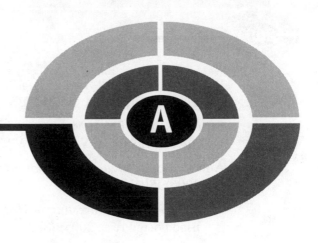

APPENDIX

Hedge Fund Resources

Books

Bill Crerend. *Fundamentals of Hedge Fund Investing: A Professional Investor's Guide,* (New York; McGraw-Hill; 1998) ISBN 0070135223.

Scott Paul Frush. *Understanding Hedge Funds,* (New York; McGraw-Hill; 2006) ISBN 0071485937.

Scott Paul Frush. *Understanding Asset Allocation,* (New York; McGraw-Hill; 2006) ISBN 007147594X.

Greg N. Gregoriou. *Funds of Hedge Funds,* (Amsterdam, Boston; Butterworth/Heinemann/Elsevier; 2006) ISBN 0750679840.

Armelle Guizot. *The Hedge Fund Compliance and Risk Management Guide,* (Hoboken, N.J.; John Wiley & Sons, Inc; 2007) ISBN 0470043571.

James R. Hedges. *Hedges on Hedge Funds: How to Successfully Analyze and Select an Investment,* (Hoboken, N.J.; Wiley; 2005) ISBN 0471625108.

Robert A. Jaeger. *All About Hedge Funds: The Easy Way to Get Started,* (New York; McGraw-Hill; 2003) ISBN 0071393935.

Sam Kirschner, Eldon Mayer, and Lee Kessler. *The Investor's Guide to Hedge Funds,* (Hoboken, N.J.; John Wiley & Sons, Inc; 2006) ISBN 0471715999.

Ann C. Logue. *Hedge Funds for Dummies,* (Indianapolis, IN; Wiley Pub., Inc; 2006) ISBN 0470049273.

Joseph G. Nicholas. *Investing in Hedge Funds: An Investor's Guide,* (New York; Bloomberg Press; 2005) ISBN 1576601846.

Joseph G. Nicholas. *Hedge Funds of Funds Investing: An Investor's Guide,* (Princeton; Bloomberg Press; 2004) ISBN 1576601242.

Matthew Ridley. *How to Invest in Hedge Funds,* (London, Sterling, VA; Kogan Page Limited; 2004) ISBN 0749440848.

Filippo Stefanini. *Investment Strategies of Hedge Funds,* (Hoboken, NJ; Wiley; 2006) ISBN 0470026278.

Daniel A. Strachman. *Getting Started in Hedge Funds,* (Hoboken, N.J.; John Wiley; 2005) ISBN 0471715441.

Vinh Q. Tran. *Evaluating Hedge Fund Performance,* (Hoboken, N.J.; John Wiley; 2006) ISBN 978047681717.

Web Sites

WSJ.com. A top source, if not the leading source, of broad financial and market information available.

HedgeWorld.com. For information on all things hedge fund–related, this is one of the best resources.

Morningstar.com. A good source for the latest market news, investment analysis, and financial happenings. From the company that assigns hedge fund rankings.

Finance.Yahoo.com. My personal favorite. An outstanding source for financial information. Covers both the depth and breadth of the market and market participants.

Bloomberg.com. Another of my personal favorites. A leading source of financial news and commentary.

HedgeFundCenter.com. Solid source of information and commentary on hedge funds.

DowJones.com. Provides an abundant source of historical information for the student of finance and investing. Top source for charting and historical prices.

HedgeFundsDemystified.com. This is the official author Web site for this book. This site provides news, articles, books, and the latest updates, with accolades received for *Hedge Funds Demystified*.

Magazines

Alpha Magazine

Absolute Return

Wall Street Journal

Kiplinger's Personal Finance

Barron's

Money

The Economist

Mutual Funds

BusinessWeek

Institutional Investor

Trader Monthly

EuroHedge

Financial Times

Fortune

Forbes

Red Herring

Smart Money

Worth

Journal of Alternative Investments

Associations

Alternative Investment Management Association (AIMA), Meadows House, 20–22 Queen Street, London W1J5PR, United Kingdom, 44–20–7659–9920, www.aima.org

Managed Funds Association, 2025 M Street NW, Suite 800, Washington, DC 20036, 202–367–1140, www.mfainfo.org

Hedge Fund Association, 2875 N.E. 191st Street, Suite 900, Aventura, FL 33180, 202–478–2000, www.thehfa.org

CFA Institute, 560 Ray C. Hunt Drive, Charlottesville, VA 22903–2981, 800–247–8132, www.CFAInstitute.org

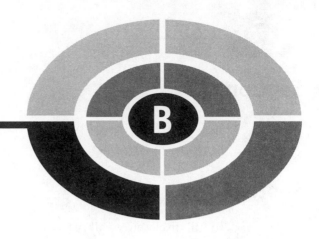

A Hedge Fund Investor's "Bill of Rights"

As a hedge fund investor, you have the right ...

Section I

To suitable, ethical, and responsible investment management

Section II

To honesty in advertising, marketing, and sales communications

Section III

To courteous, fair, and professional care and service

Section IV

To full disclosure of all risks

Section V

To thorough explanation of fees, expenses, penalties, and obligations

Section VI

To complete disclosure of conflicts of interest

Section VII

To appropriate background information on each hedge fund professional

Section VIII

To reasonable time for making investing decisions

Section IX

To accurate and truthful valuation and pricing

Section X

To sufficient access to invested capital.

Section XI

To disclosure of liquidity and redemption lockup restrictions

Section XII

To a complete, accurate, and standardized performance composite

Section XIII

To privacy, confidentiality, and safekeeping of all nonpublic personal information

Section XIV

To ask for and receive the degree of manager investing participation in the hedge fund

Section XV

To all offering, agreement, and new-account documents

Section XVI

To accurate, complete, understandable, and timely account statements and K–1 tax forms

Section XVII

To contact government regulators and industry organizations to verify employment history and investigate disciplinary records

Section XVIII

To updates of any material changes at the hedge fund company

Section XIX

To quick and just resolution of any account, service, or relationship issue

Section XX

To terminate the engagement if needed

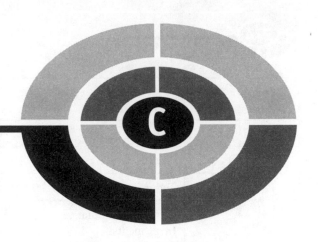

APPENDIX

Top 100 Largest Global Hedge Fund Managers

2007 Rank	2006 Rank	Firm Name	Location	Firm Capital *
1	24	JP Morgan Asset Mgmt	New York, NY	33,087
2	1	Goldman Sachs Asset Mgmt	New York, NY	32,531
3	2	Bridgewater Associates	Westport, CT	30,210
4	3	D.E. Shaw Group	New York, NY	27,300
5	4	Farallon Capital Mgmt	San Francisco, CA	26,200
6	26	Renaissance Technologies Corp.	East Setauket, NY	26,000
7	7	Och-Ziff Capital Mgmt Group	New York, NY	21,000
8	6	Barclays Global Investors	London, U.K.	18,953
9	8	Man Investments	London, U.K.	18,800

2007 Rank	2006 Rank	Firm Name	Location	Firm Capital *
10	5	ESL Investments	Greenwich, CT	17,500
11	14	GLG Partners	London, U.K.	15,833
12	9	Tudor Investment Corp.	Greenwich, CT	14,850
13	45	Citigroup Alternative Investments	New York, NY	14,081
14	33	Lansdowne Partners	London, U.K.	14,000
15	12	Campbell & Co.	Towson, MD	13,600
16	21	Atticus Capital	New York, NY	13,500
16	10	Caxton Associates	New York, NY	13,500
18	11	Citadel Investment Group	Chicago, IL	13,400
19	15	Cerberus Capital Mgmt	New York, NY	12,800
20	18	Moore Capital Mgmt	New York, NY	12,500
21	13	Perry Capital	New York, NY	12,342
22	22	Brevan Howard Asset Mgmt	London, U.K.	12,079
23	19	Angelo, Gordon & Co.	New York, NY	12,000
24	25	HBK Capital Mgmt	Dallas, TX	11,880
25	20	Soros Fund Mgmt	New York, NY	11,600
26	42	BlueCrest Capital Mgmt	London, U.K.	11,200
27	34	Sloane Robinson	London, U.K.	11,100
28	27	SAC Capital Advisors	Stamford, CT	11,000
29	23	HSBC	London, U.K.	10,946
30	48	Marshall Wace	London, U.K.	10,900
31	37	Stark Investments	St. Francis, WI	10,827
32	82	Avenue Capital Group	New York, NY	10,600
33	36	Fortress Investment Group	New York, NY	10,500

2007 Rank	2006 Rank	Firm Name	Location	Firm Capital *
34	30	Canyon Capital Advisors	Beverly Hills, CA	10,220
35	61	Bain Capital	Boston, MA	10,100
36	31	Adage Capital Mgmt	Boston, MA	10,000
36	35	Highfields Capital Mgmt	Boston, MA	10,000
36	27	Wellington Capital Mgmt Co.	Boston, MA	10,000
39	46	Gartmore Investment	London, U.K.	9,700
40	16	Maverick Capital	New York, NY	9,600
41	44	Davidson Kempner Capital Mgmt	New York, NY	9,500
41	46	The Children's Investment Fund Mgmt U.K.	London, U.K.	9,500
43	43	Cheyne Capital Mgmt (U.K.)	London, U.K.	9,203
44	—	BlueBay Asset Mgmt	London, U.K.	9,000
45	32	AQR Capital Mgmt	Greenwich, CT	8,900
46	—	Duquesne Capital Mgmt	Pittsburgh, PA	8,700
47	16	Lone Pine Capital	Greenwich, CT	8,630
48	40	York Capital Mgmt	New York, NY	8,600
49	57	Millennium Partners	New York, NY	8,400
50	—	FX Concepts	New York, NY	8,141
51	49	GMO	Boston, MA	8,092
52	38	Cantillon Capital Mgmt	New York, NY	8,043
53	58	Morgan Stanley Investment Mgmt	New York, NY	7,707
54	84	Black River Asset Mgmt	Minnetonka, MN	7,600
55	—	Winton Capital Mgmt	London, U.K.	7,410
56	50	King Street Capital Mgmt	New York, NY	7,400

2007 Rank	2006 Rank	Firm Name	Location	Firm Capital *
57	51	Elliott Mgmt Corp.	New York, NY	7,230
58	67	AllianceBernstein	New York, NY	7,200
59	—	ADI Gestion	Paris, France	7,197
60	54	TPG-Axon Capital Mgmt	New York, NY	7,168
61	62	Sparx Group Co.	Tokyo, Japan	7,139
62	100	Numeric Investors	Cambridge, MA	7,000
62	78	Tontine Associates	Greenwich, CT	7,000
64	—	Glenview Capital Mgmt	New York, NY	6,760
65	56	Marathon Asset Mgmt	New York, NY	6,500
65	41	Pequot Capital Mgmt	Westport, CT	6,500
65	64	Silver Point Capital	Greenwich, CT	6,500
68	—	Convexity Capital Mgmt	Boston, MA	6,400
69	74	Paulson & Co.	New York, NY	6,379
70	72	Eton Park Capital Mgmt	New York, NY	6,300
71	68	Alternative and Quantitative Inv. (UBS)	Zurich, Switzerland	6,156
72	59	Kingdon Capital Mgmt	New York, NY	6,139
73	64	Steel Partners	New York, NY	6,100
74	52	Baupost Group	Boston, MA	6,000
74	78	Galleon Group	New York, NY	6,000
74	—	M&G Investments	London, U.K.	6,000
74	84	QVT Financial	New York, NY	6,000
74	64	Viking Global Investors	Greenwich, CT	6,000
79	—	Polygon Investment Mgmt	London, U.K.	5,880

Appendix C

2007 Rank	2006 Rank	Firm Name	Location	Firm Capital *
80	77	Jana Partners	New York, NY	5,852
81	55	Orbis Investment Mgmt	Hamilton, Bermuda	5,826
82	97	GoldenTree Asset Mgmt	New York, NY	5,786
83	60	Fairfield Greenwich Group	New York, NY	5,743
84	53	Satellite Asset Mgmt	New York, NY	5,693
85	83	Dexia Asset Mgmt	Paris, France	5,664
86	69	CQS (U.K.)	London, U.K.	5,560
87	91	Ospraie Mgmt	New York, NY	5,500
87	84	D.B. Zwirn & Co.	New York, NY	5,500
89	—	Spinnaker Capital	London, U.K.	5,432
90	—	Highland Capital Mgmt	Dallas, TX	5,405
91	94	Appaloosa Mgmt	Chatham, NJ	5,400
92	—	Bear Stearns Asset Mgmt	New York, NY	5,373
93	75	Omega Advisors	Ncw York, NY	5,200
94	—	Harbert Mgmt Corp.	Birmingham, AL	5,180
95	72	Ellington Mgmt Group	Old Greenwich, CT	5,100
96	63	Graham Capital Mgmt	Rowayton, CT	5,000
96	—	Taconic Capital Advisors	New York, NY	5,000
96	84	Trafelet & Co.	New York, NY	5,000
99	—	RAB Capital	London, U.K.	4,891
100	80	Sandell Asset Mgmt	New York, NY	4,874

* In millions of U.S. dollars as of December 31, 2006

Source: Institutional Investor's *Alpha*, June 2007.

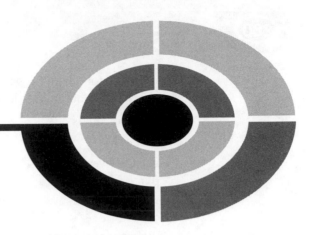

Final Exam

1. Which of the following people is credited with establishing the first hedge fund?

    a. Warren Buffet

    b. Alfred Winslow Jones

    c. George Soros

    d. Leonard Peterson

2. Event-driven hedge funds strive to profit from directional bets.

    a. True

    b. False

3. What is the name for the type of investor permitted to invest in hedge funds by the SEC?

    a. Certified

    b. Permitted

    c. Approved

    d. Accredited

4. Which of the following hedge fund styles does not directly invest in securities, but rather invests in stand-alone hedge funds?

   a. Funds of funds

   b. Tactical

   c. Event-driven

   d. Relative-value

5. A 13-F, 13-D, 13-G, and ADV are all what type of documents?

   a. Performance reporting documents

   b. Offering publications

   c. Regulatory reporting forms

   d. Typical hedge fund account statements

6. All of the following are disclosure documents each new hedge fund investor is required to receive, EXCEPT?

   a. Limited partnership agreement

   b. Offering memorandum

   c. General ownership contract

   d. Subscription agreement

7. Approximately how many hedge funds exist in the world today?

   a. 4,000

   b. 9,000

   c. 14,000

   d. 21,000

8. The typical hedge fund structure consists of hedge fund managers, considered the general partners---and investors, considered the _____ partners.

   a. Mutual

   b. Limited

   c. Associated

   d. Shareholder

9. Under which style is the *multi-strategy* strategy grouped?

   a. Tactical

   b. Event-driven

    c. Relative-value

    d. Hybrid

10. Did the SEC recently tighten or loosen their requirements for individuals to invest in hedge funds?

    a. Tighten

    b. Loosen

11. Most hedge funds registered in the United States are registered using which legal entity?

    a. Limited partnership

    b. C-corporation

    c. S-corporation

    d. Sole proprietorship

12. Which of the following return types do hedge funds strive to generate?

    a. Relative returns

    b. Capital returns

    c. Absolute returns

    d. Dynamic returns

13. Which two alternative strategies did Alfred Winslow Jones first use in his hedge fund?

    a. Selling short and leverage

    b. Leverage and arbitrage

    c. Arbitrage and market timing

    d. Market timing and selling short

14. What is the flagship company of Warren Buffet?

    a. Omaha Financial

    b. Tiger Funds

    c. Nelson Partners

    d. Berkshire Hathaway

15. What feature did Alfred Winslow Jones introduce to hedge funds?

    a. Hurdle rate safeguard

    b. Performance incentive fee

    c. Redemption fee

    d. Lock-up provision

16. Approximately how much money is presently invested in hedge funds, today?

    a. $565 billion

    b. $1.4 trillion

    c. $3.65 trillion

    d. $6.65 trillion

17. One of the primary reasons for investing in hedge funds is the reduction of volatility in an otherwise traditional portfolio.

    a. True

    b. False

18. What is the benefit of performance incentive fees to hedge fund investors?

    a. Aligns the hedge fund manager's interests with the investor's interests

    b. Eliminates lock-up provisions

    c. Stipulates specific payback schedules

    d. Guarantees provisional performance minimums

19. Restricting an investor from selling his hedge fund interest to another hedge fund investor is an example of which type of hedge fund risk?

    a. Give-away

    b. Redemption

    c. Transfer

    d. Tie-out

20. When a hedge fund in unable to finalize a transaction at pre-determined agreed terms, this is an example of which type of hedge fund risk?

    a. Credit

    b. Settlement

    c. Termination

    d. Transfer

21. When investors are unable to obtain sufficient information on hedge funds from the people who manage the funds, this is an example of which type of risk?

    a. Disclosure

    b. Information

    c. Transparency

    d. Transfer

22. What is the largest hedge fund failure in global history?

    a. Long Term Capital Management

    b. Orange County

    c. Manhattan Funds

    d. Amaranth Advisors

23. Approximately how much capital did Amaranth Advisors lose when their hedge fund crashed in 2006?

    a. $600 million

    b. $1.6 billion

    c. $3.6 billion

    d. $6.6 billion

24. In which type of market did Amaranth trade that led to their downfall?

    a. Natural gas

    b. Foreign exchange

    c. Oil

    d. Treasury bonds

25. Which external professional is responsible for the custody of hedge fund assets?

    a. Data sources

    b. Sponsors

    c. Prime brokers

    d. Financial advisors

26. Which of the following external professional is rarely used today with the start-up of hedge funds?

    a. Consultant

    b. Sponsor

    c. Marketing specialist

    d. Financial advisor

27. Who is considered the father of modern portfolio theory and received a Noble Prize for such work?

    a. Merton C. Miller

    b. Warren Buffet

    c. Myron Scholes

    d. Harry Markowitz

28. What theory says that each investment should be evaluated based on its ability to enhance the total portfolio risk-adjusted return?

    a. Asset Return Hypothesis

    b. Market Premium Theory

    c. Modern Portfolio Theory

    d. Allocation Efficiency Hypothesis

29. Which of the following represents a loan to a corporation, institution, or governmental entity?

    a. Bond

    b. Common stock

    c. Warrant

    d. Private equity

30. All of the following are considered alternative assets, EXCEPT?

    a. Commodities

    b. Convertible bonds

    c. Collectibles

    d. Private equity

31. Ownership of common stock is NOT required before an investor can sell short that same stock.

    a. True

    b. False

32. Which of the following tools allows hedge fund managers to profit in both good and bad markets?

    a. Leverage

    b. Position limits

    c. Arbitrage

    d. Selling short

33. For what purpose do hedge fund managers use leverage?

    a. To reduce the risk of the position leveraged

    b. To profit in both rising and falling markets

    c. To reduce arbitrage costs

    d. To increase assets beyond regulatory limits

34. All of the following are event-driven hedge fund strategies, EXCEPT?

    a. Merger arbitrage

    b. Opportunistic events

    c. Distressed securities

    d. Macro-centric

35. What is the aim of event-driven hedge funds?

    a. To profit from directional price movements

    b. To capture profits from specific one-time opportunities

    c. To invest according to specific principles

    d. To target small, yet certain profits

36. All of the following are considered tactical hedge funds, EXCEPT?

    a. Arbitrage

    b. Sector specific

    c. Managed futures

    d. Macro-centric

37. What is the "short interest rebate"?

    a. Difference between shares actually sold short and shares attempted to be sold short

    b. Performance premium from selling short over long only

    c. Commission returned due to selling short rather than buying long

    d. Income received from the interest earned on the proceeds of selling short

38. All of the following are relative-value hedge fund strategies, EXCEPT?
    a. Equity market neutral
    b. Fund of funds
    c. Convertible arbitrage
    d. Fixed-income arbitrage

39. Do relative-value strategies require greater than, less than, or about the same amount of leverage as do tactical strategies?
    a. Greater than
    b. Less than
    c. About the same

40. Funds of funds do NOT invest directly in securities even if attractive opportunities present themselves.
    a. True
    b. False

41. Which of the following is the primary drawback of funds of funds?
    a. Reduced diversification
    b. Improper asset allocation
    c. Extra layer of fees
    d. Minimal risk management

42. Indexing is most effective for which of the following asset classes?
    a. Large-cap stocks
    b. Small-cap stocks
    c. International stocks
    d. High-yield, fixed-income stocks

43. Risk profile includes all of the following variables, EXCEPT?
    a. Capacity to assume risk
    b. Need to assume risk
    c. Credit for risk
    d. Tolerance for risk

44. What is the name of the document investors receive to report their hedge funds earnings for tax purposes?
    a. Schedule K–1
    b. 1099-H

    c. 1040-H

    d. Schedule H–1

45. All of the following are characteristics of top hedge funds, EXCEPT?

    a. Investor-friendly provisions

    b. Strong risk management

    c. Shifting investment strategies

    d. Robust operational structure

46. All of the following are typical offering documents, EXCEPT?

    a. Limited partnership agreement

    b. Subscription agreement

    c. Offering memorandum

    d. Fund registration certification

47. What is relative performance benchmarking?

    a. Evaluating performance against dissimilar portfolios

    b. Evaluating performance against a peer group or an appropriate index

    c. Evaluating performance against properly allocated indices

    d. Evaluating performance against historical returns over the last five years

48. *Fact or Fiction*? All hedge funds employ significant leverage.

    a. Fact

    b. Fiction

49. *Fact or Fiction*? Most hedge fund strategies can be employed by common investors.

    a. Fact

    b. Fiction

50. Hedge funds are limited to how many accredited investors in each fund?

    a. 49

    b. 99

    c. 149

    d. 199

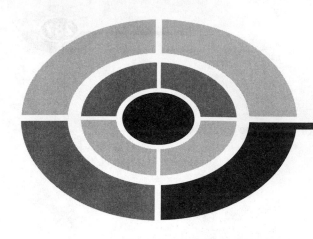

Answer Key

Chapter 1	Chapter 2	Chapter 3
1. c	1. c	1. d
2. b	2. a	2. b
3. a	3. d	3. b
4. b	4. a	4. c
5. b	5. c	5. b
6. d	6. c	6. d
7. b	7. a	7. b
8. a	8. c	8. c
9. c	9. b	9. a
10. b	10. d	10. a

Answer Key

Chapter 4	Chapter 5	Chapter 6
1. b	1. d	1. c
2. a	2. a	2. b
3. d	3. b	3. c
4. d	4. a	4. b
5. a	5. c	5. b
6. c	6. c	6. d
7. b	7. b	7. a
8. b	8. b	8. a
9. c	9. d	9. b
10. a	10. b	10. d

Chapter 7	Chapter 8	Chapter 9
1. b	1. b	1. d
2. c	2. b	2. a
3. b	3. b	3. a
4. d	4. d	4. b
5. d	5. a	5. c
6. b	6. c	6. a
7. a	7. a	7. b
8. b	8. c	8. b
9. a	9. d	9. a
10. a	10. b	10. b

Chapter 10	**Chapter 11**	**Chapter 12**
1. b	1. c	1. d
2. a	2. a	2. b
3. b	3. c	3. b
4. c	4. b	4. d
5. a	5. a	5. a
6. d	6. b	6. c
7. b	7. b	7. a
8. b	8. b	8. d
9. c	9. a	9. c
10. a	10. a	10. a

Chapter 13	**Chapter 14**	**Chapter 15**
1. b	1. d	1. b
2. b	2. b	2. b
3. d	3. b	3. d
4. b	4. c	4. c
5. c	5. b	5. c
6. a	6. d	6. a
7. a	7. a	7. b
8. b	8. a	8. c
9. b	9. a	9. d
10. a	10. c	10. a

Answer Key

Chapter 16

1. c
2. b
3. d
4. b
5. d
6. b
7. a
8. a
9. b
10. c

Chapter 17

1. b
2. a
3. b
4. a
5. c
6. a
7. b
8. b
9. b
10. a

Chapter 18

1. c
2. a
3. a
4. b
5. d
6. b
7. b
8. b
9. b
10. a

Chapter 19

1. d
2. a
3. b
4. c
5. c
6. d
7. b
8. a
9. d
10. b

Chapter 20

1. b
2. a
3. a
4. a
5. b
6. a
7. b
8. d
9. b
10. d

Final Exam Answers

1. B	17. A	34. D
2. B	18. A	35. B
3. D	19. C	36. A
4. A	20. B	37. D
5. C	21. C	38. B
6. C	22. D	39. A
7. B	23. D	40. A
8. B	24. A	41. C
9. D	25. C	42. A
10. A	26. B	43. C
11. A	27. D	44. A
12. C	28. C	45. C
13. A	29. A	46. D
14. D	30. B	47. B
15. B	31. A	48. B
16. B	32. D	49. A
	33. B	50. B

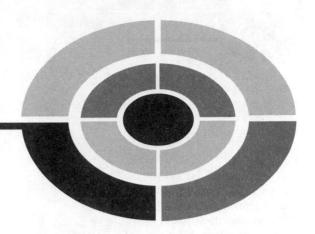

Index

Index

Index

Index

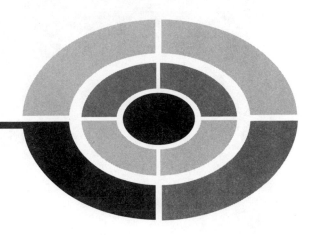

About the Author

Scott Paul Frush, CFA, CFP, is a leading authority on portfolio optimization and asset-allocation policy. He is founder and president of Frush Financial Group, a wealth management firm in Bloomfield Hills, Michigan. Frush is an accomplished financial advisor, a financial writer, publisher of the *Journal of Asset Allocation*, and a consultant on asset-allocation topics.

Frush has helped people to protect, grow, and insure their wealth for more than a decade. In 2002, he founded the Frush Financial Group to manage portfolios for individuals, affluent families, and institutions using customized and sophisticated asset-allocation solutions. Prior to founding his company, Frush worked at Jay A. Fishman Investment Counsel in Detroit, Michigan, and Stein Roe Mutual Funds in Chicago, Illinois.

Frush earned a Master of Business Administration degree in finance from the University of Notre Dame and a Bachelor of Business Administration degree in finance from Eastern Michigan University. He holds the Chartered Financial Analyst (CFA) and Certified Financial Planner (CFP) designations and is insurance licensed for life, health, property, and casualty. Frush is a member of the CFA Institute, CFA Institute Society of Detroit, National Association of Tax Professionals, and the Detroit Economic Club.

Frush is the author of *Understanding Hedge Funds* (McGraw-Hill, 2006), *Understanding Asset Allocation* (McGraw-Hill, 2006), and *Optimal Investing* (Marshall Rand, 2004) and recipient of two "Book of the Year" honors for business and investments. Frush has been quoted in or his work noted in numerous publications across the United States.

The Frush Financial Group Web site is located at www.Frush.com.